MW01055066

JOE DIMAGGIO
1914-1999

"All of baseball is deeply saddened by the passing of the Yankee Clipper, Joe DiMaggio. For several generations of fans, Joe was the personification of grace, class and dignity on the baseball diamond. His persona extended beyond the playing field and touched all our hearts. In many respects, as an immigrant's son, he represented the hopes and ideals of our great country. Major League Baseball offers its condolences not only to members of the family but to baseball fans everywhere."

—Bud Selig
Commissioner of Baseball

A Great Loss

J oe DiMaggio, an American Icon and baseball hero for the ages who was immortalized in both song and fiction, died early today at his home in Hollywood, Florida. The Yankee Clipper, honored by the Bombers on the final day of the 1998 season as baseball's greatest living player, succumbed to complications arising from a lung-cancer operation. His brother, Dominick, two grandchildren and long-time friends Morris Engelberg and Joe Nacchio were at his bedside. He was 84.

The "consummate ballplayer," DiMaggio hit .325 with 361 homers in a 13-year Hall of Fame career as Mickey Mantle's center field predecessor with the Yankees. More than anything else, however, it was his stately, dignified image that set him apart from all of his baseball contemporaries and made him one of the most respected and recognized personalities in the world.

Born November 25, 1914, in Martinez, California, the eighth of nine children of an Italian immigrant fisherman, DiMaggio honed his baseball skills on the sandlots of San Francisco and followed his older brother Vince into the Major Leagues. His younger brother, Dom, joined him in the majors, breaking in with the Red Sox in 1940.

DiMaggio is survived by his son, Joe Jr., his brother Dom and two granddaughters. The Yankees, who retired his No. 5 in 1952 and dedicated a plaque for him that is now a centerpiece of Monument Park at Yankee Stadium, have long wanted to erect a monument in his honor. Always, though, DiMaggio declined the honor. Suffice to say, with his death, his will become the fifth monument, alongside those of Babe Ruth, Lou Gehrig, Mickey Mantle and Miller Huggins, in Yankee Stadium's hallowed grounds.

—Bill Madden
March 8, 1999

Joe DiMaggio

An American Icon

Sports Publishing Inc.
www.SportsPublishingInc.com

Other Daily News Books

Big Town/Big Time: A New York Epic 1898-1998
Jets: Broadway's 30-Year Guarantee
Yogi Berra: An American Original
Yankees '98: Best Ever

DAILY ◉ NEWS

Coordinating Editors: Joseph J. Bannon, Jr., and Joanna L. Wright
Editor: Susan M. McKinney
Book Design: Terry N. Hayden
Dustjacket Design: Julie L. Denzer
Book layout: Erin J. Prescher, Jennifer L. Polson, Susan M. McKinney
Photo Editor: Angela Troisi
Research Editors: Michael G. Pearson, Terrence C. Miltner, and Victoria J. Parrillo

ISBN: 1-58261-037-1
Library of Congress Number: 99-60110

Printed in the United States.

www.SportsPublishingInc.com

Joe DiMaggio and his father, Joe Sr., study the day's catch on a fishing boat operated by Joe's brother Mike.

Joe DiMaggio

Table of Contents

Acknowledgments

When talk turns to the subject of baseball's most unbreakable records, the conversation usually winds through Pete Rose's hits, Hank Aaron's home runs, Nolan Ryan's strikeouts, Cy Young's victories, Hack Wilson's RBIs, Cal Ripken's streak and a host of other remarkable achievements. In the end, however, the talk usually comes around to Joe DiMaggio's unmatched 56-game hitting streak in the summer of 1941.

During DiMaggio's incredible streak, the *Daily News* gave its readers a front-row seat for every historic swing of the bat. In fact, it was that way during all 13 of the Yankee Clipper's glorious seasons in pinstripes. When DiMaggio and the Yanks appeared in 10 World Series, winning nine, the *Daily News* was there with full-page pictures and stories of every dramatic moment. Even now, in DiMaggio's latest, greatest battle of his life, the *Daily News* provides America with the most complete and compassionate coverage.

Bringing the career of Joe DiMaggio to life every day in the pages of the *Daily News* requires the hard work and dedication of hundreds of people at the paper. When we first approached the *Daily News* about this project, we received the overwhelming support of Ed Fay (VP/Director of Editorial Administration) and Les Goodstein (Executive Vice President/Associate Publisher). Among others at the paper who were instrumental in assisting us in this project were Lenore Schlossberg, John Polizano, Eric Meskauskas, Angela Troisi, Mike Lipack, Vincent Panzarino, Bill Martin, Faigi Rosenthal, Dawn Jackson and Scott Browne. From the *Daily News* sports department, we specifically want to acknowledge the support of editors Barry Werner and Leon Carter.

Space limitations preclude us from thanking each writer and photographer whose work appears in this book. However, wherever available, we have preserved the writers' bylines and the photographers' credits to ensure proper attribution for their work.

And finally, we are grateful for all the support and hard work of those at Sports Publishing Inc. who worked tirelessly on this project: Susan McKinney, Mike Pearson, Terrence Miltner, Julie Denzer, Terry Hayden, Jennifer Polson, Erin Prescher, Victoria Parrillo, and Scot Muncaster. Thanks also go to David Hamburg, whose final editing and proofreading were invaluable.

Joseph J. Bannon, Jr.
Joanna L. Wright
Coordinating Editors

Introduction

Golden Opportunity For Jolt From Joe

Chuck Knoblauch talked about walking the blue line. He had used the same entrance at Yankee Stadium he had always used when he was with the Twins, walked down the stairs. There in front of him was the same sign everybody sees. Left for the visitor's clubhouse. Follow the red line. Right was a blue arrow, a blue line. He went right this time. Knoblauch was already a Yankee before yesterday. Walking the blue line meant he was finally a Yankee here.

A couple of hours before the game, before another baseball season came home to the Stadium, Knoblauch stood in front of his locker, across from David Cone's.

"I always wondered what it would be like to take this walk," Knoblauch said.

He smiled and said, "Walking the blue line makes it official."

Now it was after 1 o'clock at the Stadium, maybe 10 minutes from Cone's first pitch at the Stadium, maybe twice that from when Knoblauch would lead off the bottom of the first. Here came Joe DiMaggio out of the elevator, ready to follow the blue line himself. He came after Babe Ruth at Yankee Stadium, played with both Lou Gehrig and Mickey Mantle. He will be 84 in November. He walked slowly toward another season. The line that Knoblauch officially joined yesterday, Joe DiMaggio is in front.

"I'm a little late getting down here," he said. "So many people upstairs today. They wanted some baseball stories. I told them I had at least a few to tell."

He walked down the long hallway past the press room, took a left and walked past the back door to the Yankee clubhouse. It was 1:10. He was supposed to be on the field any time now to throw out the first pitch. He had a baseball in his right hand.

At the bottom of the runway leading to the Yankee dugout, Joe DiMaggio said, "Anybody want to warm me up?"

One of the guys with him stepped back a few feet. DiMaggio tossed him the ball. The man came over, handed the ball back to him, asked if he wanted to throw a few more. The old man smiled and said, "I'm as loose as I'm going to get."

He poked a head inside the Yankee clubhouse, which was completely remodeled over the winter.

"Everything's new today, isn't it?" he said.

Everything except the great DiMaggio. He came here for the first time in 1936 and after that only became one of the magic names in the history of this place, and baseball, and American sport.

When they called for him he walked up the runway and into the sun and heard another April welcome from the Stadium and threw a strike to Joe Girardi, waved to the crowd with both hands. It is a gesture, a snapshot, that has become part of the ceremonies of the day. DiMaggio was out of breath when he came back down the runway.

"That's the most exercise I'll get all year," he said.

He walked back on the blue line and when he came to the elevator that would take him back upstairs, he suddenly found himself in the middle of all the young women from the U.S. women's hockey team that won a gold medal in Nagano. Most of them were born 25 years after DiMaggio last played a game of baseball. But when he came around the corner, all conversation stopped, all laughter. There was a new kind of excitement to the day.

Here was Joe DiMaggio, here with them.

And they felt as if they were part of the line, too.

Katie King, one of the players, introduced herself and said, "Our coach always used your name to motivate us, Mr. DiMaggio."

He asked how that was so, and King said, "Before our games leading up to the Olympics, when we'd go from city to city, he'd always tell us to make sure to have a 'Joe DiMaggio day.'"

The old man grinned. "And what exactly is a 'Joe DiMaggio day?'"

The young woman said, "He said that one time, late in the season after the Yankees clinched the pennant, somebody wanted to know why you'd played so hard that day, in a game that really didn't mean anything. And you said there might be people in the ballpark that day who might only ever see you play once, and you owed them your best."

DiMaggio said, "It was against the St. Louis Browns."

He posed for a picture with Cammi Granato, the team captain. He signed Yankee caps. One of the players leaned up and kissed him. He seemed in no hurry to go anywhere. Sixty-two years after his first April at Yankee Stadium, here was another one. He never let go of the baseball. At the head of the blue line at the Stadium, one more Joe DiMaggio day. For everyone.

April 11, 1998
By Mike Lupica

Joe DiMaggio

An American Icon

"I think there are some players who are born to play ball."

—Joe DiMaggio

Chapter 1

1934-1937

A Rising Star

*J*oseph Paul DiMaggio began his baseball career playing with the San Francisco Seals of the Pacific Coast League until the New York Yankees decided to "take a chance" on the 18-year-old phenom. Anticipation grew as fans looked to the young star to replace their beloved Bambino. DiMaggio very quickly gained an identity all his own. His businesslike demeanor on the field, along with his private grace off the field, intrigued fans around the world.

In his first years as a Yankee, DiMaggio was the subject of constant media attention and took much criticism. Unlike many Yankee greats of the past, Joe DiMaggio was a quiet, serious man who shied away from the spotlight. His first season also proved him to be "human" in that he did have a few minor struggles on the field. Because expectations were so high, criticism was abundant for the few mistakes that the young ball player did make.

Despite media and public scrutiny, DiMaggio set the precedent for his outstanding career in his first year, being named to the All-Star team, leading the league in triples, and setting AL rookie records for runs scored and triples.

The next year, he was named to the All-Star team for a second time, and led the league in home runs, runs scored, and slugging percentage. He also led AL outfielders in putouts.

Young Joe DiMaggio was becoming a superstar. ∎

1936 REGULAR SEASON

G	AB	R	H	2B	3B	HR	RBI	BB	SB	AVG.	SLG.
138	637	132	206	44	15*	29	125	24	4	.323	.576

1937 REGULAR SEASON

G	AB	R	H	2B	3B	HR	RBI	BB	SB	AVG.	SLG.
151	621	151*	215	35	15	46*	167	64	3	.346	.673*

*led American League

Ruppert Buys $75,000 Babe

By George Kenney
November 21, 1934

Babe Ruth's successor in box office and fan appeal was purchased by the Yanks today. He is Joe DiMaggio, star hitter and outfielder of the San Francisco Seals of the Pacific Coast League, who is 18 and six feet plus.

But notwithstanding that Col. Jake Ruppert took the rubber band off his millions and gave five players and $75,000 for his new exhibition piece, DiMaggio will not join the New York Yankees until the fall of 1935.

The transaction was the opening gun in the Colonel's shoot-the-works spending campaign to make the Yanks the creme de lá creme of baseball.

> Realizing that he had baseball's most sensational youngster in his clutches, Graham dictated virtually his own terms.

The names of the present Yankee players who will journey to the sunny slopes of the Pacific remained secret tonight, but it was announced that Charley Graham, owner of the Seals, would enjoy the services of three of them immediately. He will hold options on the other two.

Realizing that he had baseball's most sensational youngster in his clutches, Graham dictated virtually his own terms. He insisted that Ruppert's new Bambino remain on the Coast for another year, because in the 1934 campaign he slapped the Coast League pitchers for hits in 61 consecutive games. And Graham probably also considered that the Colonel's $75,000 purchase price wouldn't hurt DiMaggio as a drawing card in San Francisco next summer.

Manager Joe McCarthy, who went to French Lick Springs, Indiana, this morning to confer with Ruppert, verified the DiMaggio deal on his return this evening, but on orders from Ruppert, he refused to identify the players involved or to disclose the amount of cash that had changed hands. ∎

AP/Wide World Photos

Members of the DiMaggio family say goodbye to their hero, who is on his way to Florida for his first training camp with the Yankees.

Newark Gets New "Babe"

November 23, 1934

The secret report of a rival baseball scout uncovered here yesterday lent confirmation to a story that New York's new Babe Ruth—the sensational Joe DiMaggio—might prove to be a $75,000 pig in a poke.

Perhaps similar, devastating intelligence reached Col. Jack Ruppert—though 24 hours too late to save $75,000 and the five players he gave for his new exhibition piece—since that would explain the sudden announcement out of Louisville yesterday that the 20-year-old San Francisco slugger was not "ripe" for play in the Yankee Stadium outfield next spring, but would sign on with Newark, one of the Yankee farms at the end of the '35 season.

"Wrenched knee failing to respond to treatment. Eyes affected by strong floodlights in Seal Park San Francisco." This was the cryptic report sent to headquarters by the scout of a rival corporation interested in the purchase of DiMaggio. It is no secret that the Boston Red Sox, Cleveland Indians, Giants, Cubs and Dodgers at various times submitted bids. ■

DiMaggio (right) meets Col. Jacob Ruppert at training camp as manager Joe McCarthy looks on. The young star would become one of the greatest heroes in baseball.

AP/Wide World Photos

"Timid" Joe DiMaggio Spurns Yank Contract

February 3, 1936

The Yanks stopped worrying yesterday about the bashfulness of Joe DiMaggio. Their slugging acquisition from the Pacific Coast League, who is the most ballyhooed rookie since the days of Kelley and O'Toole, had been pictured as so timid he'd stand with his hat in hand for an hour before walking through a subway turnstile. They feared he'd be too frightened to play big league ball. But when he became a holdout last night they decided he had plenty of nerve—too much in fact.

In return for DiMaggio, the Yanks gave five players and $75,000. For more than a year, Coast papers have hailed him as the greatest outfielder in Coast League history. When the Yanks sent him a contract for a puny sum, Joe said "nix." Reports from San Francisco indicate he's holding out for $8,000 a year. ∎

Rookie Joe DiMaggio as a budding outfielder.

Daily News

Yanks to Open Minus Maggy

By Kevin Jones
April 6, 1936

Joe DiMaggio, the $75,000 embryo Babe Ruth and most promising newcomer of the year, landed in town alone and incapacitated yesterday and admitted he'd not be able to play for the Yankees for at least three weeks. And it may be longer, depending on his response to medical treatment. Dead Pan Joe looked gloomier than ever as he explained that the second-degree burn he suffered on his left instep while being treated for a minor sprain has failed to heal.

"It was only a bit of a sprain and I personally didn't think the diathermic machine treatment was necessary," said Joe. "There is no doubt in my mind that the infection was caused by the burn and not by the sprain." Thus Joe described the "boner" that may prove very costly to the Yank pennant hopes.

Apparently under orders not to "say too much," DiMaggio was hustled off to the Hotel New Yorker soon after his arrival at Pennsylvania Station. Ed Barrow, a business manager of the Yanks was in charge of the hustling. Once at the hotel, DiMaggio was "out" to all callers.

DiMaggio was sent to New York because the injury had Doc Painter, the trainer, and Manager McCarthy baffled. Several times the foot appeared to have healed and Joe turned out for practice, only to have the wound open again.

Doc Painter believes DiMaggio has unusually sensitive skin. He says the diathermic treatment of 20 minutes is routine for minor sprains and bruises.

DiMaggio played with the San Francisco Seals last year and was voted the most valuable player in the Pacific Coast League. He bats right-handed and in 1934 set a league record by hitting safely in 61 consecutive games. Batting .398, he led in scoring

Joe DiMaggio shows off his injured foot, which kept him off the field for a month.

runs, total hits and triples, and with Lou Gehrig, should give the Yanks a powerful one-two punch.

Should the injury prove serious, the loss of Joe's services will hit not only the Yankee bankroll, a staggering blow, but also the Yankee batting order. ∎

DiMag Hits 3, Yanks Win, 14-5

By Don Hallman
May 4, 1936

This is the story of Joseph DiMaggio, a kid of 21 from San Francisco, though it might be proper to mention that the Yankees beat St. Louis 14-5, at the Stadium yesterday. The game was pestered by rain and bad pitching—it wasn't much of a game anyway—but the 25,400 fans didn't give a whoop. They had come to see Joe DiMaggio make his first start for the Yanks; to see and to cheer—or to hoot.

Now the cheers of New York fans are not handed out to every fellow. In fact, they have subsided almost to a whisper since Babe Ruth packed his duds and went through the gates.

But yesterday they rolled in happy volume across the field and back again for a rookie—a $75,000 rookie to be sure, but only a kid stepping up to fill the vacant shoes of Big Boy Ruth.

It wasn't an easy spot, you may be sure. The Yankees had been playing bangup baseball for weeks and were in rare form, while this kid from out West had been sitting on the bench with a burned foot. The kid was on a man's errand, you might say, and he needed a little luck. His own hadn't been so hot of late.

He needed luck, and he got it—after that he went along on his own merits. Take that time in the first inning when Joe stepped to the plate to start his major league career. Crosetti had tripled and Rolfe walked.

Joe grounded to the pitcher and you could almost hear that kid cussing his luck as he beat it for

Joe Gets Going
May 3, 1936

NEW YORK YANKEES

	ab	r	h	tb	bb	so	rbi	po	a	e
Crosetti, ss	5	1	1	3	1	2	0	2	4	0
Rolfe, 3b	5	3	2	3	1	0	0	0	0	1
DIMAGGIO, lf	**6**	**3**	**3**	**5**	**0**	**1**	**1**	**1**	**0**	**0**
Gehrig, 1b	5	5	4	4	1	1	2	7	0	0
Dickey, c	3	1	0	0	2	0	1	8	1	0
Chapman, cf	4	0	4	9	0	0	3	1	0	0
Hoag, cf	0	1	0	0	0	0	0	2	0	0
Selkirk, rf	3	0	1	1	2	0	1	4	1	0
Lazzeri, 2b	5	0	1	1	0	0	2	2	2	0
Gomez, p	2	0	0	0	0	1	0	0	0	0
Murphy, p	3	0	1	1	0	0	0	0	1	0
TOTALS	41	14	17	27	7	5	10	27	9	1

first. He was an easy out, but Lady Luck whispered in Crosetti's ear to lend the boy a hand. Frankie started for home, drawing the throw as Joe reached first. Seeing he couldn't make it, Crosetti ducked back to third and Knott, starting pitcher for the Browns, threw the ball away, Crosetti scoring. Oh, it was a break all right, DiMaggio even scoring himself after Gehrig had walked and Chapman doubled.

He came up in the second inning, too, and his luck held. Rolfe had singled and Joe dropped an easy fly in center—only for some reason it dropped too fast, just a little faster than Pepper could run. It went for a single and Joe scored again on Dickey's fly to center.

Joe fanned in the fourth, but the Yanks scored two more runs anyway on Gehrig's single and Chapman's triple. Ben, by the way, got a double, two triples and a single before he was forced out in the sixth with a wrenched foot.

The sixth was something else again. It was here the fans decided Joe was OK and gave him the hand they had reserved for fellows like Ruth and Gehrig. Rolfe doubled and Joe planted a triple up against the center field boards. There wasn't any luck here; that blow would have gone for a homer in a lot of parks. Then Gehrig singled, so did Chapman. Joe had already checked in with his third run by that time, but Selkirk and Murphy, who had gone in for Gomez in the fifth, stuck in a couple of more hits to give the Yanks four runs.

Now, Joe needed just one more hand from Lady Luck in this sixth inning—and the old girl obliged. Right after he had tripled, the clouds tilted enough to stop the game. The rain threat-ened to wash that triple right off the records, and Joe needed it—it was his first in the major leagues. But after 17 minutes the rain stopped and Joe's three-bagger was safe. ∎

Now the cheers of New York fans are not handed out to every fellow. In fact, they have subsided almost to a whisper since Babe Ruth packed his duds and went through the gates. But yesterday they rolled in happy volume across the field and back again for a rookie—a $75,000 rookie to be sure, but only a kid stepping up to fill the vacant shoes of Big Boy Ruth.

DiMag Gets Homer as Yanks Win, 7-2

By Robin Harris
May 11, 1936

I n case you haven't heard, California Joey celebrated his first weekend on the Big Time yesterday by smashing the initial ball pitched to him for his first major league homer. He scored Red Rolfe and started the departing Yanks to an easy 7-2 victory over the A's.

To digress for a moment from the amazing Joe, our boys moved into the league leadership, half a game ahead of the Red Sox, who lost to Washington; 32,034 customers witnessed the agreeable spectacle. Fordham Johnny Murphy pitched excellent ball until a rush of generosity finished him in the eighth, and Bill Dickey hit his seventh four-bagger of the young season.

Perhaps all this raving about the grinning Frisco kid isn't fair to all the other Ruppert slaves, but chronologically the story of yesterday's encounter must begin with DiMaggio. Joe was as unconcerned as a fungo batter as he stepped up to face big George Turbeville, No. 1 citizen of Turbeville, N.C.

> Georgie whipped a high, fast one down the alley, and Joe leaned on it with effortless grace.

Georgie whipped a high, fast one down the alley and Joe leaned on it with effortless grace. Before you could say "Cornelius McGillicuddy" the white sphere had arrived among the screaming bargain hunters in the right-field bleachers. It was a powerful line drive, a homer in anybody's ball park, and Joe's already fanatical supporters raised a furious rumpus as he jogged around the paths.

The Yanks got another one in the second. Selkirk drove one to left center and took second when the ball slipped from Johnson's fingers as he was about to throw it. He scored on Lazzeri's burning grounder through second.

Three more came down the Yankee side in the fifth. Crosetti walked, and advanced to second on Rolfe's to first. A wild pitch put Crosetti on third, and DiMaggio, obediently sacrificing to center, brought him home. Gehrig, hit by a pitched ball for the second time, had hardly reached first before Dickey's circuit poke, landing near DiMaggio's, scored him.

This finished Turbeville and Vernon took the mound. He started the sixth by walking Selkirk and Lazzeri. He got Murphy on a foul to Hayes, and then filled the sacks by passing Crosetti. A single by Rolfe scored Selkirk, leaving the bases filled and setting the stage for something spectacular by DiMag.

But Joe can't do it every time. He's only human, and he fanned, whiffing at the last one with a grunting vehemence in the best Babe Ruth manner. Gehrig popped out on a foul to Higgins.

There was very little to say about the Athletics while all this Yankee activity was going on. Murphy had allowed only three scratch hits, and he had two out in the eighth when trouble caught up with him. Mailho, batting for Wilshere, walked, and the flustered Fordham boy handed another free ride to Johnson. Puccinelli singled and Mailho scored.

Murphy was floundering like a canoe in a typhoon by this time. By the time Pat Malone could get out of his sweater, Murph had donated Oaklies to Higgins and Warstler, forcing Johnson home. Malone fanned Dean, batting for Newsome, and the game was as good as ended. ∎

DiMaggio Crashes 2 Home Runs in 5th as Yanks Rip Sox, 18-11

By Jack Mahon
June 25, 1936

The Yankees revived that old and famous slogan of theirs, "To hell with the pitching, let's hit," here today. When the blasting was over and the dust had settled, the scoreboard read, New York 18, Chicago 11.

The principal dynamiter was slugging Joe DiMaggio, who collected two homers and two doubles and belted in five runs in one inning— equaling two records.

Joe's two circuit clouts came in the big fifth, when the Ruppert Rifles banged ten runs over the plate. He equaled the mark of Ken Williams, Hack Wilson, Bill Regan and Hank Leiber, the only others to turn the trick.

Though Fred Merkle holds the modern record of having driven in six runs in one frame, only four besides Joe ever smashed in five. They were Ty Cobb, Ray Bates, Chick Gandil and Al Simmons.

Lou Gehrig, also on a spree, passed the 100-hit mark by collecting two doubles, two singles and a walk in six trips to the plate. ■

Give DiMag a Break!

By Jack Miley
July 19, 1936

All the world is dark and dreary for young Joe DiMaggio. The proud Pisan is plunged in Stygian gloom. For the great Giuseppi isn't getting his base hits, he's bobbling that ball around in the outfield and some of the Yankee rooters are riding him. This 21-year-old San Franciscan, who was the miracle man of Mulberry Bend until he went into a tailspin up at the All-Star game in Boston two weeks ago, is learning about the fickleness of the fans. Poor Joey is heartbroken over the way his admirers have turned against him. Their cheers have changed to jeers, and DiMaggio is dismayed by this change of attitude in the folks he thought were his friends.

The Italians are the most vociferous in their booing of the Boy Wonder of the big leagues. They were the first to acclaim Joe, too. I've been going up to the Stadium this week to watch DiMaggio and it gets worse every time I wander into Ruppert's rifle range. Every time Joe comes to the plate he gets the Houston St. huzzah from the countrymen. They don't wait for him to take a cut at that apple; they give it to him in advance, long and loud. When Joey wobbles a bit out there in left field, his uncertainty is the signal for sustained abuse. The excitable fans, who used to shout their idol's praises to the house-tops, are giving him a leather-lunged lashing that isn't doing the boy a bit of good. If they keep it up and Joey doesn't prove to have plenty of iron in his spine, they're likely to ruin the most promising

> The Ruths, the Gehrigs, and the rest, have their off-days, so why shouldn't the 'Frisco flash falter momentarily?

rookie we've had in years and chase the luckless lad back to the bushes.

It is interesting the way the various groups react to the fortunes of their favorites. When DiMaggio was smashing fences with his bat and scorching the outfield turf with his breakneck saves, thousands of Italians who had never been especially interested in baseball went out to pay him tribute. They paid their way into the park all right, but they spent the money to castigate the kid they first came to honor.

I am sure the fellows who are razzing DiMaggio are hollering before they're hurt. Joe is such a splendid ball player it is ridiculous to think he's stumbling along that winding highway back to the minors. He's got too much class to collapse permanently. They've been breaking tough for Joey these last couple of weeks and he's got the fidgets. After all, the boy's been a big leaguer only a few months. The best of 'em Brody now and then. The Ruths, the Gehrigs, and the rest, have their off-days, so why shouldn't the 'Frisco flash falter momentarily? Despite his disappointing showing since the All-Star debacle, Joe is still hitting .339—and you can't do that with a feather duster! Gehrig has a $50 bet that DiMag will finish the season with .350, and I wouldn't mind having part of it. So let's lay off Giusep, and try to give the boy a helping hand instead of that old Bronx blasteroo! ■

Dear Mrs. DiMaggio

By Harry Ferguson
October 2, 1936

Louder, Mamma. Speak to him before it's too late.

You saw what happened to your Bambino Wednesday when there were two on base in the eighth inning and the rain was in his face and that Hubbell fellow was throwing Joe a wet, wobbling screwball. He hit into that double play and killed a Yankee rally when the ball game was on the fire.

That's no way for your Giuseppe to win the World Series, mamma. You didn't come all the way across the country on a slow train to watch him hit into double plays, did you? Talk to him, because he's got to go out there again tomorrow, and they throw the baseballs lots faster here than they do back home in Frisco.

He looked mighty nice out there, though, didn't he, mamma, in that grey uniform swinging a white bat through the rain? He's got a honey-smooth

> "My boy Joe will win the World Series."
> —Mrs. Rosalia DiMaggio

swing and a follow through that's as beautiful as poetry, but the Yankees aren't paying him $8,000 a year to fan the air or hit into double plays.

There used to be another Bambino who batted third for the Yankees, mamma—a big fellow named Ruth, and how that guy could hit baseballs! No hitting into double plays for him when runs were on the sacks. And every time your Giuseppe comes to bat in what those ball players call the clutch, people sort of sigh and wonder if he will do as well as the other Bambino.

Everybody has a bad day now and then, mamma, and the World Series goes best four out of seven games, so Giuseppe is going to get plenty of more chances. He wasn't the only one who was having a tough time in the rain, either. Look at that big Lou Gehrig. He couldn't even get one hit, and he's been at this business lots longer than your Bambino.

Joe DiMaggio pictured here in a San Francisco parade with his mother and niece.

So it's not too late to take Giuseppe off in the corner and talk to him. Tell him to dig his cleats in deeper and forget that this is his first year in the big leagues. Tell him to keep sending his big white bat through that sweet syrupy swing. Tell him that the Giant pitchers are scared of him and spend all their time worrying that maybe he will catch one on the end of his bat, put those thick wrists into it and break up the ball game.

Talk to him, mamma, talk to him. ■

AP/Wide World Photos

220 Grand Lost If Yanks Win 5th Game Today

October 5, 1936

If anyone doubts the honesty of organized baseball, consider this: The Yanks, if they win the series today, will be making those two destitute fellows, Horace Stoneham and Jake Ruppert, the real losers. The advance sale for the sixth game scheduled for the Polo Grounds, is $160,820.

The 24,000 unreserved grandstand and bleacher seats would net about $60,000, bringing the total receipts to about $220,000. Split 60 percent to the winner and 40 to the loser, Ruppert would lose about $132,000 and Stoneham $88,000.

The toughest part of it all is that the $160,820 for reserved and box seats is already in the till.

The players' pool, amounting to 70 percent of the $424,737 total receipts for the first four games, is not affected. The exact amount is $297,315.94. Since more Yanks share in the pot, each Yank, if the Yanks win, will collect $5,946, and $3,946 if they lose, while the Giants get $6,493 each if they win and $4,290 if they lose.

The $100,000 paid for radio broadcasting privileges is not included in these totals. This will be dumped into the general pool.

The remaining 30 percent of the players' pool, or $127,421, will be cut among the first-division clubs. The Tigers divide $31,855; the White Sox $21,236; and Washington $10,618. ■

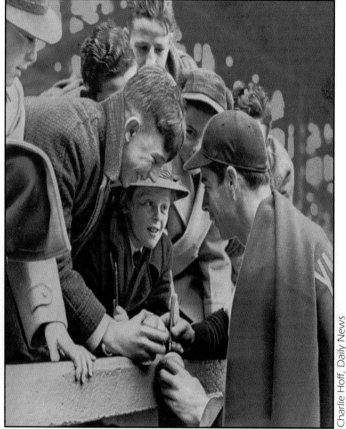

Charlie Hoff, Daily News

DiMaggio signs autographs for wide-eyed fans.

2nd Series Contest Drew 43,543 Fans

The paid attendance at the second game of the World Series yesterday was 43,543 and the total receipts were $184,962.

The players' 60 percent of the receipts was $94,330.62, bringing their pool to $182,130.69 for the two games.

The commissioner's share amounted to $27,744.30, the cut of the American and National Leagues, $31,443.54, and the share of the two New York clubs, $31,443.54.

Yanks Win Fifth Title

Seven Runs in 9th Rip Jints, 13-5

By Stuart Rogers
October 7, 1936

Hail the Yanks—new World Champs! They beat the Giants, 13-5, yesterday to win the Series, four games to two. Lefty Gomez was knocked out in the seventh inning, but Johnny Murphy appeared to pitch his team to a $54,000 victory, this being the difference between winner's share and loser's. Murphy's pitching (a) tied the old Giant-Yank feud at two series wins and two series losses each; (b) marked 20 American championships to 13 National; and (c) gave the Yanks four championships since '27 and their fifth in history. ■

World Series champion Joe DiMaggio gets in some playing time off the field after finishing a long season. DiMaggio is joined by Jack Dempsey (far right), Frank Corsett and Harry B. Smith at Dempsey's restaurant.

Bob Mortimor, Daily News

15

Italian Fans Applaud DiMag's Pay Demands

By Harry Forbes
January 31, 1937

Daily News

Joe DiMaggio, the poor Frisco fisherman's son, has 1,000,000 New York Italians solidly behind him in his holdout war with millionaire Jake Ruppert. Joe's the hero of every bambino. And the dark-eyed signorinas—ah-h-h-h-h, cara mia! Mussolini, DiMaggio, Nuvolar—there's your Roman triumvirate along Mulberry Bend. But Giuseppe—what he does for Col. Ruppert. He offered our Giuseppe only $1,000 more than the $8,500 he got last year! Signor Ruppert should give Giuseppe the $17,500 he asks.

This reporter made a tour of the lower East Side yesterday. Here's what Joe's own Italian people had to say:

Joseph Carillo, 17, of 115 Mott St., C.C.N.Y.: "Joe DiMaggio was the greatest rookie of all time. Why shouldn't he get more money?"

Frankie Infanta, 16, of 111 Mott St., Stuyvesant H.S.: "He is the greatest batter and fielder that ever played baseball. He will be robbed if Mr. Ruppert doesn't give him $17,500."

> "Joe DiMaggio was the greatest rookie of all time. Why shouldn't he get more money?"

Louis Petta, 17, of 208 Grand St., Seward Park H.S.: "I saw Joe play when I was in the bleachers last summer. Boy, he can certainly make the tough ones look easy. I hope he gets all the dough he wants."

Arthur Kimball, 414 E. 79th St., playground director: "The kids I take care of are all crazy about DiMaggio. He's their idol. I think he should get $17,500 this year."

Terry Sergi, 18, of 56 Elizabeth St., Haaron H.S. "DiMaggio should get more than $17,500. He's worth $100,000."

Tony Biondolillo, 15, of 137 Mott St., Haaron H.S.: "I like to play ball and watching Joe makes me do better. He is generous just asking for $17,500." ∎

DiMaggio in Fold at Record $15,000

By Bob Brumby
March 13, 1937

Joe DiMaggio gave up the holdout ghost yesterday. The Yank outfielder wired from San Francisco that he would accept the club's offer of $15,000. It was a $6,500 increase for the popular Italian slugger who made good sensationally his first year in big time. Jake Ruppert, usually about as garrulous as a sphinx with laryngitis, was so pleased he actually verified the terms.

With DiMag in the herd, only Lou Gehrig and Red Ruffing remain unroped. Ruffing is asking $18,000, which is $3,000 more than the Yanks are willing to pay. Gehrig craves $40,000 and a two-year contract. Ruppert has offered him $36,000 for one year. Joe asked for $17,500.

DiMaggio is reported in great shape. He has gained poundage and tips the beam at about 200. Last year he collected 206 hits for an average of .323. He belted 15 triples, 44 doubles and drove in 125 runs in 138 games played. He was third in fielding averages and first in assists with 22.

The 15 grand paycheck makes Joe the highest salaried second-year man in baseball as well as top money man among Yank outfielders. He'll leave today by plane for St. Pete. ■

Joe DiMaggio Loses Tonsils and Adenoids
April 17, 1937

Joe DiMaggio, center fielder for the New York Yankees, underwent an operation for the removal of his tonsils and adenoids yesterday at noon in Lenox Hill Hospital.

Dr. Gerard Oberender, Colonel Jacob Ruppert's physician, performed the operation and said it was entirely successful. DiMaggio, the doctor said, was resting comfortably and would remain in the hospital for "a few days."

It may be nearly a month, however, before DiMaggio can play ball. Even so, it is a question whether the removal of his tonsils relieved the neuritis in his right shoulder. The tonsillectomy was performed only because it might cure the ailing arm.

This is the second year since DiMaggio joined the Yankees in 1936 that he has been an invalid at the start of the season. He was out of the first 17 games last year with a burned foot.

DiMag, in '37 Bow, Whacks 3 Hits to Down Red Sox, 3-2

By Jack Smith
May 2, 1937

J oe DiMaggio blazoned his Italian moniker across Stadium skies in his first start with the Yankees yesterday.

The belting beauty slapped three straight hits as the champs beat the Red Sox, 3-2, before 34,381 welcoming fans. Joe scored two runs himself and collected the blow that accounted for the third. Bump Hadley and Pat Malone donated valuable aid to the San Franciscan's seasonal debut by holding the visitors to three safeties. Bump yielded all three before being relieved by Pat with the bases loaded and two out in the eighth.

DiMaggio played as if he had been in the line-up all year. After Rolfe had singled to center and Cramer booted DiMaggio's hit, Rolfe scored. Joe rollicked to second on the misplay and headed homeward when Dickey lined another one-bagger to center.

In the sixth, Joe scored what proved the winning run. He singled to center to start the frame, legged to third on Gehrig's double, and was forced home after walks to Lazzeri and Hoag. ■

AP/Wide World Photos

Joe DiMaggio shakes hands with brother Vince DiMaggio of the Boston Bees in March 1937. Vince would later go on to play for the Red Sox.

Yanks Win, Tie

Down Browns, 16-9; Draw, 8-8

By Jack Smith
June 14, 1937

Whatta day! Whatta bizness! The Yanks played a double-header with the Browns here today, won the first game, 16-9, scoring seven runs in the ninth, and deadlocked the second, 8-8, in eleven innings, after Joe DiMaggio had homered with two out in the ninth. It was Joe's third homer of the game.

The Yanks scored 24 runs, made 31 hits, including five homers, three triples and five doubles, but in spite of it all lost ground to the White Sox and now lead by only half a game.

DiMaggio collected three homers in the second game in three consecutive times at bat, running his total to 14 for the season, and nine in the last nine games. He also ran his hitting streak to 15 straight games. ∎

Yanks Win in Riot, 16-2; DiMag Clouts 2, Lou 1

by Jack Smith
July 10, 1937

Joe DiMaggio belted two home runs, a triple, a double, a single, drew a pass and batted in seven runs! Jake Powell and Joe Kuhel slugged each other with bare fists and were bounced by indignant umpires! Monte Pearson won his sixth victory! Whew! Before we run out of exclamation points, we better break down and tell you our Yankees pounded a 16-2 win over the Senators at the Stadium during yesterday's sultry afternoon.

Babe Ruth's home run record of 60 is now within striking distance of Signor DiMaggio. The Italian hit homers in the first and sixth innings to boost his gross to 22.

DiMaggio trudged to the plate six times. He homered with none on in the first, tripled with Rolfe aboard in the third, walked with the bases full in the fourth, homered with none on in the sixth, singled with Pearson on in the seventh and doubled with the bases full in the eighth.

The Senators scored with two out in the first on successive singles by Kuhel, Stone and Travis. DiMaggio's first homer tied the score in the Yanks' first. Neither side scored in the second inning but from the third on, the Yank bats worked overtime. In the third, Pearson singled, Rolfe tripled, DiMaggio tripled and Gehrig singled. Result, four runs. In the fourth, singles by Goag and Crosetti, walks to Rolfe and DiMaggio, coupled with Gehrig's single and Almada's error, netted four runs.

The Yanks scored one in the fifth, two in the sixth, when DiMaggio and Gehrig homered in succession, one in the seventh and four more in the eighth. The victory was Pearson's sixth of the season with no defeats and kept him at the top of the league hurlers. He fanned five but was troubled with control. Not one of the Senators' 11 hits went for extra bases.

Off the field, teammates Lou Gehrig, Joe DiMaggio and Bill Dickey (L-R) are all smiles, but when they get on the field, these guys carry a different expression.

The Powerhouse

By Jimmy Powers
August 24, 1937

DiMaggio and Gehrig, teammates and rivals, what are their feelings toward each other? I doubt if anyone will truly know. For nine years Lou labored in the shadow of Ruth. There was an all-too-short intermision of unshared glory and headlines. Then a California rookie, modest, slightly adenoidal, appeared. Camera shutters clicked. Newsreelers thrust sound boxes at him. The town welcomed a new hero. If Gehrig bears resentment, he fails to show it. The two are not pals. Gehrig rooms with Dickey; eats, fishes and swims with him. DiMaggio is a loner. One night he attends movies with Rolfe, the next with Powell. On the third he may go alone. The two stars do not jockey each other. When one homers, the other does not congratulate him. Both are strictly business. Hits mean one thing—money.

They respect each other, Gehrig says: "DiMaggio is the greatest hitter I know." Joe thinks the same of Lou. Both are sincere. Asked who would win the slugging derby Lou replied: "I don't know. Don't care. But there's no thrill like poking the ball out of the park. When I go up there I try to meet the ball. If I get a home run, so much the better." DiMaggio confides: "I don't know that I will beat Gehrig this year. I'd like to. When I'm at the plate I swing like the rest of 'em. Confidentially—I won't break Ruth's record!" ∎

AP/Wide World Photos

Joe DiMaggio (right), is introduced to the legendary Babe Ruth by NY sportswriter Bill Corum (center).

Babe Picks Successor

August 29, 1937

Outfielder Joe DiMaggio and catcher Rudy York are Babe Ruth's selections as his possible slugging successors, the one-time home run king said today.

The Babe, en route by bus to play in an upstate golf tournament, took time out from signing autographs to tell reporters:

"This DiMaggio boy sure looks like a natural to become the No. 1 hitter in the game, but you can't overlook that young Tigers catcher Rudy York."

He picked the Cubs as the National League's World Series entry, and said the American League winner was "in the bag," without mentioning his former team, the circuit-leading Yankees.

Fifth All-New York Series

October 6, 1937

This is the fifth All-New York Series. The Giants copped in '21 and '22: The Yanks in '23 and '36. This year, as last, the battle will be between a slugging Yank team bolstered by a better Gomez and a tough Ruffing and a Giant team with an air-tight defense, Hubbell and the prize freshman pitcher of the year, Slim Melton.

The Yanks overpowered the American League and won going away by 13 games. The Giants battled down the stretch with the Cubs, finally clinching the flag three days before the season ended. Those picking the Giants point out that the Yanks have been in a slump and will not pull out in time while the Giants have been going at top-speed for six weeks. On the other hand, Yank rooters feel Dickey,

This is the fifth All-New York Series. The Giants... won in '21 and '22: The Yanks...in '23 and '36.

Gehrig and DiMaggio will get to the Giants' southpaws sometime during the series. They point out that a good defense cannot stop home-run hitting.

About 800 cops, under the direction of Inspector Joe DeMartino, will police the Stadium. Six hundred patrolmen will be on foot. In addition, 40 mounties and six mounted sergeants will see that the crowd "keeps moving." A score of detectives will mingle with the throng looking for the usual dips. ∎

Yanks 2-1 Favorites

October 5, 1937

Series odds, *according to Robert Green & Co., Wall St. commission house, are:

2-1	**Yanks win Series.**
7-1	**Yanks won't win four straight.**
20-1	**Giants won't win four straight.**
7-5	**Yanks win first game.**
7-5	**Yanks win second.**
9-2	**Giants won't win first two.**

*Regardless of pitchers

Champions!
Yanks Win Final, 4-2

Hoag, DiMaggio Hit Homers

By Jack Smith
October 11, 1937

CHAMPS! For the second straight year, the Yanks are baseball's best, a murderous, cocky crew, exploding all opposition. They earned the title yesterday at the Polo Grounds as Lefty Gomez battled his way to a 4-2 victory over the scrappy Giants in the World Series final. Lefty had to battle. The Giants were different from those who blew three straight. They were a team which had to be beaten. They wouldn't beat themselves. They fought every minute. They lost because Gomez was out there, a man who wouldn't be beat, a pitcher who thrived when the going was toughest.

Hoag's homer scored the first run. Melton had turned back the Yanks in the first. With two on, Hoag led off the second and trotted around as the ball landed in a front box of the upper right field stands. DiMag scored the next run. There were two out in the third. DiMag caught the pitch squarely and rifled it over the left stands. The ball struck a flagpole, a yard away from the foul line and bounced back on the field, but it was a homer.

Melton pitched nicely in the fourth, facing only three Yanks and keeping the game tied. Yank power exploded again in the fifth. Lazzeri was up first, he clouted the second pitch into deep center field. It was a high, towering drive, and almost dropped into the bleachers. Leiber raced, making a desperate stab, but the ball fell for a triple.

Next, Gomez was up. The Giant infield crept in as Melton wound up. The ball came in high and inside. Lefty swung, the ball trickled past Melton. Whitehead dove for it, but missed. Lazzeri scored. Gomez had driven in the winning run. If the Giants had retired Gomez, there might have been no score. It didn't matter that Gehrig's double in the same inning drove Gomez across with the fourth and final run.

From then on, drama piled on drama. Spines tingled on almost every pitch by Gomez. The Giants could have won the game a dozen times. McCarthy could have removed Gomez and been justified. But he knew Gomez.

Drama was missing in the ninth, where it belonged. Bases weren't loaded with two strikes on the home run slugger. Gomez faced only three men. Whitehead flied to DiMaggio, Lazzeri trapped Berger's bouncer and threw to first. The Giants beefed, claiming Dickey tipped Berger's bat. After a conference with his fellow umps, Ormsby stuck to his decision and Berger was out. Gomez himself made the final putout as he covered first on Moore's roller to Gehrig.

The Yanks' four-games-to-one triumph marked their second successive victory in baseball's heavy money battle and their sixth since the war. They won previously in 1923, 1927, 1928, 1932 and 1936.

This establishes an all-time record. The Yanks broke a tie with the Red Sox and Athletics, each of whom was victorious in five series. The Yanks now have captured 20 of their last 25 series games and no club in either league, in two years, has even seriously challenged their supremacy. ∎

> CHAMPS! For the second straight year, the Yanks are baseball's best, a murderous, cocky crew, exploding all opposition.

"I'm just a ballplayer with one ambition and that is to give all I've got to help my ballclub win. I've never played any other way."
—Joe DiMaggio

Chapter 2

1938-1940

Becoming a Legend

*A*fter holding out on his contract and missing the first 12 games of the 1938 season, Joe DiMaggio finally gave in to Jacob Ruppert's "ultimatum" of a $25,000 salary. DiMag's ties to gambling guru Joe Gould also raised eyebrows among Yankee officials, but Joe held firm on his statement that the two were just casual "pals."

In 1939, all eyes continued to be on DiMaggio as his serious nature was studied and scrutinized. His private life off the field was in the spotlight as he married Hollywood starlet Dorothy Arnold on November 19, 1939, in a very public and overcrowded ceremony.

On the field, DiMaggio's play continued to be both cheered and jeered as fans struggled to understand the Clipper's style. In the end, though, respect was all that fans had for him, as Joltin' Joe led his team to World Series championships in 1938 and 1939. He also was voted the American League MVP for the first time in his career in 1939 and led the league in batting average in 1939 and 1940.

Meanwhile, after a long struggle with ALS, fellow Yankee great Lou Gehrig benched himself, ending his consecutive-game streak at 2,130 in 1939. ■

1938 REGULAR SEASON

G	AB	R	H	2B	3B	HR	RBI	BB	SB	AVG.	SLG.
145	599	129	194	32	13	32	140	59	6	.324	.581

1939 REGULAR SEASON

G	AB	R	H	2B	3B	HR	RBI	BB	SB	AVG.	SLG.
120	462	108	176	32	6	30	126	52	3	.381*	.671

1940 REGULAR SEASON

G	AB	R	H	2B	3B	HR	RBI	BB	SB	AVG.	SLG.
132	508	93	179	28	9	31	133	61	1	.352*	.626

*led American League

DiMaggio "Signs!" Reports Saturday

By Jack Mahon
April 21, 1938

Joe DiMaggio ended his "publicity" holdout when the Yankee office announced yesterday the slugging Italian outfielder had agreed to accept Col. Jake Ruppert's $25,000 "ultimatum." DiMaggio promptly left San Francisco. He will arrive here Saturday, and will confer with Ruppert on Monday, when he is expected to sign a "prop contract" for the benefit of newsreel photographers at Jake's Third Ave. brewery.

If Joe's condition is satisfactory to Manager Joe McCarthy, he probably will make his first start Tuesday or Wednesday against the Athletics in Philadelphia.

Uncle Egbert Barrow broke down and confessed Joe had finally seen the light. DiMaggio called him at the Yankees' New York office and said he was willing to play for 25 G's.

As Ed tells it, he refused to be misled by this startling change of heart on the part of his star pupil and told Joe, "Don't write—telegraph Jacob Ruppert."

Joe did so and wired "Accept your terms. Leaving San Francisco today." When Barrow got the confirmation, he promptly called Boston to inform McCarthy and slumbering newspapermen of the "big news."

Barrow indignantly denied Ruppert had offered Joe any more than $25,000. "There were no bonus offers or anything else discussed," he said. "The conversation was brief. You can't talk for long on the long distance, you know. Joe didn't say anything other than he had decided to play and would be satisfied with $25,000. Of course he will lose his pay until he is ready to play.

Ed didn't know how much Joe would sacrifice, though the amount has been estimated at $162 per day. Thus ends another typical baseball ballyhoo stunt. The end, appropriately, came on an off day, just prior to the opening of the Yankees' home season with the Senators at the Stadium tomorrow.

May we be so rash as to suggest, however, that the signing is a "build-up" for the first Sunday game of the year? DiMaggio's supposed "excessive demands" and Ruppert's repeated "final offers" have had the fans all steamed up during the past few months. There are almost as many hoping to see Joe flop as there are others joyfully welcoming him back.

The Yankees, remember, were shut out with three hits by the Dodgers and lost two of three exhibition games to them last week. They lost two of their first three season games to the Red Sox, suffering a two-hit shutout on Tuesday.

Then, as every passing day enhanced his great "holdout" value, DiMaggio (who demanded $40,000, then $30,000 and not a penny less!) suddenly decides to sign for 25 G's. Perhaps it's that old team spirit!

P.S. Joe's "publicity holdout" began January 21, '38. The *News* of January 6 announced he had signed in July '37 for—of all things—$25,000! ∎

> Uncle Egbert Barrow broke down and confessed Joe had finally seen the light. DiMaggio called him at the Yankees' New York office and said he was willing to play for 25 Gs.

AP/Wide World Photos

Joe DiMaggio, left, stellar slugger and outfielder of the Yankees, comes to grips with the Yankee boss, Col. Jacob Ruppert, right. After holding out for $40,000, he signed for $25,000 on April 25, 1938, in New York. The beaming face above the pair belongs to Ed Barrow, Yankee secretary.

Landis May Probe Gould-DiMag Duo

By Dick McCann
April 28, 1938

Joe Gould's alleged connection with Joe DiMaggio may be aired by Judge Landis, it was reported here today. The Commissioner is also interested in the talk that racing interests may have something to do with the Yankee outfielder's career, it was said.

Gould, manager of Jimmy Braddock and also known as an "inside man" on several sports activities in the East, has glibly denied he has any interests in DiMaggio. "We're just pals," Gould declared.

Gould recently admitted, however, that he had advised DiMaggio to sign for the $25,000 offered by the Yanks.

When DiMaggio arrived in New York to join the Yanks, after his so-called "holdout," he was spirited off the train in Newark by Gould and went immediately to Braddock's New York restaurant for breakfast.

Ever evasive, Landis said, "This is the first time I have heard of it." However, it is believed the probe is already under way.

Several years ago Landis forced the late Charles Stoneham, owner of the Giants, and John McGraw to relinquish their interests in a Havana race track. ■

DiMaggio's ties to "inside man" Joe Gould, pictured here, raised some eyebrows in the Yankee organization.

Daily News

DiMag Sparks Yankees to Victory

By Jack Smith
May 7, 1938

As DiMag goes, so go the Yanks. This is more than a trick—trickle of words—it's fact. One week ago, the 'Frisco wonder stepped into the lineup. His team was in fourth place. They had played shabby, disheartening .500 ball. With Joe DiMag came new life, new spirit, eager enthusiasm. Joe belted three homers, the Yanks won four out of five. Today, rarin' to go against the Tigers at Yankee Stadium, they stand one and a half games from first place.

How much does DiMaggio mean to the Yanks? On the record, Joe represents the difference between an easily won pennant and a long, tough battle. It is no coincidence that the Yanks have surged from the second division to second place since the appearance of 'Frisco's favorite son in the batting box.

The Yanks engaged in 12 games without DiMaggio. During that stretch they played .500 ball, were shut out once, held to one run twice and hit only four homers. Rolfe and Dickey were the only hitters over .300. Gehrig was in the worst slump of his career. Selkirk, Henrich, Crosetti and Gordon were in the doldrums. The Yanks scored only 48 runs in those games, never going into double figures, for an average of four per game.

Notice the difference in the figures for the six games in which DiMag has played. The Yanks won five of the six for .833, collecting 34 runs, an average of 5.6 per game. They have a four-game victory streak. They raised their total of homers to 11, hitting round-trippers in five straight games. ■

> How much does DiMaggio mean to the Yanks? On the record, Joe represents the difference between an easily won pennant and a long, tough battle.

Fans line up for Joe DiMaggio's autograph after a game.

Charles Hoff, Daily News

Jeers or Cheers?

By Bob Brumby
May 30, 1938

Mike Angelo splashed some pretty fair oil on canvas during his heyday, and it's too bad the great Italian isn't around. He could teach his fellow countryman, Joe DiMaggio, something about color and, though even his closest friends won't tell Giuseppe, color is something he is fresh out of. When Joe was jeered at the Stadium after finally reporting, many attributed the Bronx serenade to the San Franciscan's so-called "holdout." But it seems obvious the resentment lay deeper in the hearts of the half-a-buck prompters in the bleachers.

Today Joe must face his public and the sullen Italian, like the culprit in Monday morning court, knows he's got something coming, but not just what. His dogtrot into center field may bring cheers or it may rouse jeers. More than likely the iconoclastic element will be in the majority, for only as short a time ago as Saturday, the $25,000 slugger went hitless in five tries. He better not repeat that peccadillo today before the capacity crowd sure to jam the Stadium when the desiccated Yanks match bats with the gaudy Red Sox. If our hero is so thoughtless, some of the ruder citizens perched in the sun pavilion may crown Joseph with a bit of his favorite vegetable, known in the better circles of Mulberry Bend as broccoli.

Joe is a magnificent athlete and a very likable companion when you get to know him. Realizing this, and that sports fans want their idols to be flesh and blood human beings, it seems a shame DiMaggio doesn't cash in on this elementary and latent asset. For instance, recently at the Stadium, Joe slapped a terrific double into left field. Trying to stretch the hit into a three-bagger, DiMaggio was nabbed at third. He made a daring slide and the raucous cheers died into sympathetic silence. The stage was set for a bit of drama. But Joe, instead of showing the slightest vestige of emotion, merely climbed to his feet, dusted his pantaloons and strode to the dugout.

Every one, down to the pug-nosed urchin peeping through a keyhole, knows DiMaggio has never "soldiered" in his life. He is always in there giving his best, working in sweet coordination with his teammates on the field. Yet he definitely loses much popularity because the fans feel Joe is merely out there doing a job of work.

The fans aren't too dumb to realize that baseball is purely, and not so simply, a commercial enterprise and that players are bartered like watermelons at a camp meeting. Still, the average fan, like you or me or Master Joe Doakes, likes to think the athletes are playing a game and not clerking behind a ribbon counter. DiMaggio spends a lot of time around Hollywood. Maybe eventually he will pick up some histrionic finesse. We hope so, for he's a nice guy and a great ball player.

Powerhouse

By Jimmy Powers
October 1, 1938

Morning mail:
"Try to understand Joe DiMaggio a little bit better than you do, Jimmy, and you will find him a pretty nice young man. It is unfair to mention Greenberg-for-DiMaggio because there are 2,000,000 Jews in New York and naturally you received a bigger response when you asked if they'd prefer a change. Of course they would. Can you really blame Joe for trying for more money? His only mistake was holding out too long when his teammates needed him. He's made up for it. Be fair."

I think I do understand Joe DiMaggio. He and Bill Terry are alike in many respects. They frankly look upon baseball as a business. They believe their batting and fielding averages should speak for themselves. They are not "smoothies" in the sense that they know when to turn on a smile for the photos, wave a friendly hand at a cheering grandstand, or suppress annoyance at a jostling crowd of autograph hounds.

I think both are short-sighted in this, for the extra effort is slight and it reaps fat dividends.

Lately both have made belated attempts to appease "the mob," but it is evident their hearts are not in their handshakes.

Joe DiMaggio is a great ball player. He has a fine arm, a keen eye, diamond brains and power. Joe should be sitting on top of the world. Naturally he feels underpaid with his $25,000 salary.

"So, I'm only worth 25 G's, eh?" he probably mumbled to himself. "Well, that's the kind of ball I'll give 'em, $25,000 worth, and not a penny more."

Another mistake Joe made was his clash with Tony Lazzeri and Frank Crosetti when he first came up. The older Italians made friendly overtures, but Joe would have little to do with them.

"Leave him alone, boys," said Tony one afternoon. "He knows it all."

Unconsciously, Poosh-Em-Up was right. Joe DID know it all.

So you can see how Joe went. Sudden fame, never a tough year, minor jealousies on the part of dugout companions, a premature agreement in '37 to sign for $25,000, discontent with his contract and then—Joe Gould!

Joe DiMaggio was warned by his bosses that it was impolitic to be seen, not in the company of Joe Gould particularly, but in the company of the leading lights of the fight racket, the professional gamblers, fixers, touts, ex-convicts, house referees, grafters and assorted hoodlums who make up the fringe of pugilistic "society."

To the young man from the Coast these were probably glamour figures on the outskirts of a sort of Edward G. Robinson underworld.

Stubbornly, he refused to part company with them. Out of mistaken loyalty to his pal, Joe Gould, he stuck.

In justice to a young outfielder it must be written that he was too young to appreciate the import of the Black Sox scandal. The business office tried to point out that it would be just as fatal for the Yankee star to be seen dining in the same restaurant at the same table with Sam Boston or Abe Attell as it would for Umpire Beans Reardon to go poker-playing with George Weinberg.

Is it any wonder that when DiMaggio kept doggedly growling, "My pals are my pals, and what I do after I leave the clubhouse is my business" that Ruppert and Barrow and McCarthy threw up their hands in despair.

In a way, Joe is right. In a way, the club is right. And meanwhile Greenberg-for-DiMaggio talk grows and grows. The Italian's friends along Cauliflower Row and his other, and far more loyal, fans along Mulberry Bend, wonder what the hell has happened and is somebody crazy to even think of trading off a great star like old Joe? ∎

Yankees Whip Cubs, 8-3

Win Third Straight World Series

By Hy Turkin
October 10, 1938

WINNER AND STILL CHAMPION—THE YANKS! Making experts of all who dubbed them the greatest team in baseball history, the New Yorkers completed their coup at the Stadium yesterday. They crushed the Cubs, 8-3, to sweep the series and become the first club to win three straight world titles. Chicago again was outhit, outpitched, outfielded, outpowered. Even the 59,847 customers grimaced at the shambles. The Butcher Boys of Broadway slaughtered six pitchers for 11 hits (18 total bases), with at least one for each swinger. Red Ruffing encored his strong-arm triumph of last Wednesday. With the affair on the verge of becoming a contest, the Brewer's Big Horses rode over four flingers in the eighth for four runs. Arm-sore Dizzy Dean finally had to be flagged from the bullpen to save the Cubs from further humiliation.

At the head of the hickory brigade was Frankie Crosetti. The Series hero—all his binges have gone for extra bases, all his fielding plays have been four-star spectacles—clouted a double and triple to score four runs. Baby-Face Henrich was the only Yank to find the home-run range.

Big Bill Lee, humbled by Ruffing in the opener, bowed again. He hurled the first three frames and allowed three tainted tallies. Then followed a powerless pitching parade, including Root, Page, French, Carleton and Dean.

In the home half of the eighth, the Baseball Gods got out the hurdy-gurdy and made the Cubs dancing fools. The losers staged a woeful exhibition that must have made bench-riding Manager Hartnett itch to get to the mound.

> In the home half of the eighth, the Baseball Gods got out the hurdy-gurdy and made the Cubs dancing fools.

The bat-around rally began with Henrich's fly to center. Then came the first base hit yielded by Rookie Vance Page. It was DiMaggio's savage single to left.

To end the rough-house by passing Gordon to get to the pitcher. But the fun was only beginning. Another wild pitch permitted Hoag to reach third. Gordon stole second while the catcher held the ball. When Ruffing received a ticket, loading the sacks, Dizzy Dean climbed over the bullpen gate.

The crowd ceased its derisive pastime of littering the field with confettied scorecards and newspapers, and wildly acclaimed the Great One. Mr. $185,000 faced Crosetti, whose homer had cost him the second game. Frank continued his hex by lifting a high fly which Demaree failed to reach after a mad rush inward. The ball fell for a two-run double. End of the massacre came when Collins collared Rolfe's liner. ■

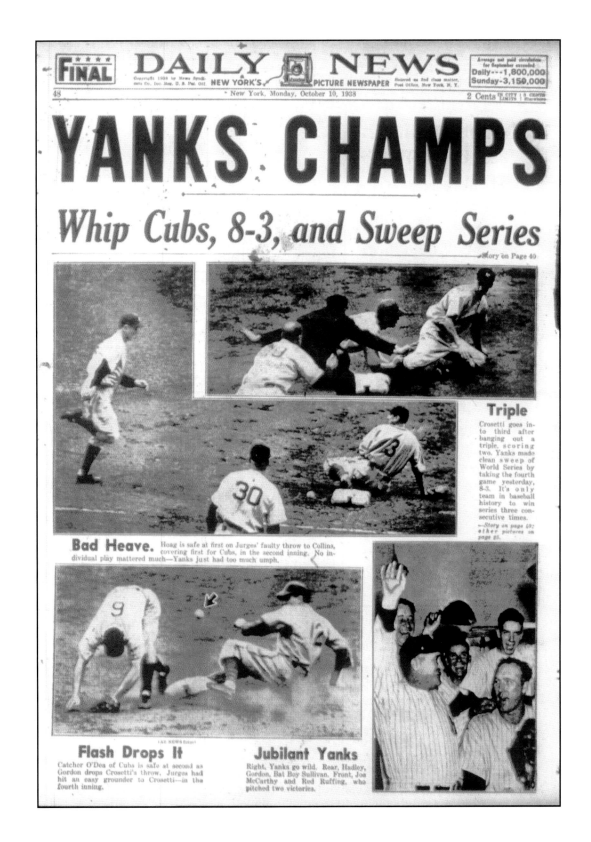

Joe DiMaggio to Marry Blonde Movie Actress

April 26, 1939

Dead Pan Joe DiMaggio, the New York Yankees' slugging outfielder, is in love with Dorothy Arnold, 21, slender, deep-voiced blonde of the movies, and before many more months have passed they'll be Mr. and Mrs.

Dorothy's inability to keep the secret any longer set the wires abuzzing today and elicited a response from Joe that made it appear, for a time, that he was playing holdout at love.

Joe, who was busy getting two hits and two runs in four times at bat against the Athletics in New York, finally straightened everything out this way:

"There is no official engagement, but we may get married next fall, or possibly winter, depending on how everything goes."

And Dorothy said:

"It seems silly to be talking this way about so intimate a thing as love, but I guess that's what happens when you get engaged to somebody very important. We really aren't formally engaged. I haven't a ring or anything. It's just understood."

Dorothy, who is on contract at the Universal Studio, said she met Joe in New York in August 1937, while she was "just sort of scenery" in a picture Joe made at the Biograph Studio in the Bronx.

"'That's a nice looking fellow,' I said," she related. "'Who is he?' Everybody looked startled and somebody said, 'Why, that's Joe DiMaggio,' and I said, 'So what?' So you see, I fell in love with him before I knew he was a celebrity. We started going around together and the first thing we knew—at least I knew—it was getting hotter."■

Hollywood starlet Dorothy Arnold cheers on husband-to-be Joe DiMaggio.

Daily News

DiMag Hurt, Yanks Lose to Nats, 3-1

By Jack Smith
April 30, 1939

Lady Luck continued to walk arm and arm with our Yanks yesterday, despite a 3-1 shellacking handed to them by Lefty Gomez of the Senators at the Stadium. Joe DiMaggio, the champs' belting beauty, narrowly escaped serious injury—the third Yank to outfeint fate in four days—when he crashed to the slippery turf in the third inning. He was chasing Bobby Estalella's line drive which bounded to his right. As he turned, his spikes caught in the wet grass and he fell on his back. He rolled over in anguish and climbed slowly to his feet. Limping painfully off the field, DiMaggio appeared to be badly hurt, with possibly a broken bone in the million-dollar legs.

Doc Painter, Yankee trainer, and fellow players rushed to the stricken player's aid. Then, while the crowd waited in stunned silence, DiMaggio was helped to the clubhouse where club physician Robert E. Walsh made a cursory examination before taking him to St. Elizabeth's Hospital.

Word spread among the 11,473 fans that DiMaggio had broken his leg and would be out for a month or more. Then good old Dame Luck walked into the picture, smiled benignly as she did when it appeared Red Ruffing and Flash Gordon were doomed by injuries earlier in the week—and X-ray examination at the hospital proved Joe had suffered only a separation of leg muscles from the bone.

He probably will be able to play again in a week or ten days, which brought a sigh of relief both to the fans and manager McCarthy.

DiMaggio was happiest of the lot.

"I thought I heard a bone snap as I nose-dived," Joe said during the clubhouse exam, "and I said to myself, boy, hellzapoppin again down in that ol' leg (he missed the '34 season in the Pacific Coast League due to a knee injury) and was I glad when those X-rays told a different tale."

After leaving the hospital in the company of Dr. Walsh, DiMaggio was able to return to his hotel, though the leg was swollen considerably above the knee. He will remain here for treatment when the Yanks leave on their first Western trip Monday. ■

> "I thought I heard a bone snap as I nose-dived," Joe said during the clubhouse exam, "and I said to myself, boy, hellzapoppin again down in that ol' leg (he missed the '34 season in the Pacific Coast League due to a knee injury) and was I glad when those X-rays told a different tale."

Paralysis Ends Gehrig's Career

By Jimmy Powers
June 22, 1939

A tiny "polio" germ that gets into the spinal cord, dulls the reflexes and slows down all the motor nerves of the arms and legs has definitely ended the playing career of Lou Gehrig.

Gehrig arrived at Yankee Stadium yesterday at 12:30 p.m. and greeted newspapermen with a cheery smile. He held an envelope in his hand. It was the sealed verdict of doctors from the famed Mayo Clinic at Rochester, Minnesota, where Lou had undergone a triple-checked examination. Lou went into the clubhouse where other Yanks, in various stages of undress, set up a great cheer of greeting. Lou then entered manager McCarthy's office with president Ed Barrow. A few minutes later, McCarthy called reporters in.

"Gentlemen," began Barrow solemnly, "we have bad news. Gehrig has infantile paralysis. The technical word for his illness is chronic poliomyelitis. Gehrig has been given a chart of exercises and a list of doctors by the Mayo Clinic. Lou will be given treatment throughout the summer, as the list covers all cities the Yankees will visit. The report recommends that Lou abandon any hope of continuing as an active player."

Lou was tight-lipped and his handsome face was drawn as Barrow told of the strange scourge that so mysteriously ended his career. Louis was 36 last Monday. He will be kept on the active player list and paid his full salary of $35,000 for the rest of the season. Then he will probably be given his unconditional release.

Later, in the clubhouse, Gehrig sat lacing his dusty, spiked shoes, confiding quietly in big Bill Dickey, his pal and roommate on the road. Trying to be courteous but very patiently anxious to avoid irritating questions, Louis said he had only a list of exercises to take. No medicine. And he did not know the details of the treatments he was to receive.

"I don't know any more than you do," he said. "They told me the doctors I'm to visit in each city have been advised and I'll find out more when I report to them."

Gehrig said the doctors did not tell him when he contracted the chronic infantile paralysis. Or where. He feels that he has had it for at least two years and he believes the disease can be checked and that it will not get any worse.

Lou first felt something was wrong when he had connected squarely with a ball and failed to drive it out of the park. He was known for his terrific power at the plate in the setting of his 2,130 consecutive games record. When he walked off the field, voluntarily benching himself in Detroit May 2, he said he felt "weak as a baby."

At Rochester, Minnesota, it was learned that Lou received the verdict "bravely." He gave no evidence that he felt depressed when he attended an informal birthday party there. And one of his last acts at the airport was to smile, shake hands with a small boy and autograph a ten-cent baseball for him.

"I am ready to adjust myself to this new condition in my life," he told his examining chief physician.

Thus ends the most amazing career in modern baseball. Lou Gehrig came up as a wide-eyed schoolboy pitcher and hero of Commerce High. Later he pitched and played the outfield for Columbia University.

Following his graduation, Lou played with Hartford. He was brought to the Yankees in '23 and

> "I am ready to adjust myself to this new condition in my life."
> —Lou Gehrig

As his teammates warm up, Lou Gehrig looks on after taking to the bench on May 2, 1939, at his own request. This marked the end of Gehrig's consecutive-game streak at 2,130.

played in 13 games. Shipped back to Hartford, Lou batted .369 the next season.

On June 1, 1925, Miller Huggins signaled for the big German youth to pinch-hit for Paul (Pee Wee) Wanninger, the regular shortstop, and Lou singled. The next day he replaced Wally Pipp at first base.

From that June day down through the years of blazing heat, aching muscles, dim grey dampness and heart-breaking defeat, the Iron Horse lumbered—a steady, dependable workman, a tower of strength and an inspiration to his teammates.

For 14 years, through all sorts of baseball luck, the big fellow was out there, cajoling and driving his mates and lending his fiery competitive spirit to the building of the greatest team baseball has ever known. Then, last fall, as the Yankees prepared to sweep to the third straight world championship, the spring began to go from the big fellow's step. He found it hard to get around and the baseball reporters saw the shadows lengthening over his determined head.

This year, however, Lou was back there again. But when the time came, neither the baseball writ-

ers, his manager nor his teammates had to tell him. As the Yankees prepared to open a Western invasion at Briggs Stadium, Detroit, Lou told manager McCarthy, personally, that he wanted to bench himself—for the good of the team. Then, and only then, did the Iron Horse stop after 2,130 consecutive games—the longest streak in baseball history.

And so yesterday, as his silent teammates went forth to meet the White Sox in the second game of their series, the Big Fellow was still out there with them. He didn't take part in the practice, being content to sit in a cool part of the dugout and watch the headline heroes of today on their way to a record-breaking fourth straight pennant.

And framed there, shielded from the roar of the crowd, Lou Gehrig will sit for the rest of the summer and watch his last baseball year roll by. ■

Yankees Rip Reds, 7-3, for 3d in Row with Four Homers

By Hy Turkin and Harry Forbes
October 8, 1939

Home run lightning from Yankee bats spread crackling terror over Cincinnati today, the Bronx high voltage crew bolting to their third-straight World Series decision over the Reds, 7-3. A sellout crowd of 32,723, watching the first Series game there in 20 years, was stunned by the celestial exhibition of power. Rookie Charley Keller blasted two homers into the right field bleachers, each time with one aboard. Big Bill Dickey cracked one to right center. And when Joe DiMaggio zoomed one over the center field fence, the ball ricocheted off the curbstone and skipped up York St., where it was retrieved by scrambling youngsters almost 600 feet from home plate.

In moving to within a game of their fourth straight world championship, the Yanks struck infrequently, but wisely and too well. Exactly five hits kayoed Junior Thompson, rookie right hander who had never been in a fall classic (and probably wishes he still retained that distinction). Lee Grissom and

Whitey Moore pitched hitless relief ball by retiring the last 13 men in order.

The Reds rang up twice as many hits, but all ten were singles. ∎

Joe DiMaggio slides safely into the plate with the run that tied the score in the ninth inning of the fourth and final game of the 1939 World Series at Crosley Field in Cincinnati.

AP/Wide World Photos

Yanks Win 4th

By Hy Turkin and Harry Forbes
October 9, 1939

Cincinnati—The Yankees won their fourth straight world championship here this afternoon. For the second successive year they swept the series in four games and today left the Reds a battered and disillusioned wreck of what was once a fighting ball team. Dissipating a two-run lead in the ninth inning and committing four vital errors when they had a great chance to salvage one game in the series, the Reds completely folded. The Yankees crashed through in the tenth inning, ran the bases like madmen, and were presented with a 7-4 victory just as 32,794 thought Cincinnati could prevent the humiliation of losing every game.

Billy Myers became one of the greatest goats in the history of the World Series. He fumbled a certain double-play throw in the ninth inning which should have gotten Bucky Walters out of a jam and easily enabled the Reds to win in regulation time. And, in the tenth, the Reds shortstop made another important fumble which completed the downfall. The utter collapse was illustrated in bold relief a moment later when Joe DiMaggio circled the bases on a single without stopping and Ernie Lombardi let the ball lie two feet from the plate without making a move for it.

He was through—and so were a once-gallant band of Reds.

Up to the time of the downfall, the Reds had outfought the champions. They overcame a two-run deficit to take the lead in the seventh. It seemed certain that Walters, who relieved Paul Derringer when the latter was lifted for a hitter in the big Red inning, could hold the lead. But his teammates couldn't stand the terrific pressure and, like every club before them, fell apart at the seams. When victory was almost theirs, they fumbled grounders, threw to the wrong bases and, as Lombardi so vividly illustrated, just plain quit in the face of baseball's greatest collection of stars.

Once again Charley Keller wears the hero's laurel. The classic's greatest individual star hit his third homer in two days in the seventh inning to break a scoreless deadlock. He started the ninth-inning rally with a single and reached base in the final frame on Myers' second error.

Bill Dickey, the game's greatest catcher, also continued to share the spotlight with the youngster who was playing for the University of Maryland only three years ago. Dickey followed the 23-year-old outfielder's homer with another blast of his own, his second in as many days. Dickey's was only the third hit off Derringer—but Paul was two runs behind.

For Oral Hildebrand and Steve Sundra had collaborated to check the Reds, despite their tendency to yield hits. Hildebrand, who started, had to stop in the fourth because of a pain in his side.

But the Reds weren't through. Rolfe almost became the goat when he booted McCormick's smash in the seventh. Lombardi struck out, but Simmons, who supplanted Craft in the fifth when the latter had an upset stomach, doubled. McCormick scored on Berger's infield out. After Myers walked, Hershberger, ex-Yankee farmhand, got a pinch-hit single, DiMaggio just failing to make a shoestring catch. Simmons scored the tying

> The utter collapse was illustrated in bold relief a moment later when Joe DiMaggio circled the bases on a single without stopping and Ernie Lombardi let the ball lie two feet from the plate without making a move for it.

39

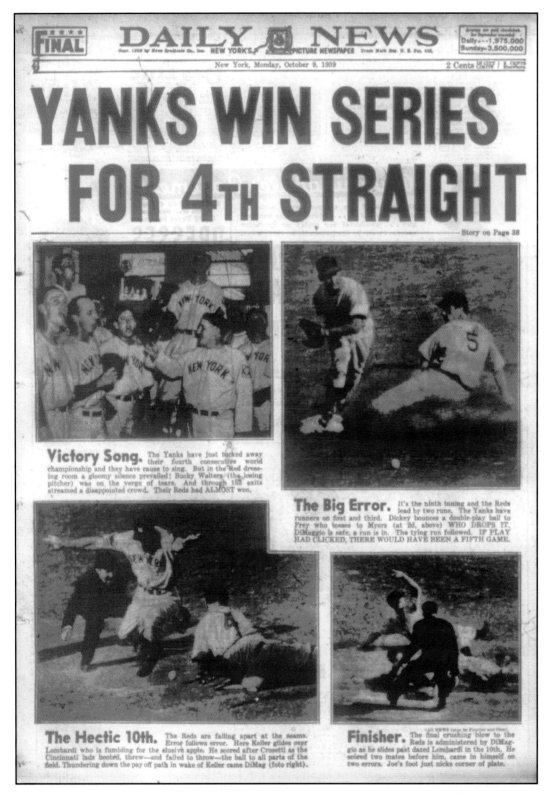

DAILY NEWS

FINAL

New York's PICTURE NEWSPAPER

New York, Monday, October 9, 1939   2 Cents

YANKS WIN SERIES FOR 4TH STRAIGHT

Story on Page 38

Victory Song. The Yanks have just tucked away their fourth consecutive world championship and they have cause to sing. But in the Red dressing room a gloomy silence prevailed; Bucky Walters (the losing pitcher) was on the verge of tears. And through the exits streamed a disappointed crowd. Their Reds had ALMOST won.

The Big Error. It's the ninth inning and the Reds lead by two runs. The Yanks have runners on first and third. Dickey bounces a double-play ball to Frey who tosses to Myers (at 2d, above) WHO DROPS IT. DiMaggio is safe, a run is in. The tying run followed. IF PLAY HAD CLICKED, THERE WOULD HAVE BEEN A FIFTH GAME.

The Hectic 10th. The Reds are falling apart at the seams. Error follows error. Here Keller glides over Lombardi who is fumbling for the elusive apple. He scored after Crosetti as the Cincinnati lads booted, threw—and failed to throw—the ball to all parts of the field. Thundering down the pay off path in wake of Keller came DiMag (foto right).

Finisher. The final crushing blow to the Reds is administered by DiMaggio as he slides past dazed Lombardi in the 10th. He scored two mates before him, came in himself on two errors. Joe's foot just nicks corner of plate.

Then came the collapse. Keller and DiMaggio singled in the ninth. Dickey hit a roller to Frey and Myers missed the easy toss as Keller romped home. That was the break. DiMaggio reached third on Selkirk's drive to Goodman. Gordon then singled, DiMaggio kicking the ball from Lombardi's grasp as he slid into the plate.

Crosetti started the tenth with a walk and Rolfe sacrificed. Myers muffed Keller's easy grounder and Walters was in another terrific jam. DiMaggio singled to right and the farce reached its hilarious height—for Goodman let the ball roll through his leap. When he recovered, McCormick relayed the ball to the plate but Keller easily followed Crosetti over, again kicking Lombardi's outstretched hand.

Here's the picture. The big catcher rolled on the dirt in front of the dish. DiMaggio galloped around the bases. Homeward he came, with the ball within arm's reach of the catcher. Lombardi made a last-minute attempt to get the pellet and tag DiMag, but Joe slid across and Lombardi once again sat, apparently realizing the futility of it all.

It was the end. ■

run and Werber drove Myers home to give the Reds a 3-2 lead. Murphy stopped the rally by nailing Lonnie Frey, who didn't get a hit in any game.

Murphy, credited with the victory, yielded another run in the eighth when Goodman doubled, McCormick sacrificed and Lombardi singled.

DiMag Best in AL; Foxx 2d, Feller 3d

By Harry Forbes
October 25, 1939

Joe DiMaggio, for four years acknowledged the greatest player in baseball by fan and expert alike, finally received official recognition yesterday when he was voted the Most Valuable Player in the American League. In receiving an honor long overdue, the 24-year-old slugger from San Francisco's Fisherman's Wharf, received 280 points out of a possible 336 in the annual vote of the Baseball Writers' Association of America and will receive *The Sporting News* award next season.

DiMaggio, who led the league in batting with .381, drew 15 first-place votes from the 24 participating writers (three from each city), three for second, three for third, one for fourth and two for fifth. For three years DiMaggio, whose arrival with the Yankees in 1936 started them on their unsurpassed streak of four successive World Championships, has been shunned when the postseason honor was awarded.

For the past four seasons, no player has been more valuable to his club than the slugging Italian. His successive batting averages have been .323, .346, and .324 before his personal high of '39, when he failed to reach the coveted .400 goal because of his usual September slump added to this mark was a record of 126 runs batted in, 176 hits, including 30 homers, six triples and 32 doubles and 107 runs scored.

Jimmie Foxx, who won the award for the third time last year, finished second in the balloting with 170. ■

Mayor F. H. La Guardia of New York is shown presenting Joe DiMaggio with a gold watch and the award as the AL MVP during the 1939 season.

AP/Wide World Photos

Fans Swamp Church as DiMaggio Weds

November 20, 1939

Joe DiMaggio and Dorothy Arnold were married today in St. Peter and Paul Cathedral, and San Francisco's North Beach Italian population turned out for the show in a carnival spirit that jammed streets and broke police lines.

The wedding of the star New York Yankee outfielder and the Hollywood starlet brought thousands of laughing Italians to the cathedral. Standing room was at a premium in the church and the crowd overflowed into adjacent Washington Square.

Even the wedding party had to battle the crowd for 15 minutes to get inside the church. One woman fainted in the crush at the doorway. Although the wedding was called for 2 p.m., the bridesmaids could not get in until 2:14 and Miss Arnold and her father were even later.

Vince DiMaggio, brother of the bridegroom and an outfielder for the Cincinnati Reds, got locked out when police closed the doors. He and his wife later got in at a side door.

Miss Arnold was Protestant, but last Thursday was accepted into the Catholic faith and the service was read on the altar by Father Parolin.

Joe's brothers Vince and Dominic, both ball players, were ushers, and brother Tom, who always speaks for the famous family, was best man. Joe's four sisters were bridesmaids.

AP/Wide World Photos

Joe DiMaggio and his bride, the former Dorothy Arnold, cut their cake after their very public wedding ceremony in San Francisco.

DiMaggio Joins Yankees Camp, One Week Late

Old Glove and Young Bride Make Trip from Coast; Star "Ready in 10 Days"

By Rud Rennie
March 12, 1940

Joe DiMaggio, the Yankees' outstanding star, reported to camp today, a week late, and hastened to make up for lost time. He got into his uniform and took a light workout at Huggins Field while the team was in Tampa playing the Reds.

DiMaggio drove from San Francisco with his bride, the former Dorothy Arnold, and took up residence on the beach at Passagrille. It took him five days to make the trip.

Writers, greeting the arrival, remarked immediately that Joe looks younger. There was no explanation for this unless it's DiMaggio's "married life must agree with me."

The lean DiMag said he weighs 194 pounds, the same as at the end of last season. "What I want to do first," he said, "is get my leg in shape. I figure I'll be ready in ten days."

Someone reminded him that the All-Star game in Tampa was next Sunday. "Oh, yeah," he said. "I want to play in that, but I don't know whether I'll be ready."

> "What I want to do first is get my leg in shape. I figure I'll be ready in 10 days."
> —Joe DiMaggio

He picked up three gloves, two new ones and an old one, all patched and torn. "I guess I'll use a new one down here," he said, "and save that old one for the regular games. I feel comfortable with that glove. It's ripped because I catch the ball up in the webbing and the glove takes a beating that way. But it feels like an old rag and I like it. I never really wear a glove. I just let it hang on my hand."■

DiMag warms up at spring training camp after driving from San Francisco with his new bride.

AP/Wide World Photos

DiMaggio's Return to Duty Indefinite

Doctor Says Yankee Ace May Play within Week, but Joe Is Not So Hopeful

April 28, 1940

Joe DiMaggio's hopes of returning to the Yankee line-up in a few days were given a jolt today following an examination of his right knee injured in a preseason exhibition game with the Dodgers.

Dr. George Bennett, Baltimore bone specialist, said Joe might be able to play within a week, but the world champion's ace outfielder was not so optimistic. DiMaggio underwent the examination at Baltimore this morning, but was back with the Yanks when they opened a two-game series with the Senators.

"All I know," said Joe, "is that I can't run and the doctor told me not to try until the leg felt perfectly O.K. I was getting worried, so I decided to find out just what was the matter. It may be some time before I return to action."

Dr. Bennett, however, said the 1939 American League batting champion was well on the way to recovery.

"DiMaggio has an ordinary injury that any athlete would suffer from a wrenched knee," said the specialist. "His condition warrants no special treatment, and if proper care is taken Joe should be back in the line-up in a very short time." ■

> "All I know," said Joe, "is that I can't run and the doctor told me not to try until the leg felt perfectly O.K. I was getting worried, so I decided to find out just what was the matter. It may be some time before I return to action."

DiMaggio Wins Batting Crown in AL Again

Yankee Outfielder Leads with .352
Greenberg's 41 Homers Top Circuit

By Rud Rennie
December 18, 1940

The reason for the failure of the Yankees in their quest for their fifth straight pennant can be found in the official American League batting averages, released yesterday. The Yankees had only two regular players, Joe DiMaggio and Tommy Henrich, batting over .300. Henrich appeared in only 90 games. And the team was last in batting, with an average of .259. Even the A's outhit the Yankees.

Babe Ruth shows Billy Jurges (left)
and DiMaggio (center) a thing or
two about batting.

Virtually the entire team, noted for its power, fell into an inexplicable slump. Bill Dickey, Joe Gordon, Charlie Keller, Red Rolfe, George Selkirk were all off form. That lusty pinch-hitting pitcher, Red Ruffing, wound up with a measly .124 and Frank Crosetti, the regular shortstop, batted a cool .194.

If all the boys had been hitting, winning the pennant this year would have been a cinch for the Yankees. As it was, they scared the life out of the Detroit Tigers and the Cleveland Indians with a September drive.

In this drive DiMaggio went on a batting spree which carried him past Rip Radcliff of the Browns, and Luke Appling of the White Sox, into the batting championship for the second year in succession.

DiMaggio led the league with .352. This was 29 points under his average in 1939, but it was enough to top such good hitters as Radcliff, Appling, Ted Williams and Jimmie Foxx of Boston, and Barney McCosky and Hank Greenberg of Detroit.

When it was all over, Appling was second with .348, Williams was third with .344, Radcliff, who had led the league for the greater part of the year, was fourth with .342, and McCosky and Greenberg were tied for fifth place at .340. Foxx, one of the league's really great batters, slipped down to .297.

Even with his September drive, DiMaggio would not have won the batting championship if he had not had a spell in July in which he batted safely in 23 consecutive games. He finished his year with 179 hits, 31 home runs and a total of 318 bases. ■

No. 5 "The Yankee Clipper".

Chapter 3

1941

The Magical Season

Nineteen hundred forty-one was truly a momentous year in American and world history. Under third-term President Franklin Delano Roosevelt, the United States officially entered World War II after Japanese warplanes blasted the port of Pearl Harbor, the Philippines, and Wake and Guam Islands. Three days later, as allies of Japan, Germany and Italy declared war on America.

Stateside, the Federal Communications Commission licensed its first two commercial TV stations—NBC and CBS—in New York City. On the radio airwaves and in big band dance halls, Glenn Miller's "Chattanooga Choo Choo" topped the hit parade. And, on the big screen, The Maltese Falcon, Citizen Kane and Walt Disney's Dumbo *captivated American moviegoers.*

At the various sports stadiums, there were headline makers, too. The Chicago Bears won the National Football League championship, defeating the New York Giants, 37-9. Joe Louis, "The Brown Bomber," defended his heavyweight boxing title on multiple occasions. And on the baseball diamond, while rookies Stan Musial and Phil Rizzuto made their debuts, Ted Williams of the Boston Red Sox helped the American League All-Stars beat the Nationals with a dramatic home run in the bottom of the ninth. When the season ended, "The Splendid Splinter" had compiled a .406 batting average. No player has since eclipsed the .400 mark.

However, the biggest story in sports was authored by the Yankees' Joe DiMaggio with his magical 56-game hitting streak. Here are the details of his greatest individual season. ∎

1941 REGULAR SEASON

G	AB	R	H	2B	3B	HR	RBI	BB	SB	AVG.	SLG.
139	541	122	193	43	11	30	125*	76	4	.357	.643

*tied American League

DiMag Gets $35,000; Reports Next Week

By Jack Smith
March 7, 1941

The Coast-to-Coast purse-string tug-of-war between Joe DiMaggio and Ed Barrow heaved to a happy ending here today when it was announced the slugging outfielder and his boss had agreed on terms. From his San Francisco restaurant, DiMag notified Barrow in New York he would leave home tomorrow and would reach camp early next week.

With the Yanks' usual secrecy, terms were not revealed, but camp guessers estimated Joe managed to wheedle a $2,000 raise out of his bosses and will receive $35,000 for his '41 efforts. He had been reported asking $40,000.

First in power, popularity and prestige among his teammates, DiMag again was the last to surrender in the wage war. This, in itself, was a defeat for Barrow, who had been determined to have the star center fielder in camp for the first day of training, hoping that, with sufficient conditioning, Joe would be in shape to play a full season. Last year, Joe missed 22 games and the year before 34 games.

However, lackadaisical DiMag, who despises the sweaty efforts of spring training, will again miss some valuable hours under the St. Petersburg sun. Joe already has lost five days of training and will hardly be ready to play exhibition games until the middle of next week.

This starts Joe's sixth year with the club—six profitable seasons as both the records and his bank account prove. His lifetime batting average (.343) is second only to Jimmie Foxx's (.344) among active players. For five consecutive seasons, he has driven in 125 or more runs and hit 24 or more homers. Excepting Bob Feller, he's the best gate attraction in the game. ∎

> This starts Joe's sixth year with the club—six profitable seasons as both the records and his bank account prove. His lifetime batting average (.343) is second only to Jimmie Foxx's (.344) among active players.

The 56-Game Hitting Streak Begins . . .

Yankees Lose 5th in Row as Chisox Romp, 13-1

By Dick McCann
May 16, 1941

The Yankees held secret practice at the Stadium yesterday morning, and they should've made the ball game that followed a secret, too. During the afternoon, the White Sox handed them their fifth straight beating by the ghastly score of 13-1. The defeat, besides disgusting the 9,040 hooting and hissing customers, dumped the Yanks beneath the .500 mark.

Their only run was rationed in the first, which Phil Rizzuto opened with a convincing double to right. Red Rolfe and Charley Keller flied out, but Joe DiMaggio got his first hit in three days, a single to left that scored Rizzuto. ■

New York Yankees' Batting Order the Day Joe DiMaggio's Streak Began

May 15, 1941

Phil Rizzuto, shortstop
Red Rolfe, third base
Charlie Keller, left field
Joe DiMaggio, center field
Joe Gordon, first base
Warren Rosar, catcher
Stanley Bordagaray, right field
Jerry Priddy, second base
Ernie Bonham, pitcher

Longest Yankee Consecutive-Game Hitting Streaks

(Before DiMaggio's 1941 streak)

33 games . . . Harold Chase, 1907
29 games . . . Roger Peckinpaugh, 1919
29 games . . . Earle Combs, 1931
26 games . . . Babe Ruth, 1921
23 games . . . Joe DiMaggio, 1940
22 games . . . Joe DiMaggio, 1937
21 games . . . Wally Pipp, 1923

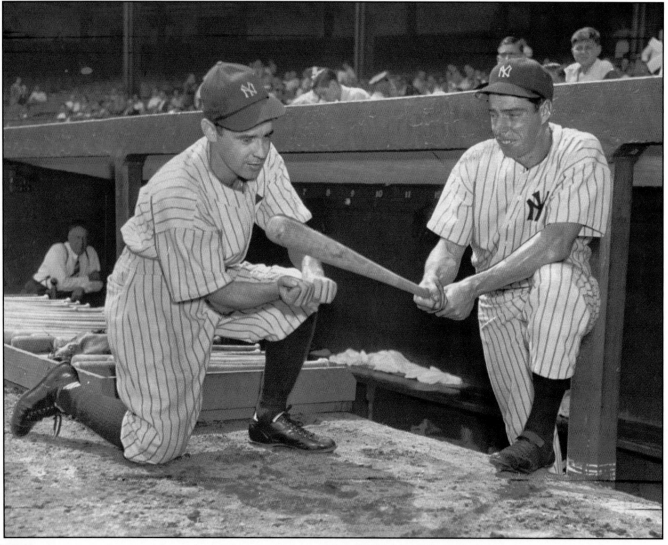

Daily News

Joe DiMaggio gives some hitting tips to Daily News reporter Joe Mathias.

Gehrig Funeral This Morning

By Dick McCann
June 4, 1941

With his city's flags fluttering at half-staff and the whole town mourning him, funeral services will be held at 10 o'clock this morning for Lou Gehrig at Christ Episcopal Church.

The services will be private, with only his family, a few fast friends and some distinguished members of the baseball and civic worlds present. The Rev. Gerald V. Barry, Christ Church pastor, will officiate.

Following the services, the remains will be cremated at Fresh Pond Crematory, Middle Village, L.I. This is believed to be the fulfillment of one of Lou's last requests.

Last night, the once-powerful body of the man who played 2,130 consecutive games for the Yanks, from June 2, 1925, until May 2, 1939, lay in state at Christ Church in the Riverdale section of the Bronx. While an unbroken stream of heartbroken fans came to console at the Gehrig home, 5,000 fans forming a line three blocks long, filed past the bier between 8 and 10 p.m.

Among those who viewed Gehrig's body was Babe Ruth who stood with bowed head in front of the remains of his former teammate. Ruth broke down and cried. He was led to another room where it was several minutes before he regained his composure.

Lou was laid out in a blue business suit with a fine pencil stripe. Reports that he had wasted away in his last days seemed false. There were a few gray hairs at his temples. And his dimpled face seemed to have a trace of a smile of thankfulness that the

National Baseball Hall of Fame

Henry Louis Gehrig, 1903-1941.

painful ordeal of the past two years was done with.

Radio, which roared out Gehrig's name in every household through the land during his sensational World Series performances with the Yanks, paid him a last tribute at 6:45 o'clock last night when the NBC radio network took mourning fans around the circuit to hear Lou's former teammates, former AL foes, and other baseball figures pay tribute to his memory. Heard on the program were Dickey, Red Ruffing, Lefty Gomez and Joe DiMaggio, speaking from Briggs Stadium in Detroit, where the stunned Yanks were beaten by the Tigers.

There were small boys who had scurried after him for autographs, and old men who had grudgingly admitted that he was better than the best of the old-timers. There were grimy-fisted truck-drivers, still in their working clothes; and richly-dressed corporation presidents. It was, in fact, the typical kind of a crowd that surged to the Yankee Stadium in the days when Gehrig was setting his slugging and durability records which probably never will be broken and certainly never forgotten. ∎

Yankee legend Lou Gehrig died after suffering for two years with the degenerative disease ALS (amyotrophic lateral sclerosis), now known as Lou Gehrig's Disease. Family, friends and fans paid tribute to him as they mourned the loss of one of their heroes.

Sox Stop Yanks, 8-7;
DiMag Hits in 30th

By Jack Smith
June 18, 1941

Alas, poor winning streak! It looked nice for awhile, shiny and promising, stretched to eight straight games by the surging Yanks. But last evening it lay shattered on the Stadium diamond, blasted, 8-7, by the White Sox before 10,442 mourners. Only Joe DiMaggio salvaged consolation from the afternoon. A lucky, bad hop single in the seventh extended his hitting skein to 30 consecutive games. Joe probably would have given up even that though for the chance to spear Myril Hoag's looping single which drove in the winning run for the Sox in the ninth. ■

The picture-perfect stroke of
Joe DiMaggio.

Cobb Pulling for DiMag to Break Sisler's Mark

By Dick McCann
June 24, 1941

Ty Cobb is rooting for Joe DiMaggio to break George Sisler's 19-year-old record of hitting safely in 41 consecutive games. "A better fellow couldn't do it," said the one-time Georgia Peach yesterday as he stepped out here en route to Boston for the first of his series of charity golf matches with Babe Ruth. They play Thursday in the Hub and then tangle again at Fresh Meadow Country Club Friday.

"I like to see records broken," Cobb, who holds many of them, said. "The idea of a fellow having a chance to break a record increases interest in baseball. Of course, like Sisler, I like to see a genuine star break the records and not a fly-by-night sensation."

DiMaggio, Cobb said, is one of the greatest players of all time. Asked to name an all-time, all-star team, Cobb picked Joe Jackson, Tris Speaker and Babe Ruth in his outfield, but hastened to add:

"DiMaggio is wonderful. Would he hit the dead ball? He'd hit anything. He would be a great star at any time in the history of the game. He is one of the greatest hitters, quickest fielders, surest throwers, and fastest runners I've seen."

Cobb, who was all of those things and more himself, mused a moment and took the time to study him. Since retiring, he has picked up some 22 pounds. His face fattened a bit to lessen the hawky look he had. His eyes, that glared balefully at opponents, twinkle with bright blueness in his ruddy, healthy face. There's a bit of gray and a bit of baldness about him. The old-timers say he was ill-tempered and hard to talk to. But he must've changed a lot. Now he talks pleasantly—almost anxious to be of help. And he chuckles a lot and laughs softly when a memory of this or that flickers across the movie-screen of his mind. ∎

Ty Cobb

DiMag Seeking Hits—Not Record Hitting Streak

By Dick McCann
June 25, 1941

You do—or you don't. That's the cool philosophy of Joe DiMaggio as he hammers along the highway of his hitting streak. The slugging Yankee outfielder is absolutely unworried about his string which yesterday was dramatically stretched to 36 consecutive games, five shy of the all-time record set by George Sisler in '22.

"Why should I worry?" says Joe. "The only time to worry is when you're not hitting. I'm not worried now—I'm happy. It's no strain to keep on hitting—it's a strain not to be hitting. That's when your nerves get jumpy."

These wise words were uttered before yesterday's Browns-Yanks game at the Stadium where Joe was held hitless until his last turn at bat. His coolness under fire proved he meant what he was talking about.

Most players are superstitious about streaks. They keep doing the same little things they did the day a string started, or they keep wearing the same baseball suit or necktie, or shoes. They're afraid to stop what they've been doing for fear it'll stop the streak, too. In fact, they usually don't like to talk about their streaks. As you know, it is an unwritten law of baseball never to discuss a no-hitter when it is in the making.

Before the game, we asked DiMag if he'd mind talking about his streak.

"Heck, no," the lanky, quiet, likable guy said with a wry smile. "Talking's not going to stop it. No,

> "Why should I worry? The only time to worry is when you're not hitting. I'm not worried now—I'm happy. It's no strain to keep on hitting—it's a strain not to be hitting. That's when your nerves get jumpy."

I'm not superstitious. Hoodoos aren't going to stop me—a pitcher will, and hoodoos aren't going to help me. A little luck, of course, but mainly it's up to me to keep swinging."

But isn't there some little trick or habit you've been following since the streak started?

DiMag grinned pleasantly, "Just one—go up there and swing."

How does Joe explain the streak following his worst batting slump since coming into the big leagues?

Joe shrugged the broad shoulders that provide the power for his punches at the plate. "I dunno." But, he added, "to tell the truth, I wasn't hitting bad during that slump—I was nailing the ball good but I just couldn't buy a base hit. Line drives went right to fielders. Now the line drives fall where they ain't. I guess that's the explanation."

DiMag says luck levels off evenly throughout the season. "You get lucky hits, and then you get robbed of real ones. The other day I got a lucky hit when the ball bounced over Luke Appling's head. That was the luckiest hit in my streak. But then, later that day, Taft Wright leaned into the boxes for what he told me later was a sure homer. That's the way those things go."

DiMag, of course, is an old hand at hitting streaks. Back in '33, in his first season in organized baseball, Joe hit safely in 61 games with the San Francisco Seals of the Pacific Coast League. This streak, eight shy of the minor league record of 69,

Left to right: Bill Dickey, Joe DiMaggio and Tommy Henrich.

was started May 28 and ended July 23.

"I can remember the day it ended as if it were only yesterday," Joe said. "Ed Walsh, whose dad was a great pitcher with the White Sox years ago, stopped me. Funny thing, I won the game that day, too.

"My manager, Jim Caeney, tried to make things easier for me and put me in the lead-off spot so I'd get more chances to bat. Heck, I didn't hit a ball good all day until the ninth when I came up with a man on third, one out and the score tied. I hit a fly into left field and the runner scored with the winning run.

"It'll suit me fine," said Joe, and all knew he meant it, "if my streak ends the same way—us winning a ball game...That's all that matters."■

> "It'll suit me fine if my streak ends the same way—us winning a ball game. That's all that matters."
> —Joe DiMaggio

Asked by sportswriters why he didn't walk DiMaggio in his final at-bat after Joe D had been hitless in his first three tries, St. Louis Browns pitcher Bob Muncrief replied: "That wouldn't have been fair—to him or to me. Hell, he's the greatest player I ever saw."

June 26, 1941: Joltin' Joe's streak becomes a team effort for the Yankees. Heading into the eighth inning, DiMaggio, who is hitless thus far, is scheduled to bat fourth. Red Rolfe walks and Tommy Henrich bunts to keep from hitting into a double play. This strategy succeeds as DiMaggio doubles in his final at-bat to extend his hitting streak to 39 games.

June 28, 1941: Joe DiMaggio walks in his first at-bat, and on a 3-0 pitch in his second at-bat, slaps an outside delivery between pitcher Johnny Babich's legs for a single. That extends Joe's hitting streak to 40 games, the second-longest ever in American League history.

Mrs. Dorothy DiMaggio smiles as her husband homers to extend his hitting streak to a record 45 games.

Daily News

Yanks Win 2

Joe Doubles in 1st, Singles in 2d; Mates Cop, 9-4, 7-5

By Jack Smith
June 30, 1941

Through the sweat and grime of one of the hottest days of the year, Joe DiMaggio carried his sensational batting streak to 42 consecutive games, a new modern record, here this afternoon. As the Yanks swept a double-header with the Senators, 9-4 and 7-5, a capacity crowd of 31,000 sweltering customers sat on seat's edge as DiMag was stopped in the early innings of each battle before coming through. Third time at bat in the opener he slashed a double off Dutch Leonard to tie George Sisler's record of 41 straight, established in 1922. Fourth time at bat in the finale, he whisked a line single off Arnold Anderson to stamp a new record into the books.

Though the Yanks also stretched their team homer streak to 25 consecutive games, DiMaggio and his struggle for a new record were the whole show. Not since May 12 at the Stadium, when Mel Harder blanked him, has Joe failed to connect at least once. With the modern record now his, the poker-faced outfielder is aiming at the all-time mark of 44 straight set by Wee Willie Keeler in 1897. He can tie it Tuesday at the Stadium when the Yanks face the Red Sox in a double-header.

Both Joe's hits this afternoon were well-thumped blows. He almost tore Leonard's leg off with the record-tying double in the opener. Then, in the nightcap, he slammed a solid single over George Archie's outstretched hands into left field. There were no flukes about these blows. They were record breakers in every way.

Too bad Joe didn't have a hand in extending the homer streak. He left that to Tommy Henrich, Joe Gordon and Charlie Keller. Henrich was the streak saver in the opener. When he stepped to the plate with one on and one out in the ninth, the Yanks still hadn't collected their daily four-bagger. But Tommy came through with a wallop over the right field fence. It was his 14th. In the finale, they didn't wait so long. Gordon walloped his into the left field seats in the second inning and in the fourth, Keller clouted a 440-footer into the same sector. It was No. 12 for Joe and No. 16 for Charley.

Lucky for the fans, they had DiMag's streak to keep them happy. The games were pretty punk. The opener was okay for four frames as Ruffing and Leonard flipped shutout ball. But in the fifth, Gordon singled and Rizzuto and Ruffing doubled for the big blows of a three-run outburst. They added three more in the sixth which DiMag started with his double. The only other hit was a single but an error and a wild pitch helped out.

Ruff allowed only one scratch hit in the first five innings. Another scratch safety by Archie started his downfall with one out in the Senator sixth. He disposed of Cramer but Lewis and Vernon doubled and Early tripled for four runs before Johnny Murphy took the mound.

The pitching was effective in the nightcap too. At the end of the fourth they were tied, 4-4. This was the last frame for Sid Hudson, the Senator starter who had fanned DiMag twice. Anderson relieved him and was clouted for winning runs. A single by Gordon, walks to Rizzuto and Silestri followed by a pinch hit single by George Selkirk gave the Yanks two in the sixth while DiMag's record-breaking single followed by Keller's triple notched the final run in the seventh. ∎

> Both Joe's hits this afternoon were well-thumped blows . . . There were no flukes about these blows. They were record breakers in every way.

Yanks Win, 7-2, 9-2

DiMag Ties Keeler's Mark in 2d game

By Jack Smith
July 2, 1941

Forty-four consecutive games! Joe DiMaggio's sensational batting streak soared to that all-time record yesterday at the Stadium where 52,832 DiMag-drawn fans clustered to watch the Yanks twice drub the Red Sox, 7-2 and 9-2. Not since 1897, when Wee Willie Keeler established the all-time mark, has a major leaguer hit safely in so many games. Joe did it with two hits in the first game and another in his first time at bat in the rain-shortened five-inning nightcap. Bill Dahlen, George Sisler, Ty Cobb, all great streak hitters of the past, have been left behind. And this afternoon, at the Stadium, the great Yank outfielder can reach a mark never before attained in the 101-year history of the game.

They were no fluke blows that kept his streak intact yesterday. Though his first hit in the opener was a questionable single, he followed with a clean blow next time at bat and duplicated the first trip to the dish in the nightcap. A couple of veteran right-handers, Mike Ryba and Jack Wilson, were the victims. ∎

Daily News

Joe DiMaggio proudly displays the status of his hitting streak.

Major League Baseball's Consecutive-Game Hitting Streaks (before 1941)

44 games ... Willie Keeler, 1897

41 games ... George Sisler, 1922

40 games ... Ty Cobb, 1911

35 games ... Ty Cobb, 1917

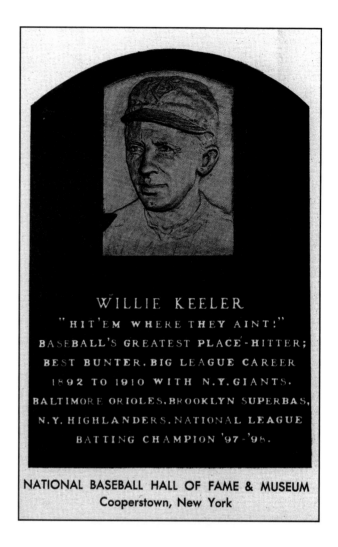

WILLIE KEELER
"HIT'EM WHERE THEY AINT!"
BASEBALL'S GREATEST PLACE-HITTER;
BEST BUNTER. BIG LEAGUE CAREER
1892 TO 1910 WITH N.Y. GIANTS.
BALTIMORE ORIOLES. BROOKLYN SUPERBAS,
N.Y. HIGHLANDERS. NATIONAL LEAGUE
BATTING CHAMPION '97-'98.

NATIONAL BASEBALL HALL OF FAME & MUSEUM
Cooperstown, New York

Daily News

(Left) Pete Rose of the Cincinnati Reds tied Willie Keeler's National League record by hitting in 44 consecutive games during the 1978 season.

DiMag Sets All-Time Record with Homers; Yanks Win, 8-4

By Jack Smith
July 3, 1941

Twice robbed of hits by his foes' fancy fielding, Joe DiMaggio yesterday decided the only thing to do was to bang the ball where the boys couldn't get at it. So, in the fifth inning, and on his third visit to the plate, DiMag clouted a cloud-scraping homer deep into the Stadium left field lodges to stretch his hitting streak to a new all-time record of 45 straight games. It was Joe's 18th homer and 100th hit of the season, and he now leads the AL in four-masters. The Yankees won the game, clubbing the Red Sox, 8-4, and increased their league lead over the idle Indians to three full games. But the 8,682 fans had cheers only for DiMag.

The rafters of "the House that Ruth Built" rumbled with their roars every time DiMag came to bat. They groaned and moaned when Stan Spence, Bosox right fielder, raced far to his right and leaped high for DiMag's first-inning fly. They fussed and fretted when Jim Tabor, Bosox third baseman, hopped behind third to stab DiMag's sizzling grounder and threw him out by two steps in the third. They booed Pitcher Newsome when Dick's first two pitches were balls in the fifth—they were fearful Joe wouldn't get a whack at the ball.

And then they went wild when Joe slammed the streak-stretching homer. As his long legs carried him laughing around the bases, he left in his dusty wake the broken hits of Willie Keeler's 44-year-old record of hitting safely in 44 straight games. Every consecutive game in which DiMag gets a hit now, he breaks his own record.

After the game, most of the fans spilled onto the field and swarmed the sweaty, swarthy swatter as he galloped in from center field to the dugout. One quick-handed youth snatched Joe's cap and raced toward the right field bullpen exit. Mike Ryba, veteran Sox pitcher, dumped him with a foot-ballish block in short right. But the lad lateralled the cap to a pal who did some fancy running until cornered by a couple of panting ushers. The cap then was restored to Joe's noble brow.

DiMag's homer came in the middle of a six-run Yankee splurge in the fifth. Charley Keller's 17th homer—a 380-foot smash into the right field bleachers in the second—and Rolfe's infield hit, Henrich's single and DiMag's infield out in the third had given the Yanks a 2-0 lead when they clinched the game in the fifth. ∎

> As his long legs carried him laughing around the bases, he left in his dusty wake the broken hits of Willie Keeler's 44-year-old record of hitting safely in 44 straight games.

Daily News

Joe DiMaggio crosses the plate after hitting a home run against Philadelphia, extending his consecutive-game hitting streak to 46 games.

Yanks Win, 8-4, 3-1; DiMag Hits in Both

By Dick McCann
July 7, 1941

A season-record crowd of 60,948 fans came to pay tribute to an old hero and stayed to cheer a new one at Yankee Stadium yesterday. The huge turnout for Lou Gehrig Memorial Day was treated to one of the most spectacular one-man exhibitions in recent years by Joe DiMaggio. DiMag stretched his hitting streak to the groaning point of 48 games with six smashing safeties and matched his hitting with brilliant, unbelievable fielding as the Yankees won both games from the Athletics, 8-4, 3-1. The double triumph, which the Yanks had pledged to Lou, their old captain, increased their AL lead to three-and-a-half games as the second-place Indians lost to Chicago.

The Yanks have now won nine straight, 13 out of 14 and 23 out of 26 games.

DiMaggio was a superman. Not content with spanking three singles and a double in the first game and a 410-foot run-scoring triple and a single in the rain-spattered nightcap, he robbed the A's of as many hits as he made.

But, truly, most of the Yanks played all-out on Gehrig Day. Sharing some of the spotlight with

> DiMaggio was a superman. Not content with spanking three singles and a double in the first game and a 410-foot run-scoring triple and a single in the rain-spattered night-cap, he robbed the A's of as many hits as he made.

DiMag in the opener were Bill Dickey, who blasted a three-run homer and a single; Red Rolfe, who smashed a four-master and three singles; and Ernie Bonham, who hurled one-hit ball through five and two-thirds innings of spectacular relief to gain his fifth triumph against two defeats.

In the nightcap, DiMaggio wasted no time continuing his hitting streak. Coming to bat with two out and Henrich on first in the first, DiMag tripled. In the third he came up with two out and Rolfe, who had walked, on second. Joe promptly singled him home. Rizzuto's inning-opening triple and Sturm's single scored the final Yank run in the seventh.

DiMaggio was brutal to enemy batters. He made no less than eight breathtaking catches. Twice, he robbed Johnson of sure-fire extra-basers. In the opener, Joe raced over to the center field exit to make a leaping, one-handed catch of Johnson's 410-foot wallop. In the nightcap, speeding through the rain and slosh, Joe snared Johnson's ninth-inning smash over his shoulder. ∎

July 8, 1941: The American League wins the All-Star Game, 7-5, at Detroit's Briggs Stadium as Ted Williams swats a dramatic home run with two out and two on base in the bottom of the ninth inning. Joe and Dom DiMaggio become the first brothers to play in the same All-Star Game; Dom singles, Joe doubles.

All-Star brothers Dom and Joe DiMaggio.

Yanks Rip Tribe, 10-3

DiMag Gets 3 Hits to Stretch
Hitting Streak to 56 in a Row

By Jack Smith
July 17, 1941

The Yanks stretched their league lead to six full games here this afternoon by trimming the Indians, 10-3, before a crowd of about 14,000. A four-run Yank outburst in the fifth finished the Indians for the afternoon as Joe DiMaggio chipped in with three hits, prolonging his batting streak to 56 consecutive games. Atley Donald went the distance for the Yanks, while Al Milnar, Indian starter, was relieved after the fifth. Charley Keller slammed homer No. 20 in the fourth and Jeff Heath hammered No. 13 in the sixth. ∎

AP/Wide World Photos

Joe DiMaggio singles in the first inning against the Cleveland Indians on July 16, 1941, extending his hitting streak to 56 consecutive games.

DI MAG'S STREAK ENDED IN 57TH GAME

FINAL

Story on Page 42

DAILY NEWS

New York's Picture Newspaper

New York, Friday, July 18, 1941

2 Cents

THE LARGEST CIRCULATION IN AMERICA

Second Draft Is On. (Associated Press Wirefoto) Here's scene in Washington as second peacetime draft began. Staff Sergt. Robert W. Shackleton is drawing the number, and Lieut.-Col. Charles Morris is guiding his hand. Far right is Secretary of Navy Frank Knox. At left (dark striped suit) is Brig.-Gen. Lewis Hershey, acting Selective Service director. —*Story on page 2, other pictures on page 3 and 24.*

Daily News

TRIVIA ABOUT JOE DIMAGGIO'S 56-GAME HITTING STREAK

- Collected one hit in a game 34 times
- Collected two hits in a game 13 times
- Collected three hits in a game five times
- Collected four hits in a game four times
- Had a batting average of .408 during the streak (91 of 223)
- Among his 91 hits during the streak were 16 doubles, three triples and 15 home runs
- Had a hit against all seven American League opponents
- Had hits against three future Hall of Fame pitchers: Boston's Lefty Grove (1 of 4), Cleveland's Bob Feller (3 of 6) and Detroit's Hal Newhouser (2 of 10)
- In the game after the streak ended, DiMaggio began a second consecutive-game hitting streak that reached 16—altogether 72 out of 73 games

Stopped!

DiMaggio Streak Dies in Cleveland

By Jack Smith
July 17, 1941

One of the greatest feats in the history of baseball—Joe DiMaggio's 56-game hitting streak—ended under the gleaming arclights of huge Municipal Stadium here tonight. The largest crowd ever to see a night game, 67,468 roaring fans, sat tensely through nine spectacular innings that ended with the Yankees beating the second-place Indians, 4-3.

In four trips to the plate, the great Yankee outfielder failed to get the ball out of the infield, drawing one walk and slapping three infield grounders. It was the end of a streak that surpassed by 12 games the previous all-time high for the major leagues and was the driving force in a Yankee surge that carried them from fourth place into the seven-game lead they now hold.

Joe's streak started more than two months ago, on May 15, when he punched a single into right field off southpaw Ed Smith of the White Sox. During that time, he faced every team in the league at least once and teed off on every kind of hurling until the combined work of lefty Al Smith and righthander Jim Bagby stopped him tonight.

DiMaggio was robbed the first time up when he smashed a sizzling grounder toward third. The Indians' third baseman, Ken Keltner, speared it close to the foul line with a great backhand stab and threw him out at first by two steps.

Joe walked on a 3-2 pitch in the fourth and, in the seventh, whacked the first pitch back to Keltner again. Against Bagby he slapped an easy grounder to Boudreau for an inning-ending double play.

The game itself was dramatic enough without the added feature of DiMaggio. For six innings, it was a blistering duel between Smith and Lefty Gomez. Rolfe's infield hit and a foul-line double by Henrich gave the Yankees a run in the first that the Indians didn't match until the fourth, when Gee Walker clouted an inside-the-park homer that stopped rolling only when it hit the fence 463 feet away.

Smith had allowed only two hits as he started the seventh. Henrich and DiMag were infield outs. The third out was not so easy. It didn't come until after Joe Gordon wafted his 15th homer over Walker's lunging hands and into the left-field stands 335 feet from the plate.

That should have been the tipoff that Smitty was tiring. He couldn't get past the eighth. Keller led off with a liner to center that Weatherly played into a triple. After Keltner threw out Rizzuto, Gomez lined a 3-2 pitch to left, scoring Keller. Sturm dropped a single in center and Rolfe banged a double to right, scoring Gomez. A walk to Henrich filled the bases, finished Smith and brought DiMaggio to the plate to face Bagby.

It was not Joe's night. He sent an easy grounder to Boudreau, who flipped to Mack, forcing Henrich. Mack pivoted and fired to Grimes for the double play. ∎

Yankees 4, Indians 3

YANKEES

	AB	R	H	TB	BB	RBI	PO	A	E
STURM, 1B	4	0	1	1	0	0	10	2	0
ROLFE, 3B	4	1	2	3	0	1	2	2	0
HENRICH, RF	3	0	1	2	1	1	4	0	0
DIMAGGIO, OF	3	0	0	0	1	0	2	0	0
GORDON, 3B	4	1	2	5	0	1	0	2	0
ROSAR, C	4	0	0	0	0	0	0	1	0
KELLER, LF	3	1	1	3	1	0	0	0	0
RIZZUTO, SS	4	0	0	0	0	0	2	1	0
GOMEZ, P	4	1	1	1	0	1	2	1	0
MURPHY, P	0	0	0	0	0	0	0	1	0
TEAM	33	4	8	15	3	4	27	10	0

INDIANS

	AB	R	H	TB	BB	RBI	PO	A	E
WEATHERLY, OF	5	0	1	1	0	0	4	0	0
KELTNER, 3B	3	0	1	1	1	0	1	4	0
BOUDREAU, SS	3	0	0	0	0	0	0	2	0
HEATH, RF	4	0	0	0	0	0	0	0	0
WALKER, LF	3	2	2	5	1	1	1	0	0
GRIMES, 1B	3	1	1	1	1	0	12	0	0
MACK, 2B	3	0	0	0	0	0	4	7	0
ROSENTHAL, PH	1	0	1	3	0	2	0	0	0
HEMSLEY, C	3	0	1	1	0	0	5	1	0
TROSKY, PH	1	0	0	0	0	0	0	0	0
SMITH, P	3	0	0	0	0	0	0	0	0
BAGBY, P	0	0	0	0	0	0	0	0	0
CAMPBELL, PH	1	0	0	0	0	0	0	0	0
TEAM	33	3	7	12	3	3	27	14	0

"Quite a Strain," Joe Admits, Glad It's Over

By Jack Smith
July 18, 1941

There was nothing glum or crestfallen about Joe DiMaggio here tonight as he soaped and showered himself in the dressing room after his first hitless ball game since May 15. Joe wore a smile as broad as his shoulders and shouted from the steam of the shower room to his Yank teammates, "I'm tickled to death it's all over. I'm sure proud of the record, but I might as well admit it was quite a strain. Naturally I wanted to keep it going. But as long as I didn't, I'm happy about the whole thing."

Joe draped a towel around his midsection and moved through the confusion of the dressing room towards his locker. "I'm going to do some real hitting now," he said. "No more bad balls. I've been up there trying to hit anything that came near me. Now I'm going to make those pitches come in there right over the plate. I want that batting crown and I'll have to do plenty of hitting to beat Ted Williams."

> "I'm tickled to death it's all over. I'm sure proud of the record, but I might as well admit it was quite a strain. Naturally I wanted to keep it going. But as long as I didn't, I'm happy about the whole thing."
> —Joe DiMaggio

Joe thought he had a hit first time at bat. "It was a low curve," he explained. "It must have been a strike too because I hit it pretty good. I never thought Keltner would come up with it. He actually caught it behind him. Smith pitched a swell ball game, but it was that Keltner that really stopped me."

Strangely, Joe has always hit Al Smith pretty hard. The Cleveland lefty started only one game against the Yanks this season and was knocked from the box as the Yanks won, 5-4. On June 15 at the Stadium, Smith relieved Jim Bagby in the fourth and twice retired DiMag on infield outs.

The fact that his Yankees won last night's game eased the pain of the fractured streak. You see, while in the middle of the streak and discussing his 61-game skein in the Pacific Coast League, DiMag recalled that the San Francisco team of which he was a member won the game in which he was held hitless and he added:

"If this one has to end, I hope it ends that way, too." ∎

Charles Hoff, Daily News

Before the 1966 Old Timers game at Yankee Stadium, Joe DiMaggio (left) put
a choke hold on Ken Keltner, star third baseman for the Indians. Keltner,
along with pitchers Jim Bagby Jr. and Al Smith, snapped DiMag's 56-game
hitting streak 25 years before in Cleveland.

Joe DiMaggio's

GAME	DATE	TEAM
1	5/15	White Sox
2	5/16	White Sox
3	5/17	White Sox
4	5/18	Browns
5	5/19	Browns
6	5/20	Browns
7	5/21	Tigers
8	5/22	Tigers
9	5/23	Red Sox
10	5/24	Red Sox
11	5/25	Red Sox
12	5/27	Senators
13	5/28	Senators
14	5/29	Senators
15	5/30	Red Sox
16	5/30	Red Sox
17	6/1	Indians
18	6/1	Indians
19	6/2	Indians
20	6/3	Tigers
21	6/5	Tigers
22	6/7	Browns
23	6/8	Browns
24	6/8	Browns
25	6/10	White Sox
26	6/12	White Sox
27	6/14	Indians
28	6/15	Indians
29	6/16	Indians
30	6/17	White Sox
31	6/18	White Sox
32	6/19	White Sox
33	6/20	Tigers
34	6/21	Tigers
35	6/22	Tigers
36	6/24	Browns
37	6/25	Browns
38	6/26	Browns
39	6/27	Athletics
40	6/28	Athletics
41	6/29	Senators
42	6/29	Senators
43	7/1	Red Sox
44	7/1	Red Sox
45	7/2	Red Sox
46	7/5	Athletics
47	7/6	Athletics
48	7/6	Athletics
49	7/10	Browns
50	7/11	Browns
51	7/12	Browns
52	7/13	White Sox
53	7/13	White Sox
54	7/14	White Sox
55	7/15	White Sox
56	7/16	Indians
TOTALS		

1941 Hitting Streak

PITCHER	AT-BATS	RUNS	HITS
Smith	4	0	1
Lee	4	2	2
Rigney	3	1	1
Harris	3	3	3
Galehouse	3	0	1
Auker	5	1	1
Rowe/Benton	5	0	2
McKain	4	0	1
Newsome	5	0	1
Johnson	4	2	1
Grove	4	0	1
Chase/Anderson/Carrasquel	5	3	4
Hudson	4	1	1
Sundra	3	1	1
Johnson	2	1	1
Harris	3	0	1
Milnar	4	1	1
Harder	4	0	1
Feller	4	2	2
Trout	4	1	1
Newhouse	5	1	1
Muncrief/Allen/Caster	5	2	3
Auker	4	3	2
Caster/Kramer	4	1	2
Rigney	5	1	1
Lee	4	1	2
Feller	2	0	1
Bagby	3	1	1
Milnar	5	0	1
Rigney	4	1	1
Lee	3	0	1
Smith/Rose	3	2	3
Newsome/McKain	5	3	4
Trout	4	0	1
Newhouse/Newsome	5	1	2
Muncrief	4	1	1
Galehouse	4	1	1
Auker	4	0	1
Dean	3	1	2
Babich/Harris	5	1	2
Leonard	4	1	1
Anderson	5	1	1
Harris/Ryba	4	0	2
Wilson	3	1	1
Newsome	5	1	1
Marchildon	4	2	1
Babich/Hadley	5	2	4
Knott	4	0	2
Niggeling	2	0	1
Harris/Kramer	5	1	4
Auker/Muncrief	5	1	2
Lyons/Hallett	4	2	3
Lee	4	0	1
Rigney	3	0	1
Smith	4	1	2
Milnar/Krakauskas	4	3	3
	223	55	91

DiMag Strikeout First in 43 Games
July 27, 1941

When Jack Hallett, Sox right hander, struck out Joe DiMaggio in the seventh inning of yesterday's game in the Stadium, he achieved quite a notable feat. It was the first time that Joltin' Joe had fanned in 43 games.

The last time he struck out was against Bob Muncrief of the Browns in the second game, June 8, in St. Louis. DiMaggio has struck out only eight times this season.

Batting Slump Drops DiMag Batting Average 25 Points

By Joe Trimble
August 19, 1941

A ball club 17 games in front on this date shouldn't have any worries at all, but the Yankees actually have a problem. Nothing vital enough to affect the AL pennant race, but important anyway. That's the three-week slump of Joe DiMaggio.

Since July 27 the Great Man has been in a slump that has practically ruined any chance he has to capture the league batting title for the third straight year. It also threatens his superiority in other departments of the batting business.

Since that date, DiMag's average has dropped 25 points and he is now 50 to the rear of league-leader Ted Williams. With the lanky Boston youngster continuing to hit over .400, Joe's chances of catching him are nil.

Of course, it was natural that DiMag would stumble over a few rough spots after his amazing splurge which saw him hit safely in 72 of 73 games.

But this spasm is the worst Joe has suffered in his six-year major league career. His splurge ended Sunday, August 3, when the Browns' Johnny Niggeling and Bob Harris blanked him in both ends of a doubleheader in New York.

Since then he has gone hitless in six games and has managed to get but ten hits in his last 48 at bats—an average of only .208. He went without a hit in the recent weekend series against the A's at the Stadium and has been blanked in his last nine times. The last three hurlers to embarrass him were Jack Knott, Bill Beckman and Phil Marchildon. Among them they have won 20 games while losing 27.

Joe can't explain how this terrible thing happened but is quite determined to break out on his Western trip, which was to have begun here today. However, rain made for a Blue Monday and the game was put over until tomorrow when a doubleheader will be played.■

DiMaggio Gets Humidor from His Yankee Mates

August 30, 1941

They say there is no sentiment in baseball, but that doesn't go for the members of New York's pennant-bound Yankees. Or at least it doesn't go as far as their feeling of admiration for their great teammate, Joe DiMaggio, is concerned.

Tonight the Shoreham Joe's pals gave him a little surprise party. They gathered in the suite and then engineered with Lefty Gomez to get DiMaggio down to the apartment. And then they told him how much they respected him as a ball player and as a man and gave him a trophy to commemorate his world's record 56-game hitting streak.

"The boys dug down and cashed in a few defense bonds and bought this for you, Joe," said Lefty as he handed him a silver cigar and cigarette humidor. On the cover was an engraving of DiMaggio taking his full cut at a pitch with the record—56 games—91 hits.

On the front of the box was the inscription: "Presented to Joe DiMaggio by his fellow players of the New York Yankees to express their admiration for the world's consecutive game hitting record—1941." Inside the cover the autographs of all his teammates are engraved. ∎

> "The boys dug down and cashed in a few defense bonds and bought this for you, Joe," said Lefty as he handed [DiMaggio] a silver cigar and cigarette humidor.

AP/Wide World Photos

A favorite of his teammates, Joe DiMaggio accepts congratulations from Manager Joe McCarthy (shaking hands).

Bonham Was a 'Bon Homme.' Out in center field, Joe DiMaggio has just made the last putout of the 1941 World Series, and here in the middle of the diamond the Yankee infield mobs pitcher Ernie Bonham, who hurled a sterling 4-hitter to win, 3-1, and clinch the Series for the Bronx Bombers. Left to right are: Phil Rizzuto (almost hidden), Red Rolfe, Bonham, Johnny Sturm and Joe Gordon. Bonham really overpowered the Dodgers in the clutch. Tommy Henrich blasted a homer in the fifth.

—Story on page 46; other pictures on page 47

Yankees Win Series

Bonham's 4-Hitter Bests Wyatt, 3-1

By Jack Smith
October 7, 1941

A dream that was built up during 21 years of patient, loyal waiting, burst in the creeping shadows of Ebbets Field yesterday when chubby, unheralded Ernie Bonham pitched the Yanks to a 3-1 victory over the Dodgers and to the championship of baseball's universe in the fifth game of the World Series. Except for one brief, wordy flare-up, the end came peacefully, quietly and without deep regret.

The crippled, but still battling Dodgers were baffled completely by Bonham's four-hit hurling and the crowd of 34,072 none-too-hopeful fans were gagged to silence in the fifth when Tommy Henrich lashed a home run over the right field wall.

A hero, even in defeat, was Whitlow Wyatt, veteran Dodgers right-hander, who pitched his heart out in a losing cause and refused to give up until Joe DiMaggio gracefully snared the final out. By winning the Series in five games, the proud, powerful Yanks regained the throne they held for four straight years which had been knocked from under them last year by Detroit.

It was the seventh world championship for the club and the sixth for their quiet little manager, Joe McCarthy. For the Dodgers it was the third failure in three shots at the highest goal in baseball. In the 1916 Series they were beaten by Boston and in 1920 they bowed to Cleveland.

> It was a glorious climax to a remarkable season for the Yanks. Though not favored to win the pennant, they steam-rollered all opposition in their league and clinched the flag on September 4, the earliest clinching date in history.

It was a glorious climax to a remarkable season for the Yanks. Though not favored to win the pennant, they steam-rollered all opposition in their league and clinched the flag on September 4, the earliest clinching date in history. They battled through the first three games of the World Series, winning two and losing one. They snapped up the biggest break a World Series team ever had, the third strike which got away from Mickey Owen in the fourth game, and then swept past the Dodgers in the Series finale yesterday. ∎

Deadpan Yanks Unbend as Title Is Won

By Joe Trimble
October 7, 1941

The deadpan, colorless Yanks get excited just once a year. And then, for just an hour. The hour began at 17 minutes before four yesterday afternoon when coach Art Fletcher led the World Champions in a powerful—if not too tuneful—version of "The Sidewalks of New York" as newsreel cameras ground and photographers' bulbs popped and flashed in the dressing room after the game.

They finished the song with three cheers for themselves and Joe McCarthy and then posed for all the pictures that anyone wanted to take. Hands were shaken and backs slapped and each player went up to the manager to congratulate him.

Leo Durocher, divested of all his bitterness over the Yanks' luck during the games, came in from the adjoining Dodger clubhouse half dressed and shook McCarthy warmly by the hand.

"You have a great ball club, Joe," said Leo with good grace.

> Joe DiMaggio was his usual ice-waterish self. He patiently explained his flare-up with Wyatt: "He called me a dirty (two words censored)! So I ran out to the mound to take up his challenge. I don't know which ump it was rushed in between us."

"You have a pretty good one yourself," answered the square-jawed Yank manager. "And a game one. You weren't disgraced."

Ed Barrow, Yank president, and McCarthy shook hands and posed for pictures. "This is the first time I've been in your clubhouse all season, Joe," Barrow said. "You're a great manager of a great team."

Joe's answer was simple. "I'm proud to be the boss of this great game club."

The older Yanks, to whom this business of winning a World Series is no longer a novelty, were passably quiet. With the exception of the ebullient Fletcher, they were content to let the kids do all the celebrating.

Joe DiMaggio was his usual ice-waterish self. He patiently explained his flare-up with Wyatt: "He called me a dirty (two words censored)! So I ran out to the mound to take up his challenge. I don't know which ump it was that rushed in between us." ∎

Daily News

The 1941 World-Champion New York Yankees

Kids Throw a Party At DiMag's

By Joe Trimble
October 20, 1941

Joltin' Joe DiMaggio went to a party yesterday. Not the ordinary grown-ups' kind of party with cocktails, hors d'oeuvres and fancy music. It was a kiddie party—arranged by the neighbors' children—and the Yankee slugger enjoyed himself immensely as he ate ice cream and cookies and thipped through a thraw. He signed autographs, shook each of 34 enthralled youngsters by the hand and a good time was had by all.

The affair took place in a vacant apartment of the house at 400 West End Ave., Manhattan, where Joe lives in a penthouse. It seems that the children have been ringing DiMag's doorbell off and on for months in hopes of obtaining an autographed baseball from the famous man.

Since Joe is a gracious one and likes children, he didn't mind the off-the-field attention of the kids. But the management of the apartment house figured that Joe and Dorothy, his wife, were paying enough rent to have some privacy.

So, Supt. George Brook was quite amenable to the suggestion of four of the children (Norma Fisch, 10; her sister, Gloria, 15; Philip Balsam, 15; and Stanley Goodman, 15) that they throw a party and have DiMag sign everyone's scrapbook at once.

The management, happy at such a simple solution, paid for the refreshments and provided little baseballs and bats for each of

the boys and girls—the oldest of whom was 15.

Joe entered the bunting-draped suite to the accompaniment of a familiar ditty, "Joltin' Joe DiMaggio," which blared forth from a portable phonograph. A sign of welcome hung in one of the rooms and a makeshift table had been set up on sawhorses, where the goodies were served after Yankee Joe finished autographing articles and posing for photographs.

The kids were obviously excited but hardly awestricken at being right in the same room with a celebrity. One smartie, about 15, twirled a freshly autographed ball in businesslike fashion and said, "Guess I can get quite a price for this!"

The parents of the children weren't allowed to spoil the fun. They stayed in another apartment most of the time and let Junior and Joe enjoy their party. ∎

Joe DiMaggio hosts a party for neighborhood kids at his apartment house at 400 West End Avenue.

AP/Wide World Photos

DiMaggio, of Yankees, Becomes Father of Son

Joe DiMaggio, New York Yankee outfielder, announced yesterday that his wife gave birth to a boy weighing 7 pounds 11 ounces at Doctors Hospital. The baby, he said, was born at 11:11 a.m. Mrs. DiMaggio is the former Dorothy Arnold of the stage and screen.

AP/Wide World Photos

Joe DiMaggio has great expectations for baby Joe DiMaggio III, who holds a miniature bat as his mother, Dorothy, looks on in their New York home.

DiMag Most Valuable; Ted Williams Second

By Jack Smith
November 12, 1941

Joltin' Joe DiMaggio today was returning to New York from San Francisco with a new bauble to show his baby son. Joe was bringing back the AL's Most Valuable Player award, officially announced yesterday after a ballot-for-ballot battle with Boston's Ted Williams in the closest race ever tabulated under the current method of voting. Fifteen ballots for first place and nine for second gave Joe 291 points, 37 more than his Beantown rival.

It was the second time in three years the award has gone to DiMaggio. He and Williams monopolized all but one of the ballots for first and second place as well as most of the slugging honors in the league. Eight of nine first-place votes which DiMaggio failed to cull went to Williams. The ninth was marked up for Thornton Lee, 22-game winner for the White Sox, who finished fourth in the total voting behind Bobby Feller of the Indians.

In the eyes of Baseball Writers' 24-man committee, undoubtedly the deciding factor in DiMaggio's favor was his 56-consecutive game hitting streak. In major slugging statistics, Joe topped Williams only in runs-batted-in, 125 to 120. Williams' amazing .406 batting average was 49 points better than DiMag's. His figures for homers and runs scored were also better.

Two other Yanks finished in the first twelve. Charley Keller, fifth, and Joe Gordon, seventh. This was nothing compared to the great sweep by the Dodgers, who finished one-two-three in the NL balloting and placed six men in the first eleven.

Other Yanks who placed in the voting were Bill Dickey (13th), Tommy Henrich (14th), Phil Rizzuto (20th) and Charley Ruffing (26th). Lefty Gomez, Johnny Murphy, Johnny Sturm and Marius Russo received "honorable mention."

DiMag's 56 consecutive games surpassed the best previous record for all time. When it started on May 15, the Yanks were 5 1/2 games out of first place. When Al Smith and Jim Bagby finally stopped Joe on July 17, the Yanks were comfortably entrenched in first by seven full games. ∎

1941 MVP Voting Results

1.	JOE DIMAGGIO, YANKEES	291
2.	Ted Williams, Red Sox	254
3.	Bob Feller, Indians	174
4.	Thornton Lee, White Sox	144
5.	Charlie Keller, Yankees	126
6.	Cecil Travis, Senators	101

DiMaggio Leading Athlete of '41

December 12, 1941

A group of 12 sports writers voted for Joe with the light brown bat yesterday, giving Joe DiMaggio a 3-1 margin over his nearest rival for the outstanding male athlete award of 1941. Joltin' Joe's hit parade through 56 consecutive games, which broke all major league records, won him the annual Associated Press poll.

DiMag piled up 157 points as 42 of the 82 writers gave him first place. Ted Williams, Red Sox outfielder, finished second with five first-place ballots for 74 points.

Joe Louis finished third with more first-place votes than Williams (10), but the heavyweight champ garnered only 64 points in the final standing. Following these three were Craig Wood, U.S. Open golf champ; Don Hutson, Green Bay end; Bruce Smith, Minnesota back; and Cornelius Warmerdam, pole vaulter. ■

Though Boston's Ted Williams hit .406, he still finished second in the 1941 MVP and Athlete of the Year polls to Joe DiMaggio.

"I'm quitting baseball for the duration, but that doesn't
mean that I intend to quit the Yankees cold."
—Joe DiMaggio, after deciding to enlist
for service in WWII.

Chapter 4

1942-1945

From Ballparks to Battlefields

*F*ollowing DiMaggio's momentous 1941 season, his career took a few unexpected turns. He experienced his first major batting slump during the 1942 season, and although the Yankees were the AL champions, they were defeated by the St. Louis Cardinals in the World Series. This loss would mark the Yankees' only loss in ten trips to the World Series during DiMaggio's career.

In January of 1943, it was announced that Joe would soon go from holding a bat to holding a rifle. The world was at war, and Joe, along with many other players, would leave his family and the game of baseball behind to serve his country.

While Joe never actually made it into battle during his two-and-a-half-year service, he helped to lift the spirits of many of the troops by playing in exhibition ball games throughout his service. Although DiMag had traded in his Yankee pinstripes for Uncle Sam's khaki, duty couldn't keep him off the playing field.

DiMaggio's life took another turn when his wife Dorothy won a divorce in 1944, but a stoic Joe showed little emotion to the public. DiMaggio continued to serve his country until September of 1945, when he was released on medical discharge as a result of chronic stomach ulcers.

The Clipper made his much-awaited return to the Yankees, and the stage was set to resume the battle between DiMaggio and Boston's Ted Williams for batting supremacy in the major leagues. The long-argued dispute over who was the better hitter would rage among fans for many years to come. ■

1942 REGULAR SEASON

G	AB	R	H	2B	3B	HR	RBI	BB	SB	AVG.	SLG.
154	610	123	186	29	13	21	114	68	4	.305	.498

Order DiMag to Sign for 40 G's

March 7, 1942

Joe DiMaggio has been offered $40,000 for '42 and told to sign—sign or else! This was revealed today by Yank President Ed Barrow in a long-distance call to the Yank training base just before Joe McCarthy's patched-up squad went across to Waterfront Park to nip the Cardinals, 8-7, in a 10-inning exhibition game. According to Barrow, DiMag, most important of six Yankee holdouts, was offered $40,000 last Wednesday—a $2,500 raise.

"But, today," Barrow said, "I received a call from him and he said $40,000 wasn't enough. I told him that was our final offer."

Barrow said he would arrive here next Thursday and if DiMag and the other Yank holdouts—Bill Dickey, Joe Gordon, Red Rolfe, Red Ruffing and Charley Keller—still had not agreed to terms, he

> "But today I received a call from [Joe] and he said $40,000 wasn't enough. I told him that was our final offer."
> —Yank president
> Ed Barrow

DiMaggio Signs!

After a prolonged holdout, DiMaggio wrangled an additional $2,000 from Ed Barrow and signed his 1942 contract for $42,000. Joe signed the contract in Barrow's hotel suite in St. Petersburg during the middle of the spring training season.

would announce precisely what salaries were offered to them and what they were asking.

This announcement conflicts with the Yankee policy, as stated in a letter to each of the players, that they are not to discuss their salary problems with newspapers.

DiMag was quoted at length by a news service yesterday, but Barrow said today that the Yankee slugger denied all the statements attributed to him. Briefly, Joe was quoted as saying: (1) he wanted a raise, (2) he had been offered $37,500, (3) Barrow had admitted he helped the Yanks make money last season, (4) he was tired of wrangling over his contract every year and sick of the "usual procedure" in which Barrow sent a contract containing the salary of the previous year. ■

DiMag Hits 2 Homers, Triple; Yanks Top Sox in 10th, 5-4

By Jack Smith
May 6, 1942

Like a giant rousing himself from slumber, Joe DiMaggio snapped out of his batting slump at the Stadium yesterday, hammered two homers and a tenth-inning triple which brought the Yanks a 5-4 victory over the White Sox, their fourth straight. The game-winning triple was a terrific blow in the general direction of the Fordham campus, where Hank Borowy, the winning hurler, earned his first baseball headlines.

Not even the spectacular blasting of DiMag, who lifted his homer total to four, could shove Borowy into the background. With another hurler due to be lopped off the staff, Hank needed an impressive performance to hang on to his job. He was more than impressive. He was darn near perfect. Relieving Johnny Lindell in the third, he fanned seven while pitching one-hit ball for the remaining seven and one third frames. Hank is here to stay. ∎

"There are always some kids who may be seeing me for the first time or last time. I owe them my best."
—Joe DiMaggio, when asked why he plays so hard every day

DiMag's Slump Officially Over

By Jack Smith
July 31, 1942

After climbing a ladder of base hits to the .300 mark, Joe DiMaggio looked into the future today and selected a .330 batting average as his goal for the season. With plenty of time to think it over as the Yanks arrived here for a night exhibition game with their farm hands, Joe sounded extremely hopeful when he said, "If I can make it .330 for the season, I'll be more than satisfied. The hardest job of all was getting out of the .200 bracket. I thought I would never make it."

Joe made it all right, but with no sudden splurge. His climb was steady but slow and he thinks now he has completely shaken the slump. "I felt stronger yesterday than I have in two years. I don't know what it was, but in batting practice I could sock the ball out of the country. That's the way I should feel. Of course, it's all a matter of timing. If you're not meeting the ball right, you can swing with everything you have and not get the distance. That's what I've been doing most of the season."

Snapping the slump was a gradual process. First his batting eye returned and he started poling out singles and occasional doubles. Next his timing started coming back and he began hitting for distance. The month of July has been his best so far. He was hitting a lowly .268 at the end of June. In 28 games since then, he's collected 42 hits in 111 at bats

> "The slump has taught me two things ... that anything can happen and that all pitchers are tough."
> —Joe DiMaggio

for a .378 average. Among his hits have been six homers and three triples.

Joe is anxious to reach the .330 mark for several reasons. First it will probably place him among the five leading batters and secondly it will lift him above his lowest major league average to date, the .323 of his first season with the Yanks.

"The slump has taught me two things," he explained. "That is that anything can happen and that all pitchers are tough. It gives me a headache to think of all the times I popped up on bad balls. Pitchers who didn't have a thing just lobbed the ball in there and I took care of it for them just the way they wanted me to.

"I'm also convinced the only way to get out of a slump is to stay in there and keep swinging. Nobody can help you. I'll bet at least 100 players gave me advice during the season and no two had the same idea."

Joe has been stopped only twice since the Yanks left New York 10 games ago. Al Milnar held him hitless in three trips to the plate at Cleveland while at Detroit, Dizzy Trout and Al Benton held him hitless in five trips. "That hurt, plenty," Joe moaned.

"Going 3 for 0 is not so bad but you lose an awful lot of ground when that big 5 for 0 goes into the box score." ∎

Cards Win, 4-2, Take Series

By Dick McCann
October 6, 1942

The team that wouldn't be beaten beat the team that couldn't be beaten. And, so those amazing Cardinals of St. Louis this morning are champions of all the baseball world. And the once-proud and mighty Yankees are ex-champions, thoroughly thumped, utterly routed. The rambunctious Redbirds, in their typical, never-say-die fashion, twice came from behind yesterday in the fifth game of the 1942 World Series to finally win, 4-2, in the ninth inning and thus capture the championship, four games to one, before 69,052 at Yankee Stadium.

It was the first time the Yanks had lost a Series since another audacious gang of Cardinals whipped them, four games to three, in 1926. Since then the Yanks had played in eight Series, and won them all in ridiculously easy fashion. The Yanks, who were 2-to-1 favorites and the choice of many experts to romp through the Redbirds in five or six games, were never before so severely beaten in their 13 Series appearances.

For eight innings of the first game the experts were right. The Yanks swaggered…the Cards staggered…and it looked like the National League team was again going to be humiliated in short and shameful style. But the Cards rallied in the ninth inning of the opener, almost pulled it out of the fire and were in command of the Series practically every sizzling second since.

Although the Yanks dropped the '42 Series, these young fans are still in awe of Joe DiMaggio.

In yesterday's game the Yanks relied on their star of the opener, Red Ruffing. Old Rufus, making what may be his last appearance in baseball, bid bravely for his eighth Series victory in nine games and pitched well enough to win most games.

But big Johnny Beazley, the former Golden Glover who out-sparred the Yanks in the second game, was too much for Ruff and his mates. Four Card errors put the rookie hurler in numerous jams and even had him hanging on the ropes in the last of the ninth. But the "Chain Gang" fugitive contemptuously flung himself out of each hotspot.

Once—in the fifth—two errors by the usually watertight Card infield helped the Yanks fill the bases with only one out. But Beazley, undismayed, disposed of Roy Cullenbine and the vaunted Joe DiMaggio in easy manner.

In the ninth, a booted double-play grounder enabled the Yanks to put men on first and second with none out, seriously menacing the Cards' freshly-gained lead. However, Joe Gordon, .500-batting star of last year's World Series but, unfortunately and mystifyingly, the goat of this one, was picked off second. Beazley breezily got rid of the last two bombless Bombers.

Every inning of this Series was a thriller-diller, but none was so exciting as that ninth. It will never be forgotten by the fans who may not see another Series for a long time. It was a grand one to take home and treasure among their memories.

The Cards, who featured late-inning rallies in their pell-mell dash to the NL pennant, got right off on the right foot in their last licks when Walker Cooper got his second hit of the day—a line single into center. Then came the customary capable Card sacrifice—a perfectly planted bunt in front of the plate by Johnny Hopp, moving Copper to second base.

Up strode Kurowski, the blond, Polish miner's son. Whitey had started this Series by striking out his first three times at bat against Ruffing in the opener. But ever since he was the main menace to the mighty Yanks.

In his first time at bat yesterday, Kurowski had hammered a long drive that just curved foul into the topmost tier of the left field stands. Since then he had been a somewhat ridiculous victim of Ruff's tricky let-up pitches. But this time, as the veteran loosed a slow, low pitch on the outside corner, Kurowski reached across, pulled it viciously and sent it shrieking on a clothes-line down the left field line. Charley Keller, off with the boom of the bat, charged right into the left field barrier and fell head-first into the seat as the ball sailed 10 rows back, just inside the foul pole for a two-run homer.

Joyously, Cooper and Kurowski jogged around the bases as the Card bench went as wild as a Saturday night saloon party. The grinning, white-haired Kurowski boy was bruised and breathless from the thankful thumps his mates gave him as he ducked into the dugout.

Their joy was not dimmed any when the next two Cards submitted tamely to the unruffled Ruffing. But, with the Yanks grimly taking their last licks, things suddenly became as dark and as threatening for the Cards as was the weather. ■

> Every inning of this Series was a thriller-diller, but none was so exciting as that ninth. It will never be forgotten by the fans who may not see another Series for a long time.

DiMag Plans to Enlist; Makes Up with Wife

January 14, 1943

Joe DiMaggio, the American League's great baseball player, reported yesterday he plans to join the armed forces and, at the same time, disclosed that he and his pretty wife Dorothy had patched their marital differences.

Arm in arm and smiling happily, the 28-year-old Yankee outfielder and his wife, the former Dorothy Arnold of radio and night club singing prominence, said they solved their marital problems about the time she had completed legal residence in Reno.

"We're very happy about it," said Mrs. DiMaggio.

"Everything is straightened out," grinned Joe, winner of batting championships and most valuable player awards in the American League.

"I'm going to try to get into the armed forces in the near future, just as soon as I can get a few things straightened out," continued Joe. "I really don't know which branch I'll try for, but I'll be in something pretty soon."

The DiMaggios have an infant son, 14-month-old Joseph III.

The decision to enter the armed forces means the Yankees, last year's AL champions defeated in the World Series by the Cardinals, will lose their greatest star.

"I'm quitting baseball for the duration," Joe said, then added cryptically, "but that doesn't mean I intend to quit the Yankees cold."

Joe may enlist in a naval branch. He comes from a family of fishermen and was reared in the atmosphere of the sea. His younger brother, Dominic, outfielder with the Red Sox, enlisted last year in the Coast Guard.

Permission to enlist will be necessary from Joe's draft board. He is registered in San Francisco. ■

Former Detroit Tiger Hank Greenberg talks with Joe DiMaggio. Many baseball stars served in the military during the war.

AP/World Wide Photos

Several years after completing his service in WWII, Joe DiMaggio toured Japan, illustrating his famous batting style to young Japanese diamond hopefuls.

Kid Hurler Holds DiMaggio Hitless

March 27, 1943

Private Joe DiMaggio went hitless yesterday against the stunts of a junior college pitcher, but he scored on one of two bases on balls and helped his Santa Ana Army Airmen to a 6-4 victory over Fullerton Junior College.

DiMaggio, making his first appearance on a baseball diamond since he swapped his Yankee uniform for Uncle Sam's olive drab, flied out twice.

DiMag Wires Yanks: "Get Another Flag"

By Jack Smith
April 23, 1943

Joe DiMaggio, who is shouldering a gun instead of a bat this spring, didn't forget his former buddies yesterday. From Los Angeles, the Yanks' great slugger and center fielder wired this message which was posted on the bulletin board in the clubhouse:

"Good luck and don't forget to bring home another pennant."

Though 3A in the draft, Joe volunteered for duty with the armed forces and at last reports was stationed at the Santa Ana Army Air Base. ■

Joe DiMaggio with Cpl. Zander Hollander (right) and Walter Judnich of the St. Louis Browns at Pearl Harbor in 1944.

7th Air Force Photo

Eleven 1942 Series Stars in Service

By Chris Kieran
October 3, 1943

Eleven participants of the last World Series will not be in either the Yank or Card dugout when the teams resume their torrid rivalry, but that's only because they're busy with the most serious "Series" of all …war. However, they've shown World Series form during the odd moment when service recreation programs have permitted them to engage in their old "profession."

Red Ruffing, who pitched the lone Yank victory last year, found a Fountain of Youth with the Sixth Ferrying Command team. The 38-year-old right-hander hung up the first no-hitter in his career and added a dozen other hill triumphs. Always a hitter at heart, though, he alternated in the outfield, and at last reports was sporting a .333 batting average. He was awarded the Helms Athletic Foundation award as California's outstanding athlete last July.

Sgt. Joe DiMaggio, slugging star of the Santa Ana Air Base team on the Coast, hit safely in 26 straight games. The remaining Yanks are serving in the Navy. Phil Rizzuto, whose .381 led all the Series hitters, hustled Brooklyn's Pee Wee Reese out of the shortstop job for the Norfolk Naval Training Station nine in Virginia. Lieut. Buddy Hassett has been the stand-by of the successful Cloudbuster Cadets from Chapel Hill, N.C. ∎

Sgt. Joe DiMaggio and Chief Specialist Pee Wee Reese, former Brooklyn Dodger, sign baseballs before playing each other in the Central Pacific Service Championship. Reese's Naval Hospital squad defeated DiMag's Seventh Air Force team, 5 to 4.

AP/Wide World Photos

Joe DiMaggio's Wife Wins Divorce

May 13, 1944

Actress Dorothy Arnold won a divorce yesterday from Joe DiMaggio, one-time home run slugger for the New York Yankees now in the Army, and broke into tears as she explained he "never acted like a married man."

Judge Stanley Mosk admitted he was a "great DiMaggio fan" but added that "the evidence in this case is overwhelming" and granted her a decree, $14,000 cash plus a property settlement and custody of their small son, Joseph Paul DiMaggio III.

"He always left me home alone," Miss Arnold complained, "he very rarely took me out, and spent his entire life with his men friends."

She paused to wipe tears from her eyes and once Judge Mosk halted the proceedings. The former Broadway showgirl said that her husband was ill-tempered and moody.

"He chose not to talk to me for days at a time," she testified. "Finally it came to the point where he grew very nasty and asked me to get out."

She said DiMaggio would come home around 6 or 7 a.m., except during baseball season.

"Things were better then," she added. "He ate dinners at home in those periods and occasionally took me out."

Her testimony ended with the statement that DiMaggio demonstrated a complete lack of cooperation during their entire married life. DiMaggio, a sergeant in the Air Corps, recently left his Santa Ana, California, base for a tour of the South Pacific war theater. ■

In happier times, the DiMaggios showed off Joe's record-setting ball in 1941. The couple divorced in 1944 while Joe was in the military.

AP/Wide World Photos

DiMag on Furlough, Expects No Release

By Hy Turkin
November 22, 1944

Scotching all rumors that he would be back with the Yanks next season, Sgt. Joe DiMaggio, recently arrived here on a 21-day furlough,

AP/Wide world Photos

Sgt. Joe DiMaggio gets some help from Brig. Gen. William J. Flood in sewing on his shoulder patch. DiMag said, "When this war is over, I want to play ball for the Yanks again."

told scribes yesterday: "I haven't asked for any medical discharge, I don't expect any, and from my most recent orders from the Army Air Force, it looks like I'm staying in for the duration-plus-six-months." When his current pass expires, the former Yank slugger will report to Atlantic City for rehabilitation and assignment.

Ironically, Atlantic City happens to be the likely site of the Yanks' next Spring Training. But DiMag emphasized that he's going to the seashore resort—where many hotels have been given over to Army rehabilitation work—strictly for physical training, having been weakened by nine weeks of hospitalization necessitated by an attack of stomach ulcers.

Looking slightly peaked, DiMaggio said he weighed 187 pounds, whereas his playing weight varied between 202 and 205. "Those ulcers did it, not exercise," he explained. "But I'll be all right, and when this war is over, I want to play ball for the Yanks again."

Spending his second season in khaki, Joe recalled that he played in 35 games this year and batted .410. "I saw quite a few Yanks in uniform, and they all looked great— Charley Ruffing, Bill Dickey, Ken Sears, Joe Gordon (who played shortstop for our 7th Air Force team) and Phil Rizzuto, who played third base in the Hawaiian World Series."

Just before the playoffs, DiMaggio became ill, and spent six weeks in a Honolulu hospital. Returned to San Francisco, he spent three more weeks at a hospital for medical observation and treatment. Now he thinks all he needs is some reconditioning, and he'll get that at Atlantic City. ■

Reunion Tales Irk Mrs. DiMaggio

November 22, 1944

Dorothy Arnold DiMaggio, estranged wife of the former Yankee baseball player, said yesterday that "it seems that every time we turn around somebody has us reconciled and we're getting a little bit stupid and jerky about it all."

The occasion for her latest denial was the rumor that Sgt. Joe and Dorothy would be back together because both were living at the Hotel Adams, 2 E. 86th St. Joe is in New York on furlough.

In the first place, Dorothy said, they're not living in the same suite. In the second place, she added, Joe is staying at the Adams "for the sole purpose of seeing the baby"—the couple's two-year-old son, Joseph Paul DiMaggio III. ■

Joe DiMaggio with his son, Joe III, and his former wife, Dorothy Arnold.

AP/Wide World Photos

Has Anyone Here Seen DiMaggio?

November 21, 1944

A couple of Yank baseball stars were in town yesterday, one arriving with his own fanfare, the other remaining in seclusion. The secretive one was Sgt. Joe DiMaggio, who came here over the weekend and hasn't seen prexy Ed Barrow or any scribe since maintaining the silence he has kept since landing in 'Frisco last August. Joe had been hospitalized with stomach trouble in Honolulu, but won't say whether he's slated for a medical discharge.

The ebullient Yank was Snuffy Stirnweiss, premier base-stealer, who took time off his Connecticut coaching job to drop down here and pass out cigars for the birth of his second daughter.

Ma DiMag Citizen, Pop to Try Again

December 12, 1944

Mrs. Rosalia Mercurio DiMaggio, 66, mother of baseball's three DiMaggio brothers, won her citizenship today, but Joseph Sr., 72, her husband, struck out. Superior Judge George W. Sconfielo asked the father of Joe, Dominic and Vincent to try again in three months.

Mrs. DiMaggio received her first citizenship papers two years and 10 months ago. ■

While Rosalia DiMaggio, mother of baseball great Joe DiMaggio II, won her citizenship, Joe, Sr., struck out.

DiMag Gets Exam by Army Again

December 23, 1944

Though there are persistent rumors that Sgt. Joe DiMaggio is awaiting a medical discharge, the former Yankee outfielder knows only that he is to report at the Army's rehabilitation center in Atlantic City Wednesday. He stopped by the club offices on West 42nd St. yesterday to pass the season's greetings with boss Ed Barrow, but didn't indicate that he expects to be released from service. He was recently brought to the mainland from Honolulu for treatment of a stomach condition and has been on furlough for the past couple of weeks. Should a discharge come through, DiMag will be in a convenient location to rejoin the club when it begins training at the New Jersey resort March 11. ∎

"It's obvious that I was not the same player I had been after I came out of the war. All you have to do is look at the record."
—Joe DiMaggio

Joe DiMaggio: Never the Same

March 20, 1991

The incomparable Joe DiMaggio was reaching his prime when he was called into the Army in 1943. In seven seasons prior to World War II, he averaged .330 with 30 homers and 130 RBIs. But the three years in the service took a toll on the Yankee Clipper—he had only one truly great year left.

"It's obvious that I was not the same player I had been after I came out of the war," he said. "All you have to do is look at the record. The fact was, those three years I was in the war, I was 29, 30 and 31—they would have been the prime years of my career. Do I think about what my overall record would have been had I not lost those three years? Sure. It's only natural."

"I spent my entire time in the War in Hawaii. I had developed ulcers and they put me in the special services. We played a lot of ball over there and it wasn't bad duty. When you ask what the war took out of me, I'd say not nearly as much as what it took from guys like Ted (Williams) and (Bob) Feller. They were in a lot longer."

DiMag-Williams Act Set for Long Encore

By Jack Smith
January 16, 1945

The big boys are coming back to the big leagues. The pre-war stars, the peacetime greats of the game are exchanging their service dog-tags for baseball monkey suits. Back to their old chores they come and with them a rebirth of fandom's favorite vendettas. The old rivalries are stirring again and foremost among them the long-argued, never-settled dispute; which is the greater hitter, Joe DiMaggio, slugging star of the Yanks, or Ted Williams, Boston's beanpole and the AL's only .400 hitter since '23?

The phlegmatic DiMaggio is already in civvies, planning a preliminary warmup for the season in Florida. The erratic Williams is soon to receive his discharge and is counted on heavily in boss Joe Cronin's renovation of the Red Sox.

Whatever their ultimate place among the game's hitting immortals, they are without a doubt the two top bat wielders in recent history. DiMaggio's swinging from the right side of the plate contributed one spectacular performance after another in seven major league seasons before his entry into service in

Hitting immortals Ted Williams and Joe DiMaggio pose together at Fenway Park.

AP/Wide World Photos

'42. The younger and left-handed Williams, with only three seasons of major league ball, approached heights untouched in years.

Now, back to the big stadiums and the roar of the crowds come these two diamond greats, prepared to continue their brilliant duel for honors. Now 31 and troubled with stomach ulcers, DiMag faces the harder task in regaining peak physical condition.

A bargain-basement acquisition, obtained from San Francisco in '35 for $75,000 and five players, DiMaggio has compiled a lifetime batting average of .345, leading the league in '39 with .381 and '40 with .352. He has blasted 198 homers, topping the circuit with 46 in '37. He has totaled 816 runs-batted-in, topping the loop with 125 in '41. And

The long-argued, never-settled dispute: Which is the greater hitter, Joe DiMaggio...or Ted Williams?

at Minneapolis and came up to the majors to stay in '39. Over a three-year span, he compiled a lifetime average of .356. In '39, his first in the majors, he topped all rivals with 145 runs-batted-in. He finished second to DiMag for the batting crown in '40, hitting .344. In '41, when he won the title with a .406 average, he also led in home runs, runs scored and bases on balls.

Not since the days of Ty Cobb and Napoleon Lajoie has there been such a rivalry for honors as between these two. ∎

brightest of all his achievements, one of the outstanding individual accomplishments in sports annals was his 56 consecutive game hitting streak compiled in '41.

Williams was purchased from San Diego in '37, spent '38

Past Records of Two Clouters

Who's the top man in slugging circles—Ted Williams or Joe DiMaggio? For three pre-war years, they matched slugging feats, DiMag with the Yanks, Williams with the Red Sox. With the war at an end, the duel will soon resume. Facts and figures will fly. Here are the statistics of the three seasons in which they were full-time rivals.

	G	AB	R	H	2B	3B	HR	RBI	B.AVG
1939									
Williams	149	565	131	185	44	11	31	145	.327
DiMaggio	120	462	103	176	32	6	30	126	.381
1940									
Williams	144	561	134	193	43	14	23	113	.344
DiMaggio	132	508	93	179	28	9	31	133	.352
1941									
Williams	143	436	135	185	33	3	37	120	.406
DiMaggio	139	541	122	193	43	11	30	125	.357

DiMaggio, Sr. Passes U.S. Tests

April 10, 1945

Joe DiMaggio, Sr., 71, father of the baseball-playing trio of Joseph, Vince and Dominic, passed his naturalization tests today in his second effort. Born in Palermo, Sicily, he came to the United States in 1898.

DiMag Set Free; Won't Join Yanks

September 15, 1945

Although he could make almost as much money playing the remaining 16 days of the season as he did in his two-and-a-half-year stretch in the Army, Sgt. Joe DiMaggio announced upon his medical discharge here today that he will not rejoin the Yanks until next spring.

Periodically troubled by stomach ulcers, the former $40,000-a-year slugger finally received his discharge from the AAF Don Cesar Hospital here this afternoon. DiMag intends to leave soon to confer with his new boss, Larry MacPhail, in New York and then will head for his home in San Francisco. ■

Yankees Sign DiMaggio ($42,000) and Chandler

By Jack Smith
November 29, 1945

Joe DiMaggio was officially reinstated as the second highest salaried Yank in history yesterday. The war officially ended for the West Coast Italian when Larry MacPhail revealed that he and Spud Chandler, star right-hander, had been signed to the customary documents "for some time." Joe signed at the same pay he received on his last Yank contract in '42—a cool $42,000. This has been topped only by the $80,000 peeled off for Babe Ruth in his prime.

A little leaner and a little older than when he last drew civilian pay checks, Joe grinned toothily through another coffee and sandwich session in MacPhail's Fifth Ave. office.

"I'm not going to rush into action the way Hank Greenberg did," Joe offered. "I'm going to get it, a lot of preliminary work. I'm thinking of going to Bear Mountain for a couple of weeks. Hiking through the mountains will toughen my legs. Then I'm going to St. Petersburg around the end of January. I hope to be ready for more strenuous work when spring training officially opens."

The signings actually took place at the end of the past season and, according to MacPhail, "It took only a minute to sign each." As stipulated by baseball's "GI Bill of Rights," each was tendered the same salary he received before going into service, Chandler's pay reaching in the neighborhood of $20,000 and DiMaggio's $42,000, a sum he

> He confessed that he is 10 pounds underweight, still on a diet for stomach ulcers, but nevertheless confident it will not take too long for him to get into top shape.

wrangled from Ed Barrow after a prolonged holdout.

At that time, DiMag was fresh from his brilliant 56-game hitting streak. He was demanding $42,500 from Barrow, who was offering only $40,000. Barrow finally upped the offer and DiMag signed in Barrow's hotel suite in St. Petersburg during the middle of the training season.

With DiMag, his slugging and outfielding star, and Chandler, his pitching ace, already lined up for '46, Joe McCarthy is off to a fine start toward bringing the pennant back to the Stadium. Service discharges becoming known every day are gradually piling up a huge backlog of material and by the time—about February 10—Joe calls his Spring camp to order, he'll have approximately 75 hopefuls of varying degrees of experience and talent available for duty.

MacPhail scanned the roster and reserve list yesterday and numbered 18 Yanks who have either been discharged or are about to get out. These include some who were the Yanks last season—Chandler, Ruffing, Robinson and Keller—as well as such standbys as Henrich, DiMag, Hemsley, Sears, Silvestri, Gordon, Rizzuto, Hassett, Sturm and Selkirk.

The list of 18 also includes the rookies or newcomers, Charlie Stanceu, Rinaldo Ardizoia, Herb Karpel and Hank Majeski. ∎

Whittaker, Daily News

"After you've been away from it for a couple of
years you have trouble."
—Joe DiMaggio in Spring Training

Chapter 5
1946

Getting Back in the Swing

*T*he Yankee stars seemed to have lost some of their shine during their time in the military. Joe DiMaggio wasn't immune and whether it was due to rusty skills or to injury, DiMag slumped to a batting average of .290 for the season. This was down from a seven-season average of .337 before the war.

While Joe D didn't enjoy a great year and the Yankees managed only third place, the fans didn't seem to mind, and season attendance was over two million.

With banner attendance, the Yankee ownership was flush with cash. Instead of being one of the holdouts, Joe DiMaggio was the first Yankee to sign for the 1947 season.

In addition, DiMaggio seemed to develop a new appreciation for the game and his fans during his time in the military. He signed more autographs during Spring Training in '46 than he did during entire seasons before his military service. ∎

AP/Wide World Photos

Joe DiMaggio is all smiles about reporting to Spring Training.

1946 REGULAR SEASON

G	AB	R	H	2B	3B	HR	RBI	BB	SB	AVG.	SLG.
132	503	81	146	20	8	25	95	59	1	.290	.511

DiMag Turns Student to Improve Batting

By Joe Trimble
February 19, 1946

You were standing behind the batting cage out in the scorch in a Panama sun and you were learning something. You were learning that even the greatest baseball player in the business is not good enough to stop learning. As you stood there during batting practice, Joe DiMaggio walked up, idly trailing a bat, and leaned against one of the struts which support the backstop. Phil Rizzuto was batting and DiMag watched him acutely.

"Getting a few pointers on hitting?" you asked in an attempt at some light conversation.

"Well, yes," came the answer.

You asked if it helped him to watch another player hit. He said no, but that it did help to watch what the pitcher was throwing.

"After you've been away from it for a couple of years you have trouble. Standing back here and looking through this netting of the backstop makes sense because I'm getting an idea of how the different pitches break," he added.

A moment later, Tommy Henrich was the hitter and Steve Roser, who was pitching, fired a hard one which seemed to "take off" or skip a bit away from the batter as it reached the plate. "That was a slider," Joe said.

When Henrich had finished (each batter gets three socks which land in fair territory) it was DiMaggio's turn. The crowd of about 1,000 clapped and chattered as they saw the big guy step to the plate. They knew from his pictures in the papers before the team ever came here and every new attendee at the practice is quickly told by the other fans that No. 5 is Big Joe.

> The crowd of about 1,000 clapped and chattered as they saw the big guy step to the plate. They knew from his pictures in the papers before the team ever came here and every new attendee at the practice is quickly told by the other fans that No. 5 is Big Joe.

He missed his first swing and topped a half-hit grounder over third base on his next. Then he rapped the ball hard but high to center field, an ordinary fly. The next few pitches were bad and then Joe fouled a couple. With Joe still in the batter's box, Charley Keller, the next hitter, stepped around from behind the batting cage and bent over to pick up a couple of loose bats that lay where previous hitters had thrown them.

DiMag misinterpreted his act, thinking Charley was trying to hustle him out of there much in the fashion of an annoyed poppa winding the alarm clock as a hint for a daughter's boyfriend to vamoose. "Still have another fair one to hit, Charley," Joe said.

Keller agreed and explained that he was only picking up the bats. Then he added, "Bet a coke on this next one of yours against my three for distance."

Joe accepted and crashed the next pitch over the center field fence, the ball travelling about 375 feet. The crowd roared and clapped at that and DiMag, grinning, stepped out of the box and came back again behind the cage.

"Guess you win that one easily," you said to him.

"Wait and see," he said.

We waited and Keller's second swing drove the ball just as far over the right field wall. Charley hit a grounder after that and said: "Guess we're even."

DiMaggio agreed. ∎

Hank Olen, Daily News

DiMaggio's Spring Training studies helped him get back in the groove after his military service.

Fans Just as Important as Hits to "New" DiMag

By Joe Trimble
April 28, 1946

J oe DiMaggio is the most compelling figure in baseball, the greatest player in the game and a man the multitudes have accorded the place once held by Babe Ruth. He is America's No. 1 athletic hero, and his popularity will be reflected in the AL box office returns this year. It has been predicted that this season will produce a record number of paying patrons in major league ballparks and, if this comes to pass, DiMag will be in a large measure responsible.

Most interesting thing about all this is that the player himself likes it. He thoroughly relishes being the Big Guy of the Yankees and gets as big a thrill out of pleasing the crowds as Ruth ever did. Perhaps that would seem natural but it really isn't. Fact is, the Joe DiMaggio who went away to war in 1942 disliked crowds. He disliked people. He was a loner and if need be, could be ungracious enough to let others know it. He wanted to be alone as much as Garbo did.

That was '42. Now it is different. Perhaps the three years in the Army did something for Joe DiMaggio. Perhaps they made him a better

human being. Or maybe this change would have come anyhow—merely with the development of Joe socially. Anyway, it is a happy change . . . and everyone who knows him and values his friendship is glad for it.

To have dubbed pre-war DiMag as a "sour apple" would have been harsh but awfully close to the truth. He was aloof—from the fans, the press and even his teammates. He accepted applause and derision with equanimity.

Only time he was really upset by the fans was in

Just one of many additional autograph sessions Joe DiMaggio took part in after returning from the Army.

Daily News

'42 when, with the nation at war, he became the target for unfair criticism. He was told by thoughtless fans that he ought to be in the Army, and was razzed all season long. Even though he had as much right to be deferred, at the time, as other family men, he was marked as unpatriotic. This eventually got under his skin and he enlisted after the '42 season.

There is little doubt that he matured mentally while in the service. To put it in a few words, he learned to take it. He also found out that there is a tougher life than baseball. So, upon returning this year, he was a different man.

> Fact is, the Joe DiMaggio who went away to war in 1942 disliked crowds. He disliked people. He was a loner and if need be, could be ungracious enough to let others know it. He wanted to be alone as much as Garbo did.

Baseball was no longer a job to be done. It was a game worth playing and something that could be fun. For the new DiMaggio, all life is fun.

He has even forgotten his unhappy marriage and resultant divorce from the former Dorothy Arnold, and fastens his affection upon their handsome little boy, 4 1/2-year-old Joe the Third. He lives for the kid, now, and he wants that little boy to be proud of him.

Joe's renewed interest in the game was first evident in Panama where the Yankees began training early in February. He "played up" to the fans, even to the extent of hitting homers in practice. He enjoyed it when the little Panamanian kids would run after him in the streets of the city, calling his name and asking for autographs.

He has signed more autographs this spring than he used to in a whole season before the war. In rail stations, at airports, in hotel lobbies, and of course at the ballparks, he was besieged.

One day in New Orleans before a game, teenaged boys were jumping out of the stands to get his autograph. The head groundskeeper was annoyed at this and asked DiMag not to sign for the kids.

"It is up to you to keep them off the field if you want them off," said Joe. "I'm not going to refuse when I'm asked. I don't want them going off saying that DiMaggio was the kind of guy who wouldn't give an autograph."

The Yankees played to 316,846 customers from Balboa to Brooklyn, the most fabulous Spring Training record in history. The club picked up around $150,000 at the box office, and this paid for the entire training period. Never in history has a major league club gotten off the "nut" (Spring Training expense) before the regular season began. This year the Yanks showed a profit on it—and nearly every dollar taken in was one which its owner offered for the privilege of seeing DiMaggio.

In Ruth's heyday the Yanks never managed more than a $65,000 exhibition gate, so even allowing that money is freely spent for entertainment these days— it would seem that DiMag is a greater draw than Ruth, who certainly was a more colorful person. ■

Yanks (7-3), A's (4-1) Split; DiMag Injured

By Joe Trimble
July 8, 1946

The Yankees split a double-header with the A's before a crowd of 27,169 in Philadelphia here this afternoon, but lost more than just the second game. They were deprived of the services of Joe DiMaggio for at least a week. The outfielder was injured in a slide into second base during the opener, which New York won, 7-3, on homers by Aaron Robinson and Charley Keller. Right-hander Bob Savage bested Spud Chandler in the night-cap, 4-1.

DiMag's injury, which was diagnosed as a twisted knee cartilage and a sprained ankle, came when he hustled to second on a two-bagger in the second inning. He slid and his spikes caught as he hit too close to the base and bounced past it. He managed to grab hold safely with his hand but there was no doubt that he was hurt.

After a brief massage of the knee, he limped from the field. Dr. James Pugh, A's physician, attended him and packed the leg in ice.

"It's the same cartilage that I hurt in '34," Joe explained. There was no need to take him to the hospital. The big outfielder has played in every Yankee game of the year, 44 exhibitions and 77 league games.

Johnny Lindell ran for him and scored ahead of Robbie's wallop (No. 5) over the right field fence.

DiMag had made six hits in his last 11 times at bat when his injury forced him out. For the first time in many years, the fans here rooted wildly for the Yankees. ∎

Daily News

A routine slide like this one against the Cardinals kept Joe DiMaggio out of the lineup for two weeks when he twisted his knee and sprained his ankle.

DiMag X-rayed; Out of Lineup 2 Weeks

By Joe Trimble
July 9, 1946

The fates which have bedeviled the Yankees all season took another swipe at them yesterday when it was revealed that Joe DiMaggio's banged up left knee is so out of whack that he'll be out of the lineup longer than expected—at least two weeks.

Cursory examination in Philadelphia after he sustained the injury on Sunday had led to the hopeful conclusion that he'd be back in the game in time for next Sunday's twin bill with the Tigers.

Joe's spikes caught when he slid into second base on a double in the second inning of the opener against the A's. His foot caught a portion of the base, and the cartilage on the inside of his left knee popped loose. It was a recurrence of an injury he sustained in '34 when playing with San Francisco of the Pacific Coast League.

The leg was X-rayed yesterday at a New York Hospital where Dr. S. W. Moore attended the center fielder. It was his estimate that Joe can't possibly play until the passage of two weeks' time. This means, of course, that he'll be of no value in the home stand against the West, which comprises 11 games, beginning Thursday night.

Dr. Moore fitted DiMaggio with a light plaster cast which immobilizes the knee. It is to be removed daily so that he can take diathermy treatments. It wasn't necessary for him to remain at the hospital. The X-ray of his ankle showed only a bruise, no sprain.

Johnny Lindell will have to play center field in his place—for better or worse it is hard to say. ∎

DiMaggio Throws Out Arm, Hits Homer, Then Sits

August 16, 1946

"I don't believe my arm has ever been this sore," Joe DiMaggio said gloomily in the dressing room this afternoon just after leaving today's game with the Red Sox. "It hurt from the elbow right up to the shoulder. I threw it out while trying to get Bobby Doerr going from first to third after I fielded Rudy York's hit in the fourth inning."

Assistant trainer Gus Mauch sat him under a baking lamp and said that he would have to keep hot applications on it during the night. He will try out the flipper in left field tomorrow. "I felt it coming on even before today," DiMag claimed. "But I wasn't certain until I tried to get Doerr. It hurt like the devil when I made that throw."

Joe had to make two more throws in the fifth inning and they were weak lobs. The Red Sox didn't catch on that there was anything the matter and didn't try to run on him. He told manager Dickey what was wrong and Bill agreed to take him out after he batted in the sixth. It was then that he homered.

DiMag Sets Sights on .300 in Yankee Fadeout

By Joe Trimble
August 29, 1946

There is nothing left of the Yankee ball season except the current spurt of Joe DiMaggio toward the .300 mark. That, alone, remains a feature of the team's activity as it concludes a campaign mottled with personal failure by many of the key figures.

Even DiMag, if he does hurdle the .300 line of demarcation that divides baseball's better people from their poor relations will not have totally absolved himself. His season has been bad, too. But that has been due largely to the difficulty of postwar adjustment. The big thing is that he is proving by his late drive that he isn't washed up. And, for him personally, a .300 average may save some of the slashing his salary is certain to get next winter.

Right now, Joe is a thrilling player to watch. He is hitting hard and long and looks like the guy who batted safely in 56 straight games back in '41. He was talking about that before last night's game with the Indians.

"During that streak I never had a bad day. That is, never a day where a pop-fly single or a blooper kept my string going. I was hitting the ball on the nose all the time," he recalled. "I'm doing that again now. Of course, there's an occasional popup because of poor judgment or timing, but no really bad days in which I never really get hold of a ball."

In that heroic streak, DiMag had a lot of trouble with pitchers who wanted the personal glory of being the one to stop him. "I guess Dutch Leonard was the toughest of them all," Joe says. "He simply fired those knucklers all over the place and very few of them over the plate. Most of the pitchers I faced were wary of giving me a good ball. As a result I was often forced to swing at 3-0 pitches.

"In this I had the full cooperation of Joe McCarthy, who was as anxious as I to keep it going. Ordinarily a hitter is given a 'take' sign when he has three balls and no strikes on him, but Mac told me to hit any pitch I wanted regardless of the count."

Joe did have a couple of really close calls before pitchers Al Smith, Jim Bagby and third baseman Ken Keltner combined to horsecollar him on July 17, 1941. He made it 38 in a row by just the matter of half an inch. In a game at the Stadium against the Browns he got one hit, a solid line drive off the webbing of the glove of Harlond Clift, the St. Louis third baseman.

When he finally was stopped it was Keltner who did it by making two terrific stabs of hard ground balls hit right over third base.

"Never knew I had either of them," Kenny told Joe afterward. ■

Betty's Sharp, But She Can't Stick Joe

October 6, 1946

Joe DiMaggio, New York Yankee outfielder, yesterday dismissed a Boston report that he was engaged to Betty Sharp, a night club entertainer, as "a publicity stunt."

"I've never seen the girl but twice in my life," said Joe. Miss Sharp was quoted by the *Boston Globe* as saying she and DiMaggio planned to be married and that they were looking for an apartment in Boston on the assumption that he "will be wearing a Red Sox uniform next year." DiMaggio said the whole thing was "news to me," including the implication that he would be playing for Boston. Recent rumors have linked the Yankees and Red Sox in a deal involving DiMaggio and Ted Williams.

Yankees Give Thanks, Contracts Generous

By Hy Turkin
November 27, 1946

At least two dozen Yank baseball players had an extra reason for Thanksgiving yesterday. These were the ones who received generous contracts for '47—thanks more to loyal Stadium fans who amassed a record gate this year than to their own batting and fielding feats. Joe DiMaggio and 13 others already have signed.

But those who haven't heard from Yank prexy Larry MacPhail must feel more like the turkey on Thanksgiving eve, for Larry murmured with the impact of a blunderbuss: "There will be no cuts in Yankee contracts for next year. If I feel I have to cut a player, I'm better off selling or trading him." Then he admitted there are still some he considers in the latter category.

Though the Yanks finished a sorry third, more than two million customers poured through the Bronx turnstiles, so Larry says, "Our club won't plead poverty in dealing with players. I anticipate no salary squabbles."

MacPhail admits only one player returned his contract unsigned, but says he's certain he'll come to terms soon. The man who might have been the most stubborn holdout of all, Joe DiMaggio, was first to sign! Though he was bothered by injuries and slumped to .290 after a lifetime batting average of .339 for seven seasons, DiMag wasn't cut from his '46 stipend salary. MacPhail also bagged Joe's outfield maters, Charley Keller and Tom Henrich. ∎

DiMaggio swings and misses. Despite a lower batting average than before the war, Joe remained one of the game's top athletes.

Hank Olen, Daily News

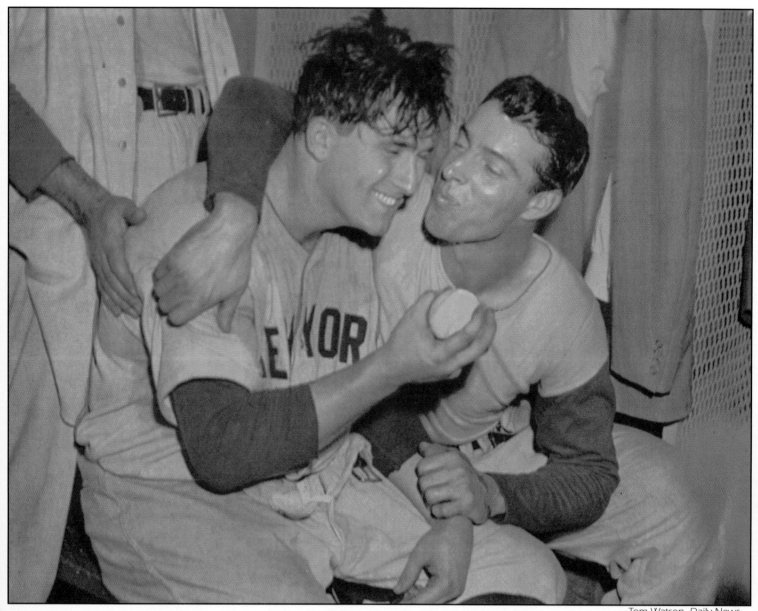

Tom Watson, Daily News

"If DiMaggio has a good season, we can win,
if he doesn't, well..."
—Bucky Harris

Chapter 6

1947

As DiMaggio Goes...

*I*n the 1920s, it was said, "As Ruth goes, so go the Yanks." In 1947, it was DiMaggio who was the team's barometer.

As DiMaggio struggled early due to a heel injury, the Yanks dropped to sixth place. In May, team president Larry MacPhail fined the recovering Yankee Clipper, along with other players, for leading a "revolt" after refusing to pose for a previously agreed-to team promotion. DiMaggio rallied the team to focus its anger at the opposing teams. The gambit worked, and in June, the Yanks launched a five-game winning streak that lifted the Bronx Bombers from sixth place to second place behind the Detroit Tigers in the space of two weeks.

After passing the Tigers, DiMaggio led the Yankees to victory in one of the most competitive World Series in history. The first World Series ever televised went seven games, with three games decided by a single run.

With a 2-1 series lead over Brooklyn, Yankee right hander Bill Bevins pitched 8 2/3 innings without giving up a hit. The only hit he allowed was the game-winning double that drove in two runs as the Dodgers evened the series at 2-2. In the fifth game, Joe hit a game-winning home run that gave the Yanks a series lead and led them to their 11th World Championship.

Unfortunately, 1947 also continued DiMaggio's history of injury troubles. An operation to remove a bone spur kept him out of uniform until April. He was limited to pinch-hitting duties in the season opener. Then he pulled a leg muscle in a July double-header in Detroit. In August, it was a torn neck muscle. During those 10 days the Clipper was sidelined, the Yanks lost four of six games. After returning to the lineup, he left the next day as his heel flared up again. Luckily by then the Yankees were safely in first place and were never threatened after taking the lead in late June. ∎

1947 REGULAR SEASON

G	AB	R	H	2B	3B	HR	RBI	BB	SB	AVG.	SLG.
141	534	97	168	31	10	20	97	64	3	.315	.522

Operate on DiMag Heel: Say Babe "Satisfactory"

By Jim McCulley
January 6, 1947

Two of the greatest ballplayers in Yankee history were confined to local hospitals yesterday and both were reported doing well after surgery. Babe Ruth was "somewhat better after an uncomfortable night" at French Hospital, where he is recovering from a neck operation for the relief of intractable, uncontrollable pain, and Joe DiMaggio underwent a minor operation for removal of a spur from his left heel at Beth David hospital.

Ruth, who has been battling a sinus infection, went under the knife Monday morning. He had been admitted to the Hospital November 26 for sinus treatment. Yesterday evening, 30 hours after the operation, his condition was pronounced satisfactory and Harry Kiely, hospital director, said that no further bulletins would be issued unless there is a radical change.

DiMag entered the hospital Monday, and Dr. Jules Gordon performed the surgery yesterday afternoon. He removed the spur, three-fourths of an inch long and half an inch wide, and also cleaned up a bursa sac that was inflamed. Dr. Gordon said that the center fielder's post-operative reaction was excellent and that Joe would be able to leave the hospital within a week. The foot must remain in a cast for one week following his departure. ∎

DiMaggio to Accompany Yanks to Puerto Rico

By Dick Young
February 8, 1947

After extricating a size 11-D foot from his mouth, Larry MacPhail recently stated that henceforth, all official announcements concerning the Yankees will come from Arthur (Red) Patterson. So, here is Arthur announcing: "Joe DiMaggio will accompany the main player group to Puerto Rico." Thus MacPhail's aired voice yesterday quashed widely spread rumors that DiMag's ailing left heel would restrict his training.

"Joe wants to go to Puerto Rico," added Patterson. "He knows that he has a better chance of getting in shape there than anywhere else."

The entire fuss arose over DiMag's rather slow recovery from an operation for the removal of a bone spur a month ago. It wasn't till the other day that Joe discarded his cane and, in view of his slight limp, it was suspected that DiMag might not make the flight to Puerto Rico February 14, but would work out with the Yankees' secondary squad at St. Petersburg.

But Patterson denies this. The reason appears obvious: Manager Bucky Harris wants DiMag under his direct scrutiny as much as possible. Joe's poor showing last season was attributed, in part, to "over-training," and Bucky wants to guard against a repetition.

In addition, the name DiMaggio pulls customers into the park for exhibition games, and MacPhail is fully aware of the fact that the fans in Puerto Rico use American money.

DiMag, Williams $64 Question as Players Leave for Camps

By Dick Young
February 9, 1947

Baseball's rush-hour is on. By train, plane, boat and car, anxious players are hurrying to Puerto Rico, to Havana, to Catalina Island and a dozen other sun-soaked paradises where a score of vital questions wait to be answered. By the end of this week, the first of the major league training camps will echo the squeaks of stiffened bones. Then, the others follow quickly until by the first of March, every pretty palm tree that majestically fringes the camp fields will take on the curved appearance of a giant question mark in the minds of the tormented managers.

For this particular spring grind, like no other for many years, holds the clues to those huge queries which were asked at the conclusion of last year, and which spell each team's success or failure for the coming campaign. Down at Puerto Rico, for instance, where the Yankees roll out their bats this

Saturday, the question that awaits an answer is: "Can Joe DiMaggio come back?"

There, under the tropical glare, as each sweat-soaked day goes by, the important reply will be pieced together, slowly but inexorably. Little by little, it will become apparent to manager Bucky Harris whether DiMag's disappointment of '46 was merely the result of a wartime layoff, or whether Joe has really "gone back" to a point where he will never again be the incomparable Yankee Clipper.

Over at Sarasota, Florida, where the AL champion Red Sox convene on February 24, the question is: "Can Ted Williams find the answer to the over-shifted defense which smeared such a sad ending on his otherwise brilliant season last year?" Will manager Joe Cronin insist that The Kid learn to hit to left to discourage such defensive finagling, or will Williams stubbornly insist upon swinging away in defiance of the gang-up act? ∎

> Down at Puerto Rico, for instance, where the Yankees roll out their bats this Saturday, the question that awaits an answer is: "Can Joe DiMaggio come back?"

DiMag Is Out for Six Weeks

By Joe Trimble
February 16, 1947

This sun-kissed fragment of tropical real estate has had some celebrated "heels" through the years, some shady characters who swaggered and swindled through Puerto Rico's turbulent political history. However, the most important one here now, not political but physical, is the left heel of Giuseppe DiMaggio.

It became quite evident today as the Yankees engaged in the first workout of the training season, that DiMag's recently operated-upon heel is mending too slowly to permit him much chance of getting in shape for the regular campaign. Dr. Mal Stevens, team physician, said this afternoon that he doubts very much if Joe will be able to engage in competitive baseball for about six weeks—if then.

"He has what is known as an open, granulating wound," Stevens explained. "There is very little that can be done for it except to let it come along of its own accord and that is going to be a tedious process. Daily treatments and dressings are necessary and any strain on it is harmful. Baseball, or even much walking, is out of the question at this time."

> "DiMaggio is the most important player on this club...and I will be guided by whatever the doctor recommends."
> —Bucky Harris, Yankee manager

Manager Bucky Harris is disappointed by the doctor's diagnosis, of course, as he is most anxious to have Joe ready for a great comeback after last year's miserable showing, when the great outfielder hit under .300 (.290) for the first time in his career.

"DiMaggio is the most important player on this club," Harris said as he supervised the workout. "I am happy Stevens is here to look after him and I will be guided by whatever the doctor recommends. In any case, Joe will not be forced to do a thing until Stevens tells me it is okay. I want him ready for the opening of the season and every game after that. I only hope this lack of training won't be too damaging."

It is apparent now that the operation for removal of the spur from his foot should have been done a lot sooner than it was, which was on January 6. However, Joe himself put it off and, much to tell, really didn't want to have it done at all, but he was so anxious to make good this year that he underwent the operation in order to remove any possibility that he might be hobbled during the season. About the only silver lining in the whole business is that he is laid up at this time—when his presence is not needed. ◾

DiMag Returns to U.S. for 2nd Heel Operation

By Joe Trimble
February 26, 1947

Yank prexy Larry MacPhail revealed today that outfielder Joe DiMaggio will undergo further surgery on his injured left heel in order to hasten recovery. Joe will leave this training camp by plane tomorrow noon and is scheduled to arrive at LaGuardia airport at 7 p.m.

The Yankee star will then go to Johns Hopkins Hospital in Baltimore for a "closure operation" and possible skin graft.

Dr. Gordon operated on DiMaggio in New York, January 6 for removal of a bone spur (calcium deposit). Dr. Mal Stevens, Yankee club physician, agreed the added surgery could be done right here, but feels perhaps it would be better if done by a plastic surgeon. So, he is sending Joe to Dr. George Bennett.

The unlucky outfielder, who has missed being in the opening-day lineup six years out of the eight he has been in the majors, was agreeable to the sugges-tion that he undergo another operation.

"I'm happy to do anything which helps," said Joe, who is irked by idleness. "I want to start the season and will do anything the doctors say I'm to do. I'm not so worried over the future, but I do want to be useful to the team. They tell me I couldn't possibly open the season if the heel were allowed to heal naturally, so I agreed to the opera-tion."

Stevens explained that the wound has healed so slowly that it's approximately two weeks behind schedule. He added, however, "It has improved tremendously during the last four days, and will be in perfect condition for operation."

The wound is a half-inch deep, and healing from the inside out in the shape of a V. It resembles a cut in a badly hit golf ball. Dr. Bennett may graft skin over the opening to aid recovery. ∎

DiMag to Be in Uniform for Opener

April 11, 1947

Although still about a month away from regular play, Joe DiMaggio will appear in a Yankee uniform when the club opens the season against the Senators in Washington Monday. Left behind when the main squad left St. Petersburg last Friday, DiMag rested his stitched left heel, which is healing faster than originally anticipated.

Trainer Gus Mauch said that the Clipper, fortified with a specially built shoe, has been run-ning as well as batting and has advanced far enough to serve as a pinch-hitter. Returning with DiMag and Mauch are Dr. Mal Stevens, club physician, and pitcher Mel Queen.

Following yesterday's workout in the Stadium, Harris nominated Floyd Bevens; Marius Russo, who is still testing his left arm; and Spud Chandler in the first of three against the Dodgers in Ebbets Field this afternoon.

Yanks "Revolt" against MacPhail

DiMaggio, Four Others Fined

By Joe Trimble
May 23, 1947

Under-the-surface bitterness between Larry MacPhail and the Yankees burst into the open yesterday, and none other than Joe DiMaggio was revealed as the leader of a player "revolt." MacPhail has fined Joe and four others for refusal to cooperate in the club's promotional ventures, Joe's paycheck being clipped for $100, those of Johnny Lindell and Aaron Robinson for $50 each and those of Charley Keller and rookie pitcher Don Johnson for $25 apiece.

DiMaggio, who is no clubhouse lawyer or Bolshevik by any means, unwittingly is cast as the leader of the "revolution" against Larry. Joe refused to pose for Army Signal Corps newsreel shots and that precipitated the fuss. Keller followed DiMag's lead, as did Lindell and Robinson. The latter pair also persuaded other players against posing.

Young Johnson was penalized for failing to go to a dinner in New Jersey after he had promised to be there and his appearance had been advertised.

DiMaggio confirmed the levying of the fine last night and said that he would take it. "There isn't anything else I can do about it. The management wanted me to pose for the Army newsreel shots during batting practice last Monday and I said I wouldn't because I needed the batting practice badly and did not want to give up that time to anything else."

The Yankee owner explained the club's side of the controversy in a phone conversation with *The News*. "DiMaggio, Keller, Robinson and Lindell were fined because they reneged on their promise to pose for the Signal Corps photographers. The club never ordered them to do it. They were asked to do so last week and agreed. The idea was that they would appear in pictures alongside soldiers wearing the new Army uniform. The point was to publicize the uniform, and the club was willing to cooperate.

President of the New York Yankees, Larry MacPhail.

Daily News

"But when the time came to do it, the players refused. Keller did so only because DiMag had balked first. He told me afterwards that it really didn't matter to him. Robinson and Lindell were fined more than Keller because they influenced others not to pose. But no one else was fined. Young Johnson simply broke an appointment on purpose and was reprimanded.

"And, incidentally, it has been the practice on this club to collect fines at the end of the season and there is a very good chance that these won't be collected then."

There appeared to be trouble brewing over the travel situation, too, due to a report that MacPhail has issued an ultimatum to the effect that any player—excepting Frank Crosetti—who refused to fly on the coming western trip would have to pay his own way. This MacPhail vehemently denied last night.

"I have never told any player that he could not take the train if he wanted to," Larry said. "No player ever has had to pay his own way and none ever will be required to by this club. And there is no truth to the story that the players who went by train on the last western trip were billed for the cost of their travel."

"The Yankee management has a contract with United Airlines which expires July 7. Until then, those who desire to fly, can. After that everyone goes by train. But there will be no penalty against anyone for refusing to fly."

The players do not get anything out of the after-dinner appearances and hate to go to banquets. This is particularly true when they've been through a

> DiMaggio, who is no clubhouse lawyer or Bolshevik by any means, unwittingly is cast as the leader of the "revolution" against Larry.

losing streak—as they were before Wednesday night's 5-0 triumph over the Tigers. Incidentally, two of the fined players were largely responsible for that victory. DiMag doubled home three runners in the first inning and later on Keller tripled in a run and scored another.

Caught right in the middle of the maelstrom is Bucky Harris. The latter has been struggling hard to keep the morale of the club up and this latest move by MacPhail may prove a staggering blow to the harassed manager. It is a pity that Larry didn't at least give Bucky a chance to talk to the players and try to enlist their cooperation before levying the fines.

His attitude seems ridiculous, something like when a little boy picks on another kid and says, "I'm bigger than you and I can lick you. I wanna be best." Strangely, the other Yankee owners, Del Webb and Dan Topping, apparently agree with MacPhail. The three held a meeting Tuesday in the Yankee offices and discussed the entire matter—including the fines—before MacPhail notified the players. Each man affected received notice of his pay deduction after Tuesday's game. News of it didn't break until yesterday when the players were to hold a protest meeting. However, due to the rain, there was no game and therefore no meeting.

Nine men refused to fly on the last western trip. They are Spud Chandler, Don Johnson, Allie Reynolds, Bill Bevens, Frank Shea, Snuffy Stirnweiss, Tom Henrich, Crosetti and coach John Schultz. The first five are the team's starting pitchers. Others who want to go back on the rails for good are Yogi Berra and Phil Rizzuto. ∎

DiMag Ignited Blazing Yanks

By Joe Trimble
May 28, 1947

In a way, this is personal and maybe it shouldn't be in the paper. But the boss said that as long as I was not busy I ought to write something nice about the Yankees for a change, maybe some explanation of their rise from sixth place to second and the five-game winning streak they carried into tonight's game here against the Senators.

Well, to me there is one man responsible for the great and wonderful change that has come over the Yankees. One guy has made the difference—one hustling, battling ball player whose spirit and drive have made a pennant contender out of a club that had all but quit on itself less than a week ago. That is Joe DiMaggio, of course.

There are a load of statistics which show how the big guy has carried the club forward. Such as his 10 hits in 10 at-bats in the four-game sweep of the Reds.

But this isn't going to be about figures. His average by the way, is .323, highest since '42. It might be higher than that if he had gotten four hits instead of three last night—and that is where the personal angle comes into this story.

You see, I am the official scorer at the Stadium; the gink who decides whether questionable plays are hits or errors. I had a tough one last night when Joe, up for the last time in the game, hit a twisting grounder to Rudy York, the whale who plays first base for Boston. York made a swipe at the ball and missed it. It caromed off his toe at right angle to the direction in which it was hit.

I thought that he should have grabbed the ball for the out. Some of the other newspapermen claimed that it hit the base just before it hit him and others said that it had so much "English" on it that it was difficult to handle and should be a hit. But I reasoned that a big league first baseman should have caught it and so called it an error.

Well, it happens that I'm a DiMaggio rooter just as hard as you are. I wish that it could have been a hit. I was even willing to concede that I might have seen it wrong. So I asked Joe about it when we were coming down on the train this morning.

"You called it right," he said. "York messed it up. I could see it all the way because I was running right down the line at him. I know it didn't hit the base before he touched it. It would have been good to have another hit, for sure, but I wouldn't want that kind. You wouldn't be honest with yourself if you'd called it a hit, either. Rudy loused it up. That's all." ■

Missing games due to injury gave DiMag time for other pursuits, like spending time with his five year old son, Joe III.

AP/Wide World Photos

*O*pening Day versus the Kansas City Royals, 1996. *Photo by Linda Cataffo*

*G*eorge Steinbrenner traditionally awards first pitch honors at all important Yankee games to DiMaggio, including this one during the 1996 World Series against the Braves. *Photo by Linda Cataffo*

Daily News cartoonist Bill Gallo shows Joe DiMaggio one of his drawings of the Yankee Clipper during DiMaggio's visit to the paper. *Photo by Pat Carroll*

Joe DiMaggio and New York Governor George Pataki participate in the parade celebrating the New York Yankees' 1996 World Championship. *Photo by Misha Erwitt*

*G*eorge Steinbrenner applauds as Joe DiMaggio is introduced at City Hall during the Yankees' World Championship celebration in 1996. *Photo by Keith Torrie*

*J*oe DiMaggio and George Steinbrenner present the Yankees' World Championship trophy to Mayor Rudolph Giuliani for display at City Hall. *Photo by Keith Torrie*

*J*oe DiMaggio performing first pitch duties at the Yankees' Opening Day in 1997. *Photo by Linda Cataffo*

*J*oe DiMaggio throws out the first pitch prior to the first interleague game between the Florida Marlins and the New York Yankees in Miami, 1997. *Photo by Marta Lavandier*

*J*oe DiMaggio attends *Time Magazine's* 75th anniversary celebration at Radio City Music Hall. *Photo by Richard Corkery*

MAGAZINE 75TH ANNIVERSARY
MARCH 3, 1998

*J*oe Torre presents Joe DiMaggio with Mayor Giuliani's proclamation on Joe DiMaggio Day, September 27, 1998. *Photo by Keith Torrie*

Office of the Mayor
CITY OF NEW YORK

Proclamation

*J*oe DiMaggio and Phil Rizzuto wave to the crowd on Joe DiMaggio Day after Rizzuto presented DiMaggio with replicas of the World Series rings that were stolen from him. *Photo by Keith Torrie*

*J*oe DiMaggio visits the City Room of the *Daily News*. *Photo by Pat Carroll*

*J*oe DiMaggio gets a hand from fans and fellow oldtimers during Oldtimer's Day ceremonies at Yankee Stadium.
Photo by John Roca

*L*es Goodstein (far left), Pete Hamill, and Bill Gallo (far right), all of the *Daily News*, share a meal with Yankee legend Joe DiMaggio. *Photo by Todd Maisel*

"Where have you gone, Joe DiMaggio?"

*T*he Graduate featured the song "Mrs. Robinson," which posed the question "Where have you gone, Joe DiMaggio?" *Embassy Pictures*

Yanks Beat Tigers, 3-0; DiMag Gets 4, Tops AL

By Joe Trimble
June 4, 1947

Years ago, they said: "As Ruth goes, so go the Yanks." Today, you've only to substitute the name Joe DiMaggio and the saying fits perfectly. When he is great, so are they—as happened again this afternoon as Big Joe assumed the batting leadership of the AL and led his club to a 3-0 victory over the first-place Tigers.

Right now Big Joe is the No. 1 hitter in the league and can be challenged only by Harry Walker in the NL. This afternoon he rattled Hal Newhouser for four straight hits before finally going out and soared his average to .368. He has hit safely in eight of his last ten times at bat; in the past 16 games he has lifted his average 126 points from the .242 it was when he began the streak on May 18.

> DiMaggio is an inspiration to the rest of the club. They just seem to pick up and go into high gear when he shows the way. In this streak...he has been superb.

He has, of course, carried the Yankees on his broad back for the past two weeks. They were in sixth place on May 20, but today are second and only two games out of the lead. They have won 10 of their last 13.

The story of today's game is not entirely DiMaggio's though, even if his bat did gain the runs needed to win. There must be some consideration of fat Frankie Shea, the Connecticut Yankee who is whistling a merry tune through the holes in the bats of AL hitters. The stout person from Naugatuck dropped his first start, 1-0, to the Red Sox even though he pitched a three-hitter. Since then, no one has hurt him.

Last time out, he defeated the Senators. Before that he shut out Detroit, 5-0, allowing four hits and beating Newhouser for the first time. Incidentally, this was Newhouser's sixth loss against five wins and he'd just as soon not pitch against Shea anymore. That's for sure.

DiMaggio is an inspiration to the rest of the club. They just seem to pick up and go into high gear when he shows the way. In this streak, perhaps the greatest of his big league career, he has been superb. In the 16 games, he has been at bat 67 times and has made 33 hits for a .493 average.

Even in his 56-game skein of '41, he wasn't as potent. Then he went many a day with only one safe hit. In this splurge he has averaged better than two per game. Until he hit into a double play in the ninth today, he was rapping an even .500 for the 16 games. You'll go through a lot of record books before you find the equal of that.

Joe made his influence on today's pastime felt early. Stirnweiss reached base on Eddie Lake's first-inning error and moved to second as Keller walked. Joe then grounded a single hard to left to send in Stirny.

Newhouser got the first two batters in the third and then had to look at DiMag's white-hot bat again. He didn't get a good look. Joe screamed a hit to left and alertly took second as Wakefield played footsie with the ball. McQuinn walked and Pilly Johnson rapped a hit to left to send in DiMag.

The other run crossed in the ninth, and to DiMag's embarrassment, he was no help at all. Henrich began the inning with the eighth Yank hit and Keller walked. Joe hit into a double play which moved Tommy to third and then later scored as White wild pitched. ∎

DiMag Rejoins Yanks for Series with A's

By Joe Trimble
August 12 ,1947

Joe DiMaggio, the biggest Yankee of 'em all, put on his creamy white uniform with the No. 5 on it last night, strode majestically to the plate and announced himself ready to return to the lineup after a week's absence due to a torn neck muscle. And every little Yankee, from Bucky Harris down to the clubhouse boy, heaved a happy sigh of relief and had a glowy feeling about the World Series riches to come.

For, without Joey, this hasn't been much of a Yankee team. While his bat has lain in the dust, the club has dropped four games out of six. As he goes, so goes the club. And when he isn't in that lineup, it ain't good. Joe was very anxious to get back into the lineup and he took batting practice with gusto before last night's game with the A's. The early ones in the crowd of about 50,000 cheered his presence on the field in the batting drill.

Joe's return—he's been missing since a week ago Sunday—permitted Yogi Berra to put his mask back on and go behind the plate, where he belongs. As a left fielder, Yogi looked like one of Olsen and Johnson's stooges—willing but hardly artistic. Yogi is the team's No. 1 catcher now, even though the hitting of Aaron Robinson has improved of late.

DiMaggio has missed 10 games this year. He was delayed due to the convalescing heel and didn't begin his season until the Yanks' fifth game of the year. Then he played right on through until he had to quit after last Sunday's match here against the Indians. He had injured himself the previous day when sliding out a triple off Bob Feller. He pulled the muscles in the right side of his neck that day and aggravated the hurt the following afternoon.

As a consequence, he didn't play here last Monday night against the A's or in Philly against them the following two days. His injury enabled him to miss last Thursday's exhibition game in Waterbury, Connecticut, and forced him out of the entire weekend series in Boston. The Yanks dropped both of those series, two games to one. They seemed to be a stumbling, unsure collection of people, not the finely coordinated club which had made a runaway of the AL race.

> Anyway, the Big Guy is back, and barring another zig where he should have zagged, should be right on the beam until the pennant is clinched.

Anyway, the Big Guy is back, and barring another zig where he should have zagged, should be right on the beam until the pennant is clinched— along about September 12. Sound like the right date?

The rest probably did Joe some good. He was in a mild slump before he was hurt and his average had dropped to .326. He wants very much to lead the league this year and now is poised for the effort to catch up with George Kell, Lou Boudreau and Luke Appling. These three currently lead him in the average.

Joe has been taking treatments at the office of Dr. Jules Gordon, currently the Yankee physician. Gordon replaced Dr. Mal Stevens, who had differences with one L.S. MacPhail. To differ with MacPhail is to wear red flannels while looking a bull in the eye. ■

Idle Yankees Win 15th Flag

By Joe Trimble
September 16, 1947

"To Joe Page!... and to all the other kids, including George McQuinn," said Bucky Harris happily in the Yankee dressing room as he toasted the Yanks' clinching of the pennant. The assurance of mathematical certainty came exactly at 3:51 P.M. when a Western Union wire flashed the final score of the Red Sox loss to Chicago in Boston. This is the 15th pennant to be won by a Yankee team—most by any club in the modern era (since 1900).

The Yanks won it while sitting in their club house but not through any fault of their own. They wanted to win it on the field, but the early afternoon rains washed out the game with the Browns just a few minutes after it had begun. So all the players could do was go into the locker room and wait until the end of the game in Boston.

Most of the players had dressed quietly by the time word of the Red Sox loss was relayed. Then all broke out in grins and photographers grabbed them for pictures. Noticeably absent were

Joe Page and Joe DiMaggio, the two men most responsible for the flag.

Page was having his ankle taped and DiMag's numerous body bruises needed attention. Someone finally remembered them and they came into the main locker room to join in the shouting.

The actual clinching margin was 13 games. And there looked to be many, many times during the season that the club would have been a certainty to be 13 behind, not ahead, on this date. This was particularly true in the early days when, after losing a three-game series to the Indians, they were in sixth place.

But these Yankees, led by Harris, inspired by the hustle and talent of DiMaggio and supported by the tremendous relief pitching of Page, came on from there. ■

Cleveland's Lou Boudreau and the Yanks' Joe DiMaggio battled each other for hitting supremacy throughout the 1947 season. In the end, however, both were passed by Boston's Ted Williams, who won his fourth AL batting crown with a .343 average.

AP/Wide World Photos

World Series Will Be Televised for First Time in Its History

September 27, 1947

The World Series will be televised for the first time in the history of baseball. It was announced yesterday by Edgar Kobak, president of the Mutual Broadcasting System, which owns the television rights. Agreement to televise the games, which had been held up by certain stipulations of A.B. Chandler, Commissioner of Baseball, was reached at a meeting yesterday.

The rights were sold for a reported figure of $65,000. A brewing company had offered to pay the original asking price of $100,000 but had been turned down by the commissioner.

Commenting on the announcement, Kobak said: "Both Mr. Chandler, the sponsors and Mutual feel that television will be greatly stimulated by making this Series available to as many baseball fans as possible who cannot attend the games. We feel that the greatest public service can be rendered on behalf of baseball by the broadcasting and television industry in making these telecasts available to all."

The Mutual network also has the exclusive rights for the play-by-play broadcasts of the Series. The games will be broadcast in this country, Canada, Hawaii and Alaska by more than 500 stations affiliated with the network.

AP/Wide World Photos

Already the subject of great fan and media attention, the World Series will receive even more exposure this year, as the Series will be shown on television for the first time ever.

Death Stills a Yankee Fan, 8

By Edward O'Neill and Henry Lee
October 1, 1947

Yesterday was going to be the biggest day in Patty Ciccarelli's life. Patty, 8, slowly dying of acute leukemia, couldn't leave his little, white-walled sickroom at 1421 Needham Avenue, Bronx, so a neighborhood radio store lent him a television set.

The elaborate installations were completed Monday and when Patty dropped off to sleep at 10 o'clock that night, he was thinking what his Yankees and his hero, Joe DiMaggio, would do to the Dodgers.

DiMag and the Yanks did all right, but Patty didn't see them. He died at 5 a.m. yesterday.

All during the day, while the television set stood unused in his room and radios blared the game up and down Needham Ave., neighborhood kids and schoolmates from P.S. 78 across the street slipped quietly into the Ciccarelli home and said good-bye to Patty.

"It's tough he couldn't have seen just one game," a nine-year old said. "He was a very particular Yankee fan."

His parents, Anthony and Mary Ciccarelli, were prostrated.

"They've been dying with him for three weeks," said an uncle, Michael Restivo.

Patty, a third-grader at P.S. 78, was stricken last July. The father, 39, an employee of the Department of Parks, took him to two hospitals, paid for many blood transfusions and called in medical consultants. They could see nothing but an early death.

> "It's tough he couldn't have seen just one game...He was a very particular Yankee fan."
> —A nine-year-old friend of Patty Ciccarelli

Patty, listening to radio play-by-play of Yankee games, was greatly concerned about the approaching Series.

Then two weeks ago, in response to an aunt's plea, Joe DiMaggio dropped in to talk baseball with Patty and autograph a bat and ball for him.

"Gee, Joe, I'm the luckiest kid in the world," Patty said.

Last Thursday, during his eighth birthday party, he thought he was pretty lucky, too. A neighborhood bakery sent around a get-well cake, his friends asked to see and touch the wonderful ball and bat. Robert Harrison, owner of Rhoda Radio Service, 1304 Castle Hill Ave., Bronx, promised the loan of a television set for the whole Series.

After that, Patty kept getting weaker. Just before the end, the doctors warned he'd sleep fitfully and then pass into a coma.

"We knew he was dying," said his uncle, "but we were hoping he'd hold out until he could see the Yankees and DiMaggio in the Series. That kid loved baseball."

Monday, he drowsed off and on during the day, and then early yesterday, he went into the coma. His parents knew it was the end. Both were at his bedside when he died, eight hours before game time.

Patty's funeral will be held Friday, with a mass at 10 a.m. in the Church of the Immaculate Conception, Gun Hill Road, Bronx, and interment in St. Raymond's Cemetery.

Daily News

Joe DiMaggio with Patty Ciccarelli two weeks before
the boy succumbed to leukemia.

Cookie Hit with 2 Out in 9th Spoils Bevens' No-Hitter, Nips Yanks, 3-2

By Dick Young
October 4, 1947

Out of the mockery and ridicule of "the worst World Series in history," the greatest baseball game ever played was born yesterday. They'll talk about it forever, those 33,443 fans who saw it. They'll say: "I was there. I saw Bill Bevens come within one out of the only Series no-hitter; I saw the winning run purposely put on base by the Yankees; I saw Cookie Lavagetto send that winning run across a moment later with a pinch-hit double off the right field wall—the only hit, but big enough to give the Brooks the 3-2 victory that put them even-up at two games apiece."

The clock read 3:51, Brooklyn Standard Time—the most emotional minute in the lives of thousands of Faithful. There was Lavagetto being mobbed—and off to the side, there was Bevens, head bowed low, walking dejectedly through the swarming crowd, and completely ignored by it. Just a few seconds earlier, he was the one everybody was planning to pat on the back. He was the one who would have been carried off the field—the only pitcher ever to toss a no-hitter in a Series.

Now he was just another loser. It didn't matter that his one-hitter had matched the other classic performances of two Cub pitchers—Ed Reulbach against the Chisox in '06 and Claude Passeau against Detroit in '45. The third one-hitter in Series annals—but Bevens was still nothing more than a loser.

Bev felt bluer than Harry Taylor had at the start of this memorable struggle. In the first five minutes, Taylor had been a momentous failure. Unable to get his sore-elbowed arm to do what his mind demanded of it, the rookie righty had thrown his team into a seemingly hopeless hole before a Yankee had been retired.

Stirnweiss had singled. So had Henrich. And then Reese had dropped Robinson's peg of Berra's bouncer, loading the bases. Then Harry walked DiMaggio on four straight serves, forcing in a run. Still nobody out, still bases full. Taylor was through; he had been a losing gamble. In one inning, the Yanks were about to blow the game wide open and clamp a 3-1 lock on the Series.

But, just as has happened so often this year, the shabby Brook pitching staff delivered a clutch performer. This time it was Hal Gregg, who had looked so mediocre in relief against the Yanks two days before. Gregg got McQuinn to pop up and then made Johnson bang a DP ball right at Reese.

Only one run out of all that mess. The Faithful regained hope. This optimism grew as DiMag was cut down at the plate attempting to score from first when Edwards threw McQuinn's dumpy third-frame single into short right. But in the next stanza, as the Yanks did their only real teeing off on Gregg, the Brook hopes drooped. Johnson poled a tremendous triple to the center field gate, and Lindell followed with a booming two-bagger high off the scoreboard in right. The Yanks' lead was now 2-0.

There was still some hope for the Brooks, based on Bevens' own wildness. The Brooks couldn't buy a hit, but they had men aboard in almost every inning, sometimes two. Altogether, Bev was to go on to issue 10 passes, just topping the undesirable Series record set by Jack Coombs of the A's in the 1910 grapple with the Cubs.

Finally, in the fifth, Bill's wildness cost him a run. He walked Jorgensen and Gregg to open the stanza. Stanky bunted them along, and Jorgy scored while Gregg was being nailed at third on Reese's grounder to Rizzuto. Pee Wee then stole second for his third swipe of the Series, and continued on to third as Berra's peg flew into center. But Robinson left him there with a whiff.

Thus, before they had a hit, the Brooks had a run. And right about now, the crowd was starting to grow no-hit conscious. A fine catch by DiMaggio, on which Joe twisted his left ankle slightly, had deprived Hermanski of a long hit in the fourth, and Henrich's leaping stab of another Hermanski clout in the eighth again saved Bill's blossoming epic.

Then the Yanks threatened to sew up the decision in the top half of the ninth. Behrman had taken over the chucking an inning earlier as a result of Gregg's being lifted for a pinch-swinger, and Hank got into a bases-bulging jam that wasn't exactly his responsibility. Lindell's lead-off hit through the left side was legit enough, but after Rizzuto forced Johnny, Bevens' bunt was heaved tardily to second by Bruce Edwards. Stirnweiss then looped a fist-hit into right center, loading the bases. Hugh Casey was rushed in.

Hugh threw one pitch, his million-dollar serve which had forced DiMag to hit into a key DP the day before. This time the low-and-away curve was jammed into the dirt by Henrich. Casey's glove flew out for a quick stab...the throw home...the relay to first . . . and the inning was over without so much as a single Yank run. Just one pitch, and Hughie was set up to become the first pitcher credited with World Series victories on successive days.

But the Brooks were still down a run entering their half of the ninth—and they still hadn't gotten so much as a single hit off Bevens. A long drive by Edwards was grabbed by Lindell against the left field wall for the first out. Bevens then served up his ninth free pass of the day—this time to Carl Furillo. Jorgenson fouled meekly to the Yanks' first-sacker McQuinn for the second out.

Now, as Bevens was just one out away from having his bronze image placed among the all-time greats in Cooperstown, came the first of several switches that were destined to make a genius of the Dodgers' Burt Shotton and an eternal second-guess target of Bucky Harris.

"Reiser batting for Casey," boomed the loud-speaker, and "Gionfriddo running for Furillo."

With the count 2-1 against Reiser, Gionfriddo broke for second and slid safely under Berra's peg. With the count now 3-1 on Reiser, Bucky Harris made a decision that would forever brand him as the most second-guessed man in baseball. The Yankee pilot signalled Berra to step out and take an intentional fourth ball from Bevens.

The "winning run" was now on first, and the sore-ankled Reiser was replaced by young Eddie Miksis. Up to the plate stepped Cookie Lavagetto, a clutch money veteran of 14 seasons. On the second pitch, Cookie drove the ball deep into the right corner.

Racing frantically toward the right field line, the Yanks' Henrich leaped, but was too late. The ball flew some six feet over Tommy's glove and banged against the wall. Gionfriddo was tearing around third and over with the tying run.

Miksis, too, was running full speed. When Henrich reached the ball, he hurried an off-balance peg to McQuinn, who whirled desperately and heaved home—too late. The speedy Miksis was already sliding over the plate with the winning run, and a big grin on his face.

With Eddie sitting on the plate like an elated kid, God's Little Green Acre erupted in bedlam at precisely 3:51. ∎

> With the count now 3-1 on Reiser, Bucky Harris made a decision that would forever brand him as the most second-guessed man in baseball.

Laud Shea;
DiMag Hit Fast One

By Joe Trimble and Jim McCulley
October 5, 1947

What a difference a day makes. The Dodgers' dressing room was a morgue after yesterday's terrific game, in startling contrast to the hilarious bedlam it had been 24 hours ago. The Yankees, of course, were happy and hollering. Mainly the Bombers used one word: "Guts," as they took a three game lead over the Brooks in this year's Series.

Trainer Eddie Froelich said it best and in one sentence, "That kid (Frank) Shea has more damned guts than the whole Dodger pitching staff."

Shea was bubbling. "Know what I'm going to do?" he asked. "I'm going to take my Series share—a winning share, that is—have it put in a big pile of $20 bills. Then I'm going to my hotel room, lock the door and throw it all up in the air. Then I'm going to wade through it and wallow around in it. I've never seen that much money in my life."

Shea and DiMaggio got most of the attention and saw more photographers' bulbs than a movie queen. DiMag said that he had hit a fast ball for his decisive homer off Barney that gave the Yanks a 2-1 victory. "It was high and inside and right where I could lose it. Into the upper tier, too. Well, I like 'em better that way. Don't like to have any doubt about it."

> DiMag said that he had hit a fast ball for his decisive homer off Barney. "It was high and inside and right where I could lose it. Into the upper tier, too. Well, I like 'em better that way. Don't like to have any doubt about it."

We brought up his two double-play grounders and he grinned. "Boy, what a bum I was on those. In fact, I was the goat until Shea threw that third strike to Lavagetto. I hit at a fast ball when Barney got me in the first and it was a curve that Casey threw."

The Yankee pitcher threw a fast ball right down the middle when Reese was called out on strikes with the bases full in the seventh. It looked like a change-of-pace pitch from the stands and he was told that.

"Gee, maybe it did. There wasn't much on it. Right at that time I was having trouble. I threw it as hard as I could, but I'm lucky he took it. It wasn't really fast."

It was after that decisive pitch that catcher Aaron Robinson came back to the bench and told Bucky Harris that Shea was losing his stuff. So Harris immediately had Joe Page warm up again. But the gritty hurler went out to knock down three Dodgers in the eighth and showed that he was strong enough to finish.

The Dodgers, grim and silent, had little to say and asked the press to leave after a few questions were asked. Burt Shotton merely said, "A pitching performance like Shea's deserves something. Not to beat Brooklyn, but it was darned fine. But we are not dead yet." ∎

Yanks Champs! Trim Flock, 5-2

By Joe Trimble
October 7, 1947

Brooklyn is a borough of three million pallbearers this morning. There, where the trees grow with equal vigor on the stately avenues of Flatbush and the sordid streets of Williamsburg, the citizens are deep in mourning. They've suffered their greatest loss—the world championship. With yesterday's 5-2 defeat in the seventh game of the Series, the dashing Dodgers died. They went down almost without a struggle under the crushing pitching of the Yankees' left-handed relief man, Joe Page, in the last of this mad set of games.

The Dodgers' last gasp came exactly at 3:49 in the bright sunshine which bathed the Stadium in glowing warmth. As McQuinn clutched the final throw, the Yanks poured from their bench and mobbed Page. They almost pulled his great left arm off and the right one, too. They grabbed and hugged him and finally swept him off the field before the fans could pour out of the seats and engulf him.

The championship was the 11th for the Yankees in 15 Series and their first since '43. It was a triumph for the new Yankee dynasty: president Larry MacPhail, who resigned after the game; manager Bucky Harris; and the players. For the disappointed Dodgers, this was their fourth failure to win the title. They flopped in '16, '20 and '41. This was the first time they'd been able to carry it to a seventh game, however.

The crowd of 71,548 lifted the total attendance to a new Series record. Exactly 389,763 saw the seven sensational games and there must be at least that many ulcers in bloom. ∎

DiMaggio Wins 1947 MVP Race

November 28, 1947

By the slimmest of margin, the Baseball Writers Association has selected the Yankees' Joe DiMaggio as the American League's most valuable player for the 1947 season. DiMag's total of 202 bested Boston's Ted Williams by a single point. The race for third place was also decided by one point, with Cleveland's Lou Boudreau edging the Yanks' Joe Page, 168 to 167. Rounding out the top five vote-getters was Detroit's George Kell.
DiMaggio joins Jimmie Foxx of Philadelphia and Boston as baseball's only three-time MVP.■

Hank Olen, Daily News

1947 American League MVP Vote Totals

Joe DiMaggio	202
Ted Williams	201
Lou Boudreau	168
Joe Page	167
George Kell	132

George McQuinn congratulates Joe DiMaggio as he crosses home plate after hitting a game-winning home run in the World Series.

Tony Lazzeri   Babe Ruth   Lou Gehrig

"It is with great pride that I welcome the champions on this day
and Babe Ruth the hero of all our baseball days."
—New York Mayor William O'Dwyer
at Yankee Stadium on Babe Ruth Day,
June 13, 1948

Chapter 7

1948

Saying Goodbye to the Babe

*D*iMaggio followed his third MVP season with yet another good year, despite increasing problems with his knees and feet. He was named to his 10th All-Star team and led the league in home runs (39) and RBIs (155). In September, he hit his 300th career home run. And, early in the season, he had the second three-homer game of his career.

The summer of 1948 was dampened by the death of Babe Ruth. The Yankee legend, who had been battling cancer for nearly two years, finally passed away on August 16. His body lay in state at Yankee Stadium for the next two days, and over 100,000 people came to pay their respects. Thousands more were still waiting in line when the Stadium gates were closed to allow the body to be taken to St. Patrick's Cathedral. On August 19, over 80,000 more fans surrounded the cathedral, cemetery and funeral route, while 6,000 mourners attended the funeral. DiMaggio served as one of the honorary pallbearers.

In October, as the World Series was being played without them, the Yankees fired manager Bucky Harris. He was replaced by Casey Stengel, who went on to win seven World Series in 12 years with the Yankees. A month later, DiMaggio again underwent surgery to have bone spurs removed from his heel. ■

Joe DiMaggio signs autographs for an entourage of fans.

Nick Petersen, Daily News

1948 REGULAR SEASON

G	AB	R	H	2B	3B	HR	RBI	BB	SB	AVG.	SLG.
153	594	110	190	26	11	39*	155*	67	1	.320	.598

*led American League

DiMag Hits 3

Yankees Whip Feller in First Game, 6-5

By Joe Trimble
May 24, 1948

An overflow audience of 78,431—largest ever to see a ball game in this city—thrilled to a tremendous and exciting contest as the Yankees edged the Indians, 6-5, in the opener today. Joe DiMaggio had his greatest day at bat in 10 years when he hit three successive homers to drive in all the New York runs and give Allie Reynolds his sixth victory.

DiMag got four of the eight Yankee hits. He singled first time up, a wasted effort. He hit into the left field stands after Keller walked in the fourth. Then Tommy Henrich walked and Keller singled before Joe crashed a 440-footer into the crowd massed on the field behind the low centerfield fence in the sixth. Both those came off Bob Feller. In the eighth, with no one on and Bob Muncrief hurling, he again hit into the crowd, this one flying about 380 feet.

This last was his tenth of the season and sixth in the past four games. It proved to be the winning run and lifted his average above .300 for the first time this season. His RBIs were raised to 33, 16 of them on this trip. Only once before, on June 13, 1937, had he socked three in one game. ∎

> Joe DiMaggio had his greatest day at bat in 10 years when he hit three successive homers to drive in all the New York runs . . .

A Sunday twin bill with the Yanks brought customers from as far away as Buffalo (180 miles) and Pittsburgh (150). They came by train and bus at excursion rates. Included was a "Joe DiMaggio Rooters Club" from Pittsburgh.

No. 3 Brings down House That Ruth Built

By Joe Trimble
June 14, 1948

The Yankee Stadium has played many thrilling scenes on its broad green stage through the years, but never one quite like yesterday's Silver Anniversary celebration when the greatest baseball player who ever lived—Babe Ruth—wore Yankee uniform No. 3 for the last time.

Flanked by 16 teammates from the first championship club that ever played at the Stadium—the '23 Yankees—and other former greats in the proud history of the club, the Babe emerged from the dugout and pigeon-toed to home plate with a bat in his hand. The roars of the crowd of 49,641 billowed from the stands of "the House That Ruth Built."

As he stood out there, he was as magnificent as ever—the top showman of them all. The crowd rose as Ed Barrow, second only to Ruth in the glorious history of the Yankees, shook hands with the Babe and then affectionately hugged him. As he patted the Babe's big back, old Ed's eyes filled up.

George Pipgras and Waite Hoyt, pitchers of the '23 team, fought back their tears, too. Handkerchiefs were in evidence through the stands as the band played "Auld Lang Syne." Lucille Manners sang it and the fans were asked to accompany her. Not many were able to because of the lumps in their throats.

The Babe stood bareheaded until the music stopped and then Mayor William O'Dwyer and Will Harridge, AL president, spoke briefly into the public address system microphone. Harridge formally accepted the Babe's uniform with these words: "As president of the American League, I declare Yankee uniform No. 3 retired. It never will be worn again in this stadium or on the road."

O'Dwyer said, "It is with great pride that I welcome the champions on this day and Babe Ruth, the hero of all our baseball days."

It wasn't known beforehand whether Ruth would speak. His voice is terribly cracked from the searing illness which almost cost him his life last year. But he said he had something to say.

He stepped to the mike, his old uniform hanging loosely from his shoulders, which are bowed from the sickness that has so sapped his strength. His voice was husky as he said: "I am proud I hit the first home run here. God knows who will hit the last one. It is great to see the men from 25 years ago back here today and it makes me feel proud to be with them." ■

Babe Ruth wears his famous No. 3 uniform for the last time on June 13, 1948. Thousands of fans at Yankee Stadium honored the Babe on the day his uniform was retired.

AP/Wide World Photos

Five Locals in All-Star Tilt

By Jack Smith
July 7, 1948

Led by Joe DiMaggio, who nailed down his centerfield berth by the widest margin tabulated, the Yanks, Giants and Dodgers placed a total of five players in the starting lineups of the All-Star Game, according to the final returns of the nationwide poll announced yesterday. In addition to DiMag, the Yanks placed George McQuinn at first base on the AL squad, while the Giants matched them with Johnny Mize at first base and Walker Cooper as catcher on the NL team. The lone Dodger entry is Pee Wee Reese, who won out over Marty Marion and Buddy Kerr in a three-way battle for the NL shortstop assignment.

The nationwide All-Star poll, which set an all-time high by recording over 4 million fan ballots, was conducted by 453 newspapers, radio stations and magazines throughout the United States, Central and South America, Puerto Rico, Cuba and the European Theatre of Occupation, which was represented by Stars and Stripes.

According to the agreement with A.B. Chandler, Commissioner of Baseball, Ford Frick, NL president, and Will Harridge, AL president, the players winning the poll will not only start the All-Star game but will play at least three innings. The remainder of the 25-player squads, including the pitchers, will be selected by the rival managers, Lippy Leo Durocher and Bucky Harris. The game will be played in St. Louis, July 13.

Fans in the Metropolitan area who forwarded more than 70,000 ballots to *The News* picked ten of the 16 positions in the balloting correctly, missing three positions in each league. In the NL, New Yorkers selected Carl Furillo of the Dodgers for center field. In the nationwide balloting, the winner was Richie Ashburn of the Phils with Bobby Thomson of the Giants second and Furillo fourth. They also

missed out by picking Willard Marshall for right field instead of Enos Slaughter, and by balloting heavily in favor of Bob Elliot at third base instead of Andy Pafko.

In the AL, New York fans went astray by naming Tommy Henrich for right field. The nationwide winner was Pat Mullin of the Tigers with Henrich second. Yogi Berra was the local choice for catcher with Buddy Rosar of the A's copping the nationwide honors. And they went wrong again in naming Cleveland's Ken Keltner at third base. George Kell of the Tigers won out on the total tabulations with Keltner second.

The honor of polling the greatest number of votes went to Ted Williams, who was named on 1,556,784 ballots. Stan Musial was second with 1,532,502. Though DiMaggio, who won the honor last year, came in third this time with 1,519,182, his margin over Hoot Evers was the widest recorded.■

An overzealous DiMaggio fan is escorted from the outfield.

Legs Wobbly, DiMaggio's Last Hope Is First Base

By Joe Trimble
July 25, 1948

The baseball life span of a major leaguer is measured not in years but in feet—his own two feet. To be more correct, it is the legs which usually fail first and force a man to hang up his glove when he still can do everything but run. Anyway, gimpy gams end careers, and even the greatest have to bow out when the underpinning fails. No exception is Joe DiMaggio.

The Yankee Clipper is having leg trouble this year—lots of it. He started to play baseball in San Francisco with the Seals when he was only 17 years of age. He is 34 now, so he has been going along continuously as an outfielder for 17 years. His three years in the Army could be excepted, but he surely wasn't resting his legs any then, either.

It is doubtful if he can go much more than another year or two as an outfielder. So if he is to continue as a major leaguer past 1950, at anything close to his comfortable rate of pay, he'll have to find himself another position . . . one where speed is not in demand. The logical place is first base, so don't be surprised if you some day look at a Yankee box score and see that the cleanup hitter is "J. DiMaggio, 1b."

DiMag is playing under the handicap of two bum legs right now. Both his heels are very sore. His left was operated on twice in 1947. A bone spur was removed the first time and a second surgery was needed to close the slow-healing incision left by the first. Now he has developed bursitis in his right heel. Currently, that is the more painful of the two. He wears sponge rubber heel supports in both shoes to ease the pain and shock of running.

There is little doubt that he'll have to have another operation next winter on the right heel. He may recover okay from that, and it is hoped that he does. But he is a sure bet to be very much slower than he is today. And if he can't move fast on his feet, then he can't play center field in this lively ball era. He can't play the outfield at all. His handicaps would affect the pitchers, who need all the outfield help they can get.

So, first base is the logical place for him to turn. No speed is needed at that position. The men who were first-sack rivals in the recent All-Star game are striking examples. Neither Johnny Mize nor George

Waters, Daily News

Manager Bucky Harris, Joe DiMaggio and other Yankees departing for Spring Training in Florida.

McQuinn can run. Yet they are able to keep going as big leaguers because fleetness is not demanded of first basemen.

DiMag's presence at first would be needed, too, by 1950. McQuinn is close to 40 years old and can hardly be expected to go on for more than one more season. And there is no one in the Yankee farm system who is a highly regarded first base possibility for the majors. Jack Phillips, a fairly good right-handed batter and thrower with Kansas

> The logical place is first base, so don't be surprised if you someday look at a Yankee box score and see that the cleanup hitter is "J. DiMaggio, 1b."

City, is the best and he was far from a smooth fielder when the Yanks had him at training camp this spring.

There is every reason to believe that his conversion to first base would be easy for DiMag. He is a graceful man, equipped with sure hands and fine baseball sense. He still is a fine hitter, aside from Ted Williams and Stan Musial, the best in the business. His batting eye is about as good as ever. But those legs are quickly failing him. ■

DiMag Back in Lineup

July 15, 1948

Most thankful for any little favor at this point, the Giants today start out West and the Yanks come home to roost in much better straits as a result of their mid-summer respite of three days. The Giants delve into a doubleheader in Pittsburgh with a refreshed pitching staff. And the Yanks begin a 15-game stand at the Stadium tonight against the Browns with a gent named Joe DiMaggio in centerfield.

By his own request, DiMaggio returns to the lineup after missing the Saturday and Sunday games in Washington. The swelling in his ailing knees has subsided and he is confident he'll be able to play every day from now on.

"These last six days off (time out for one turn at bat in the All-Star game) have been a big thing for me," Joe said yesterday after returning from St. Louis. "I needed the rest. I feel pretty good and expect to play every inning, including the doubleheaders. This is our big chance to get moving and I want to be in there to help."

If his sore heels and knees cooperate, DiMag will participate in 15 games against the Western clubs in the next 11 days. Of these, four are twin bills and three others will be played under the lights.

DiMaggio has most of his leg trouble in the second half of a double feature, following a night game. In order to favor his right heel, bothered by bursitis, he puts extraordinary pressure on his knees when compelled to make quick starts and stops.

It was after last Friday's game in the Capital that his knees swelled to such an extent he had to leave the lineup. He had played in 74 consecutive games before limping to the bench.

With DiMag back, the Yanks hope to make their pennant drive in this stand. They are only two and a half games out and, with the 1-2 teams, Cleveland and Philadelphia, about to knock each other's brains out, they'd like to feed on the bumpy Browns.

Babe Ruth, Baseball Idol, Dies

By Harry Schlegel
August 17, 1948

George Herman (Babe) Ruth, the greatest figure in American sports history, died at 8:01 last night in Memorial Hospital. The 53-year-old Babe had suffered for nearly two years from cancer, but the immediate cause of death was a pulmonary complication.

The Babe's death came less than two hours after the hospital announced—in its fourth bulletin of the day on his condition—that he was "sinking rapidly."

Earlier, at 5:10 p.m., Ruth's physician, Dr. Hayes Martin, had disclosed in a special memorandum that the chest condition had grown "worse since this morning. Condition considered more critical."

At the Babe's bedside when he died were his wife, Claire; a sister, Mrs. Wilbur Moberly, of Baltimore; and two adopted daughters, Mrs. Dorothy Sullivan and Mrs. Richard Flanders.

The Ruth family left the hospital at 9:25 p.m., by a little-used side door on York Ave. There, Mrs. Ruth and her two adopted daughters entered a car.

The family was given a police escort when they drove away.

Death for the Babe came five days after he had been placed on the hospital's critical list. But to the very end, he fought the battle of the kids—the kids who so faithfully prayed for his recovery and who hour after hour sat outside the hospital waiting for the latest word on his condition.

They, as all others, knew how close to death their hero hovered, but they welcomed every syllable of encouragement contained in the daily bulletins. They devoured every word printed about him, especially the story about his last appearance. That was on July 26 when he attended the opening of the movie "The Babe Ruth Story" at the Astor Theatre.

The body of the home run king arrived at the Universal Funeral Chapel at 1:45 a.m. escorted by two police radio cars. A crowd of about 300 stood silently along the curbs as the hearse pulled into the driveway.

A Requiem Mass was tentatively scheduled for 11 a.m. Thursday in St. Patrick's Cathedral. Definite arrangements will be announced at 11 a.m. today. ∎

The Yankees and fans stand in solemn silence at the Polo Grounds after the announcement of Babe Ruth's death.

Hank Olen, Daily News

People He Loved Say Farewell to the Babe

By Edward Dillon and Henry Lee
August 19, 1948

One hundred a minute, the Babe Ruth fans—as typical a slice of democracy as any doubleheader crowd —filed past the Babe's bier in Yankee Stadium for nine hours yesterday and last night in a grief that seemed only to deepen.

A one-legged veteran of the Italian campaign whom the Babe had placed in the pro game before the war was in line with a blind man, a boy and his dog, old women, children and celebrities.

One arm around his 14-year-old son Daniel, Baseball Commissioner A.B. Chandler looked down at the casket and wept. "I wanted my boy to see the Babe," he said.

American League president Will Harridge was there. Beau Jack, the Negro lightweight, brought his three children. An unknown grandfather lifted an eight-year-old boy as they passed the casket and said:

"Take a good look, sonny. You'll never see another man like him."

In double file past the casket, some 60,000 persons viewed the body from 10:02 a.m. till about 7 p.m. Then the gates were closed, though thousands more were patiently waiting in a line that ran for blocks from 157th St. and Ruppert Place. In all, in the two days, more than 100,000 had in person paid their respects to the 60-homer man. ∎

> One arm around his 14-year-old son Daniel, Baseball Commissioner A. B. Chandler looked down at the casket and wept. "I wanted my boy to see the Babe," he said.

Daily News

With Lou Gehrig's death in 1941 and Babe Ruth's in 1948, Yankee fans said goodbye to two baseball legends.

Throng Ignores Rain to Bid Adieu to Ruth

By Arthur Mulligan and Harry Schlegel
August 20, 1948

A crowd greater than any that ever cheered itself hoarse for him under sunny skies stood reverently silent in grayness and rain yesterday as New York paid the final tribute to its beloved Babe Ruth.

There was the governor of the nation's leading state . . . the mayors of three of its greatest cities . . . the woman who rose from a sickbed to hobble on crutches to the Mass . . . the executive who as a youngster was one of scores "healed" by a Ruthian home run . . . the kid who represented the Babe at the funeral of his discoverer, Brother Gilbert.

And there were other people, just people.

Seventy-five thousand of them alone in the area surrounding St. Patrick's Cathedral, where Cardinal Spellman presided at the Mass. Uncounted thousands along the route of the cortege. Another six thousand at Gate of Heaven Cemetery, Hawthorne, where the Babe was laid to rest.

Inside the huge Gothic edifice, 6,000 mourners filled every pew as the mahogany casket, blanketed with orchids and red roses, was borne up the aisle at 11 a.m. Behind it walked the family, quiet and composed—Babe's widow, Claire, their two adopted daughters, Mrs. Richard Flanders and Mrs. Dorothy Sullivan, and his sister, Mrs. Wilbur Moberly. ■

DiMag Flies from Ruth's Rites, Sparks Yanks Over Nats, 8-1

By Joe Trimble
August 20, 1948

The cynics among us—and there are too many—doubt the inspirational value of sports, or of a ballplayer to a ball team. But if Joe DiMaggio isn't the spark and spirit of the Yankees, then there isn't much substance to this national game of ours. The team was losing to the Senators yesterday when he came running out on the field after an airplane ride from the Babe's funeral. He went into center field immediately and, in his first time at bat, singled to start a six-run explosion in the fourth inning. The champs went on from there to win, 8-1, and sweep the three games here.

The short visit to the Capital was very profitable. While the Yankees were cleaning up the Senators, the A's and Red Sox were splitting two games in Boston over the last three days. So, in that span, the Yanks have picked up a game and a half on each of the other two Eastern contenders.

Once DiMag showed up, the Yankees went ahead and crushed Early Wynn, the Senators' pitcher. He hung around for the whole game and was plastered for 13 hits. Everybody except Charley Keller got one. It was Wynn's 14th loss, and seventh in succession.

Whittaker, Daily News

Umpire Bill Klem and Joe DiMaggio were honorary pallbearers at Babe Ruth's funeral.

Yankees Sign Stengel to 2-year Pact as Pilot

By Joe Trimble
October 13, 1948

Casey Stengel became the new manager of the Yankees yesterday when he received a two-year contract at $30,000 per season and a promise from the owners of the club that they would back him completely in his efforts to bring the team back to the pinnacle that New York fans expect it to occupy.

The 57-year-old pilot was chosen as the new field leader to succeed Bucky Harris just last Sunday night, and only after owners Del Webb and Dan Topping and general manger George Weiss had thoroughly studied the qualifications of all the men in baseball who were available.

All the players who live in this area were invited but only Joe DiMaggio and Frank Hiller showed. DiMaggio had never met Stengel formally before yesterday but he graciously stated that he looked forward to playing under Stengel. "I've seen Casey pull quite a few antics in baseball," DiMag said, grinning. ■

All Yanks Trade Bait —but DiMag, Henrich

By Dana Mozley
December 4, 1948

Armed with the intent of a David Harum and the resources of a small Rockefeller, general manager George Weiss and other top brass of the Yankees' hierarchy leave this morning for the annual minor league meeting in Minneapolis where they'll trade away every member of last year's team except Joe DiMaggio and Tommy Henrich if the occasion arises.

Weiss is most anxious to deal with any small clubs, particularly for the pitchers and second baseman he knows he needs. If the offers are reasonable—and he expects that dealing will be heavy at next week's meeting—he's willing to give up anyone except his two "untouchables." "DiMaggio and Henrich are not on the market, no matter what they might return in trade," Weiss promised yesterday.

"If anyone makes a fair offer for any of our other players, we're ready to let them go," Weiss added. "Of course, we must receive at least equal value in return—in players and not cash. We're interested in bolstering the team and will not weaken one position to benefit another. If we trade a shortstop, for instance, we must get a shortstop in return."

Although Bucky Harris (left), shown here with Yankee president Larry MacPhail, led the Yankees to a world championship in 1947, his clashes with General Manager George Weiss the next year led to his firing after the 1948 season.

Named the Yanks' new skipper after the 1948 season, Casey Stengel quickly became a favorite of the fans, the players and the media. Here he is seen in the Yankee dugout at Yankee Stadium with Joe DiMaggio, III.

AP/Wide World Photos

"I thank the good Lord that He made me a Yankee."
—Joe DiMaggio at Yankee Stadium
on Joe DiMaggio Day

Chapter 8

1949

All the Baseball in Just Half the Games

*I*n a year when the Yankees won the pennant despite a season total of 71 injuries, DiMaggio played in only 76 games of the 154-game schedule.

Losing half a season would dampen the spirits and hamper the performance of almost any player. But no one ever accused Joe DiMaggio of being just "any player." After suffering through chronic heel problems that kept him out of his Yankee pinstripes until late June, DiMaggio made his presence felt in his first series, hitting four home runs and driving in nine runs to lead the Yankees to a three-game sweep of the Boston Red Sox.

Despite his limited playing time, Joe made his 11th All-Star appearance. But this time it was as All-Star manager Lou Boudreau's special selection instead of as a fan ballot favorite.

Health problems continued to haunt DiMaggio. In September, it was a viral infec-

tion that kept him out of the lineup until the World Series. But Joltin' Joe was certainly there for the Series, hitting the winning home run in the deciding fifth game.

For his troubles, DiMaggio was well compensated. In early February, the Yankees signed DiMaggio to a package worth between $85,000 and $90,000, which made him the highest-paid Yankee. ■

AP/Wide World Photos

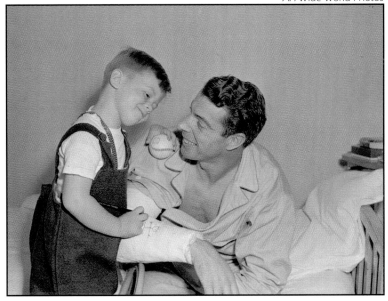

Despite injuries that kept him out of half the games in '49, DiMaggio's inspired performances when healthy sparked the Yanks to another World Series victory.

1949 REGULAR SEASON

G	AB	R	H	2B	3B	HR	RBI	BB	SB	AVG.	SLG.
76	272	58	94	14	6	14	67	55	0	.346	.596*

*led American League

DiMag's 85-90G Tops Ruth's Highest Salary

By Dana Mozley
February 9, 1949

I n recognition of both his playing skills and box-office magnetism, Joe DiMaggio yesterday was officially revealed to have signed the biggest pact of his career—a one-year, $85,000 to $90,000 bite of the Yankee payroll that makes him the highest paid player in the club's history. The pact was originally agreed upon during the World Series, as disclosed exclusively by *The News*.

The announcement that the 34-year-old star had penned the new contract came on the 55th birthday of the late Babe Ruth, who, until yesterday, was the

---

Joe DiMaggio makes the most expensive pen stroke in Yankees history by signing his name to a contract believed to be worth between $85,000 and $90,000.

AP/Wide World Photos

> The announcement that [DiMaggio] had penned the new contract came on the 55th birthday of the late Babe Ruth, who, until yesterday, was the highest salaried Yankee of them all.

highest salaried Yankee of them all. The Bambino made $80,000 in 1931 and 1932. DiMaggio's best previous income was the $70,000 he drew last summer.

Although neither DiMaggio nor the club would disclose the terms of the pact, it was generally regarded that the Clipper will receive a base pay of $60,000 plus a series of bonuses based on home attendance that should add another $25,000 to $30,000. Last year, his pay was $50,000 and his bonuses about $20,000.

DiMaggio was beaming after the official signing ceremonies in the club's plush Fifth Ave. offices. "I'm very happy about the whole thing," he said. "This is by far the best contract I've ever had."

Owner Dan Topping was in an expansive mood, too. "We are both very happy and all I can tell you is that Joe got a darned good raise over last year," he admitted.

This was DiMaggio's 11th contract with the Yankees, who first paid him $7,500 as a rookie in 1936. In 10 years, his pay checks have totaled $345,750 and he has picked up an additional $40,809.20 for World Series engagements.

Only one other player in all baseball history has received more than $90,000 for a single season. Hank Greenberg, in his one-year tenure at Pittsburgh two seasons ago, made slightly more than $100,000 via salary and substantial bonus arrangements. Unless Ted Williams can talk Tom Yawkey into giving him a large boost, which is unlikely, DiMaggio's salary will be the largest in the majors this season. The Bosox belter is now the only top-drawer player yet to sign. Last year, he received about $75,000.

Cleveland shortstop-manager Lou Boudreau has already contracted for $75,000 for each of the next two years, without any bonus incentives. ∎

Big Dough, DiMaggio

February 9, 1949

We're no sports experts, or even the owners of a crystal ball. So we're not going to enter the current guessing game as to whether Mr. Joe DiMaggio of the New York Yankee baseball team is going to get a 1949 salary of $85,000 or $90,000 or (biggest estimate) 100 grand.

It seems certain that the Yankee Clipper is going to haul down more dough than the $80,000 Babe Ruth got in his record seasons of 1931 and 1932.

But we'd still like to point out to Joe's customers, and ours, too, that in real cash the late Babe is still the champ. The Bambino got his, remember, when a buck was still a buck, and before our New Deal spenders and taxers took to grabbing their cut of all incomes before we taxpayers even got our paws on it.

Good luck, anyway Joe. Get out there and really slug this year, for the Yankees and Uncle Sam.

Joe's Heel Still Hurts in First Stadium Test

By Joe Trimble
May 24, 1949

The spirit was willing, but the flesh was weak—and Joe DiMaggio's "Achilles Heel" still hurts. Blisters on his hands from whacking the ball last night further incapacitate the great Yankee slugger today and make his return to active play more problematic than ever.

Taking his first workout in six weeks, the Clipper went through a lengthy, but not intense, batting practice before last night's arc tilt at the Stadium.

It was the first time since April 11 that Joe had been in uniform. At that time his right heel, ailing since a winter operation, kicked up such a fuss he had to quit for treatment.

The Clipper belted several into the stands last night, one off the weak tosses of Frank Crosetti and a couple off the slants of Fred Sanford. He also jogged lightly in the specially constructed shoes which have spikes on the soles only.

He grimaced with the pain, however, when he put too much pressure on the healing extremity and when he finished he wore a relieved smile.

"I didn't do much and it felt all right," Joe said. "I'm going to take it easy. I'll be out again tomorrow and every day, but I won't be able to bat for a couple of days because of the blisters."

Yankee officials said that, despite the pain in the ailing heel, it is possible Joe may be jolting again within two weeks. Dr. Sidney Gainor, Yankee physician, said, "There's a chance he'll be back within that time. It depends on how the heel comes along."

From Joe's attitude and the fine hand he received from the customers, it seems as though it's going to be difficult to keep him grounded. "This suit feels so good I think I'll wear it to bed," Joe said. "I'm in uniform to stay." ∎

AP/Wide World Photos

Joe DiMaggio makes his first appearance in uniform in the 1949 season after suffering heel problems.

DiMag Hits HR, Single; Yanks Nip BoSox, 5-4

June 29, 1949
By Joe Trimble

Casey Stengel waited 25 years to manage a ballplayer as good as Joe DiMaggio, and he found out tonight what a privilege he had been missing. The Yankee Clipper, finest player of his time, made a magnificent debut this evening before the largest night game audience in Boston history. Joe, in his first game of the season, hit a homer and a single as the Yankees shaded the Red Sox, 5-4.

The crowd of 36,228 gave the sore-heeled center fielder a rousing welcome the first time he came to bat. Joe responded by lining a curve thrown by lefty Maurice McDermott to left-center for a single. Two outs later, Johnny Lindell drew a pass and then Hank Bauer stroked a homer against the screen atop the left field fence.

DiMag's next opportunity came in the third, with two out and Rizzuto on through a single. McDermott, a blazing fast-baller who reminds folks in this town of Lefty Grove, tried to buzz one past the Big Guy. It crashed high against the screen. In view of the fact that Allie Reynolds eventually gave up the four runs, the Clipper's blast was the margin of difference in the ball game. So, in a manner of speaking, you could say Joe won the first one he played in.

DiMag was his old, sturdy self in centerfield and on the bases. He didn't favor the calcified right heel which caused him to miss almost half the season and threatened to retire him permanently. He handled six fielding chances nicely, two of them

smashes he had to move quickly for.

He ran fast to first on his single, hoping to stretch it if the ball had eluded one of the outfielders. And, after drawing a base on balls in the eighth, he slid hard into shortstop Vern Stephens to break up an apparent double play at second.

The $90,000 outfielder seemed confident the heel could take all the punishment he could give it. Joe isn't the sort of player who loafs. He hustled hard all night. If the heel doesn't pain him from this effort, the Yankees have much hope of retaining their lead, and even of extending the 4 1/2 game margin. ■

Making his debut in June, after missing April and May due to heel injuries, DiMaggio crosses the plate after hitting a home run in his first at-bat.

Daily News

DiMaggio Named to 11th All-Star Squad

July 3, 1949

Joltin' Joe DiMaggio, now in a roaring comeback after being a fixture among the Yankee halt and lame, will be back doing business as usual at the All-Star stand in Brooklyn July 12.

The Yankee Clipper today was named to the AL squad in a special appointment by All-Star manager Lou Boudreau of the Indians.

DiMaggio, named to 10 previous All-Star contests, didn't get a tumble in the recent poll of 4,637,000 fans for the simple reason that the "grand-stand coaches" figured the only way he could get to the game was in a wheelchair. So Boudreau used his prerogative of selecting whomever he chose beyond the eight non-pitching starters picked by the fans.

Boudreau, in a statement released through the American League office, emphasized that picking DiMaggio was just a matter of honoring a great player. He invited Joe to join the squad more than two weeks ago, well before he bounced out of the crippled list with his big war club booming this week.

"DiMaggio said he would like to be on the All-Star squad," explained Boudreau. "I felt he belonged on it, even though he had not played because of injury (for the Yankees' first 65 games), and I wanted him on the team I'm to manage.

"He's a great star who deserved to be named this year just as he deserved to be named to 10 previous teams."

Under the mandate of the fans, Boudreau must play the outfield of Boston's Ted Williams and Dom DiMaggio in left and center, and the Yankees' Tom Henrich in right for the first three innings.

Thus, the prospect is that Joe will come into the game as a replacement for "little brother" Dom, who did a whale of a job maintaining DiMaggio prestige during Joe's injured-heel convalescing respite.

DiMaggio's skein of All-Star selections since he came up to the Yankees from the San Francisco Seals in '36 was interrupted only by the war when he was in service, 1943-44-45. He was on the squad but failed to play in '46 and last year appeared as an All-Star pinch hitter.

DiMag batted .212 in All-Star play, belting one homer and driving across three runs. ∎

DiMag Clouts Home Run for Sick Boy

August 6, 1949

Yesterday Joe DiMaggio visited the hospital bed of Michael Rosenthal, 10, of Liberty, N.Y., who had just undergone his third major operation in 24 days.

"I'll try to hit a home run for you tomorrow, Mike," said the Yankee star. "I haven't hit one in some time and I'll be swinging for you."

Today DiMaggio connected for a homer in the fourth inning of the first game of a doubleheader against the Browns.

DiMag Glad He's a Yank; Gets Shower of Sedans

By Jim McCulley
October 2, 1949

There have been hundreds of "Days" for ball players, but never anything to match the one in which this city and the ball fans of the nation yesterday honored Joe DiMaggio, who received gifts valued at over $5,000 as well as the sum of $7,500, which was donated, in his name, to the Heart and Cancer funds.

The Yankee Clipper, in an extremely well-delivered speech of acceptance, said simply: "I thank the good Lord that He made me a Yankee."

Mayor O'Dwyer, who had officially declared this "Joe DiMaggio Day" in the city, congratulated Joe, and the ball player, the greatest of his time, answered: "When I left San Francisco to come to the big leagues, Lefty O'Doul, manager on the Coast, told me that New York City was the friendliest place in the world and that I shouldn't be afraid. My mother told me the same thing. They were right. I found that out then and I know it even better today."

Mama DiMaggio came out on the field near the microphone set up at home plate, joining Joe and brother Dom, who was called for by the crowd after Joe referred to "The little guy in center field, who takes base hits away from me all year." Then Joe Jr., aged seven, also joined the family group, as photographers popped their bulbs in a cascade of brilliance which reminded you of an electric sign on Broadway.

Joe, who feels he is a poor speaker and doesn't like to talk before a crowd, paced the dressing room floor nervously, chain-smoking as he waited to go "on stage." Through the open door, we could hear Mel Allen, whose microphone was set out at home plate, introducing speakers and announcing the gifts.

"I wish I could save the energy I'm using up right now," he grinned as he did a "squads left" around the little table which sits in the middle of the room.

"Why don't you sing a song or something to relax," we suggested.

He laughed and said: "Gee, I hope I can finish this whole day singing a song."

Joe's opening remarks were the only part of the speech he rehearsed. "I haven't choked up very much in a long time," he said. "But I'm sure doing it today."

The crowd applauded wildly every time he stopped to get his breath and most of all when Mrs. DiMaggio stepped up and kissed first Dom, then Joe.

DiMag spoke of his appreciation of the three managers he had played under (Joe McCarthy, Bucky Harris and Casey Stengel), saying, "They all taught me something."

The Red Sox and Yankee players were grouped behind him and he lauded the "enemy" and McCarthy. "If we can't win today and tomorrow, then I want Joe McCarthy to know that I am glad that he is the guy who does."

McCarthy then leaped out of the dugout, ran up and shook Joe's hand warmly as the packed stadium gave Marse Joe his greatest cheer since he left the Yankees in 1946.

The Clipper received over sixty gifts, including a Cadillac sedan from the people of the city. One of the finest presents was a four-year scholarship at a New York City college or university for a boy of Joe's selection. This was donated by the Italian newspaper *Il Progresso*. There also was a speed boat, contributed by New Haven fans.

Oddest were 300 gallons of ice cream and a taxi ride from Newark which a cab company there gave fans from that city to the stadium. The cabs were placarded with the words "This ride is on Joe D." ■

Yankee Medical Box Score:

71 Injuries; Yogi out 9; DiMag out 78

By Joe Trimble
October 1, 1949

The Yankees are a credit to their league, to American sport and, most particularly, to the medical profession. Never in the history of the major leagues has a ball club used so much medication, bandages and splints and still survived to win a flag.

They had a fever chart to match every box score, from Spring Training on. During the regular season, starting April 19 and ending in the great victory last Sunday night, 71 different injuries came in sickening succession and nearly every one knocked a player out of the lineup.

Most banged up of all was Yogi Berra, who was either sick or hurt on nine different occasions. Tommy Henrich couldn't equal Berra's visits to the infirmary, but he had the more grievous injuries. Old Reliable sustained a broken toe, lacerated stomach and ribs, bruised elbow and two broken vertebrae in his back.

Joe DiMaggio missed the most games, the Clipper being able to take part in only 76 of the 154-game schedule because of spurs on his heels, pulled shoulder muscles and a virus infection, at different times. ∎

DiMag Comeback Tops All in Poll

January 5, 1950

Joe DiMaggio, who rose from a sickbed to spark the Yankees to another pennant and world championship, made sports' greatest comeback in 1949. Twenty first-place votes in the AP's annual year-end poll went to the Bronx Bomber who thereby barely nosed out the Yankee team as a whole, which drew 19. To make the Yank imprint even stronger, Manager Casey Stengel received six votes to tie for third-place honors with the LSU football team.

Hank Olen, Daily News

The Yankees greet Joe D. after he hits a home run at Ebbets Field in the 1949 World Series.

Yanks Win '49 Championship

Take 5th Series Game under Arcs, 10-6

By Dick Young
October 10, 1949

By order of Commissioner Chandler, they turned the Ebbets Field lights on at 4:50 yesterday afternoon—but by that time none of the 33,711 fans who sat in on that unprecedented action could see the Brooks, anyway. They saw only the Yankees—the world's champion Yankees—who had by then wrapped up their 12th title by bloodying the NL challengers, 10-6.

The powerful arcs, used for the first time in a big league daytime tilt, were employed to cut the dusk that was gripping the field at the start of the final frame, but they served, just as much, to spotlight the mighty "Team of Destiny" in the same manner that Hollywood actors are glamorized at big events.

Among those stars who made it look so easy by sweeping three straight to take the Series at four games to one, the bright lights focused on Joe DiMaggio, who, snapping out of his pernicious slump, crashed a homer; on rookie Gene Woodling, who cracked three straight hits; on Vic Raschi, who came back to win on two days' rest and did a gritty job of it till he tired in the seventh, and, of course, of Joe Page, the inevitable Joe Page, who ended the thing from the hill, just as he had done against the Dodgers two years before.

And, perhaps, some of the refracted light trickled

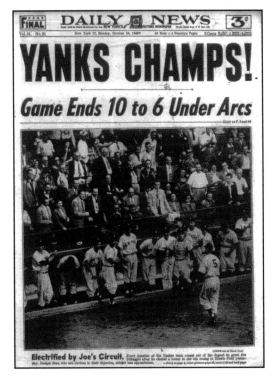

Electrified by Joe's Circuit.

onto a few Brooks—fellows like Gil Hodges, who tried, but much too late, to keep his club alive with the three-run homer that routed Raschi, and Duke Snider, who ripped off his goatskin with three spectacular catches and two hits.

But Gil's circuit and Snider's grabs could not compensate for the extreme deficiency of the Dodger hurlers. This, the classic that was called "The Pitchers' Series" because of the overpowering hurling that marked the first two games, wound up as the "pitchers' series" because the Brooks used nothing but pitchers in trying to stop the flow of blood. Six moundsmen, as many as had ever been used in a single series game, were thrown into the affair by manager Burt Shotton—and two more were toiling rapidly in the bullpen in the final moments as the Brooks were striving to overcome the remaining four runs of their huge early deficit.

But they had started from too far back. At one time the Yankees led, 10-1, which is as good a way as any of illustrating the fact that the Dodgers were hardly in the battle—despite the comparative closeness of the final score. They weren't in it because, in addition to the Yankees' 11 hits, Brook chuckers gave up the eight walks. ■

"If I can't do it right, I don't want to play any longer."

—Joe DiMaggio

Chapter 9

1950-51

Calling It a Career

*I*nstead of being accused of overstaying his welcome in "The Show," Joe DiMaggio bowed out after the 1951 season. He claimed he wasn't performing at his best and so he retired. But there was plenty of evidence that he hadn't used up everything. Just the previous season, in 1950, Joltin' Joe hit three home runs in a game against the Washington Senators. He also hit a game-winning home run in the second game of the 1950 World Series—after popping out in his six previous Series at-bats.

For the second year in a row, DiMaggio was the highest-paid player in baseball, with a contract for $100,000. ■

Tom Watson, Daily News

Joe DiMaggio celebrates winning the 1951 World Series by rubbing the head of Yogi Berra.

1950 REGULAR SEASON

G	AB	R	H	2B	3B	HR	RBI	BB	SB	AVG.	SLG.
139	525	114	158	33	10	32	122	80	0	.301	.585

1951 REGULAR SEASON

G	AB	R	H	2B	3B	HR	RBI	BB	SB	AVG.	SLG.
116	415	72	109	22	4	12	71	61	0	.263	.422

DiMag Signs for 100 Gs

By Dana Mozley
January 25, 1950

Heavier and healthier than at any time since the War, Joe DiMaggio yesterday was also just about as happy as any one man can be when he sat down amidst pomp and ceremony to offer his special services to the Yankees for 1950. For the second straight year, he signed for $100,000—baseball's highest salary figure.

Neither DiMaggio nor general manager George Weiss would offer any details of the new contract, completed in the Yankees' plush Fifth Ave. offices, but there was no doubt it is a replica of last year's. It will run for a one-year term, on a straight salary basis.

Although there had been a movement in the club's management to start slashing DiMag's pay-check this year, the 35-year-old center fielder hinted himself, that there was no change. When asked if he'd do as well financially as last year, he quickly answered: "I would say 'yes.'"

With another $100,000 paycheck, DiMaggio finally passes his first half-million on his 12th contract with the club. Although he started off slowly—$7,500 in 1936—his 1950 salary boosts his total major league income to $545,750. Add another $46,335.67 for eight World Series shares and he approaches $600,000.

While he's one year older, DiMaggio feels several years younger than he did in 1949, when his in-spired leadership and great clutch hitting helped furnish the Yanks with another AL pennant and

The Powerhouse

By Jimmy Powers
January 29, 1950

The inequities of baseball salaries have long intrigued us. Take the recent signings of Joe DiMaggio and Jackie Robinson. Joe was paid $100,000, Robinson, $35,000. There's something manifestly unfair here. Robinson is the best hitter in his league. He is the best base-stealer. He is a definite box office draw, especially in cities with a large negro population. And he plays every day.

DiMaggio is worth every penny of his salary. But DiMaggio is prone to injury, and there are days and weeks on end when he is not in the lineup. Sometimes he is not even in the ballpark. So, to our mind, Robinson is not getting the salary he rates.

The fact that Robinson can hustle out of season and make money on the radio, as an electrical appliance salesman or a movie star, is beside the point.

It was recently revealed in court that the St. Louis Cardinals, who have a larger pay-roll than the Dodgers, and a smaller attendance total, made a profit of $1,600,000 last year. We can assume the Dodger profit was larger.

We have Larry MacPhail's own word for it that in four years he drew $2,000,000 from the Yankees. Bill Veeck and the late Bob Hannegan also were paid fantastic sums, considering services rendered.

The way we see it, the Yankees can afford to pay DiMaggio $100,000, and the Dodgers can well afford to pay Jackie Robinson $100,000, too.

Just what do you think Branch Rickey would be paying DiMaggio if Joltin' Joe were a Dodger and had appeared in only 76 games for Brooklyn last Summer?

> DiMag credits his mother's good home cooking and golf with making him a new man this Winter: "Between them, I've gotten my weight up to 202 pounds and my legs and feet in wonderful shape."

world championship. He played in only 76 games last year—none before June 28—but this time he expects to be in 154 of them.

"I'm not kidding when I tell you that I feel better right now than any time since the War," DiMag said. "My heels are now 100% perfect and I'm heavier than I've been since 1942. For a change, I'm going to open this next season and I plan to play right on through."

A few minutes earlier, DiMag had everyone worried. When asked to say something for the news reels, he jokingly said: "I feel like Old Man River, but the water is knocking at my door." In the next breath, he straightened himself out by admitting, "I want to play on at least two more championship teams."

DiMag credits his mother's good home cooking and golf with making him a new man this Winter. "Between them," he said, "I've gotten my weight up to 202 pounds and my legs and feet in wonderful shape.

"I finished the last World Series at 179 pounds and haven't been up to 200 since the War. I'd like to go to camp weighing about 212 and get down to 205 or 207. That's what I weighed in 1937 when I had my best year" (.346, 46 homers and 167 RBIs).

Although doctors tell him that his heel worries are now over, DiMag is still wearing the specially constructed shoes he wore last year off the field to ease the pain. He'll also continue to wear the special baseball shoes made for him.

"I don't see why I should take them off now," he explained. "They're comfortable."

DiMaggio wouldn't predict what he'd do on the field next year, but his 1949 record speaks for itself. Although sidelined with a recurrent heel injury from Spring Training till he broke in with a game-winning homer at Fenway Park, June 28, he hit .346 between aches and pains from then on. In 76 games—he sat out three weeks with virus pneumonia near the season's end—he batted in 67 important runs. ■

Yanks Paste Indians, 8-2;
DiMag Gets 2,000th Hit
June 21, 1950

The 52,733 at Municipal Stadium were disappointed this evening as the Yankees broke the Indians' six-game winning streak with an 8-2 whipping. But the customers gained some solace in that they were privileged to witness Joe DiMaggio's 2,000th major league hit. The Clipper nudged a grounder through short in the seventh inning off reliever Marino Pieretti and was handed the ball as a souvenir after it was returned from the outfield.

Pieretti walked over to Joe at first, flipped the ball to him, then shook hands with him. That hit meant a lot to DiMag and the ball will go to his eight-year-old son as a memento of a famous dad. It meant nothing as far as the ball game was concerned, because the Tribe was well beaten by that time. It was the 11th New York hit and drove home the seventh run.

Nats Touch Up Sanford; DiMag Moves to First Base

By Joe Trimble
July 4, 1950

A juggled batting order and the appearance of Joe DiMaggio as a first baseman didn't harm the Yankees any today. But the presence of Fred Sanford in the pitcher's box did. The erratic right-hander was there only because Casey Stengel had no one else and his inability to pitch enabled the Senators to breeze to a 7-2 victory.

This was their fifth win in eight meetings between the two clubs and the Nats are the only ones to hold a seasonal edge over the champs. Sanford surprised everyone by hurling four hitless innings at the beginning. But he blew up and was pounded to the showers as the home team broke a 1-1 tie by scoring four runs in the sixth inning.

DiMaggio looked fairly good, though a bit confused at times because of his unfamiliarity with the new position. He handled 13 chances without an error—11 throws and two grounders. One of the tosses, a near-wild throw by reliever Tom Ferrick in the eighth, was a tough one. Joe leaped high for it and, with a continuing motion, tagged the runner, Sherry Robertson. It was a dandy play, proof that a good ballplayer can play anywhere. ■

All-Star Hoodoo Hits AL: Williams, DiMag Hurt

July 12, 1950

The All-Star Game injury jinx struck at the American League's greatest pair of hitters of the generation, so neither Ted Williams of the Red Sox nor Joe DiMaggio of the Yanks is likely to be available when the pennant race starts again Thursday. Ted jammed his elbow when he ran into the concrete wall in the first inning. DiMag pulled a groin muscle as he grounded into the game ending double play.

Yankee Broadcaster Casts DiMaggio Vote

July 17, 1950

Latest ballot received in *The News* poll for the All-Star Game is a live wire from Mel Allen. There's a fellow who knows whereof he speaks because (1) Mel has broadcast nine All-Star Games and (2) he is paid about $75,000 annually for his assorted sportscasts.

"Your fans are right on the ball when they put Joe DiMaggio on the top of the AL outfield list," wired Allen from St Louis, where he is currently bleeding with the Yankees. "Sure, he's in a horrible slump right now. But his batting average doesn't discourage the fans...nor does it fool the opposing pitchers. DiMag still draws a tremendous number of walks, and despite a .243 average he has driven in more runs than almost anyone in the National League.

"DiMaggio does a dozen important things that never appear in a box score, but certainly help his team. The fact that he hasn't let his hitting slump affect his other departments of play is further proof he's a real pro, in fact, he's the greatest all-around player I've ever seen."

62,825 See Yanks Rip Tigers, 14-5

July 22, 1950

The 62,823 fans at the Stadium last night got a surprise when the batting order for the big game with the Tigers showed Johnny Mize hitting cleanup for the Yankees with Joe DiMaggio dropped to fifth position. But before the night was over, the customers and the battered Bengals had looked at two cleanup men. Each of the veteran sluggers made four hits in the 14-5 avalanche, Mize capturing the crowd with two more homers as well.

The big fellow, who was cast off by the Giants last August and unwanted by the Yankees only three weeks ago, is on the wildest hitting splurge of his career. In the last four games, he has smashed 13 hits in 15 times at bat. Five have been homers, one a double, and he has seven singles. He has drawn three passes, so in 18 appearances at the plate, he has been on base 16 times.

The victory was the 12th in the last 15 decisions for the Bombers and cut Detroit's lead to a game and a half. If they can sweep the three-game series, the Yanks will be in first place by Sunday night. And if Mize keeps on going, they'll never get out of there.

Johnny got started in the three-game set with the Browns. With DiMag absent and ill, Mize batted cleanup and went wild. Casey Stengel refused to derail him by dropping him out of the fourth slot when Joe returned last night. So Joe, for only the second time in 13 years, batted out of his favorite spot—a spot he had inherited from the late Lou Gehrig on May 4, 1939, two days after the Iron Horse broke his 2,130-game endurance streak. ■

Yanks Call on DiMag to Lead Victory Push

By Joe Trimble
August 19, 1950

Joe DiMaggio found himself in one of the toughest spots of his fulsome major league career when he stepped back into the lineup against the Athletics here this evening. The great but fading star knew that he must supply the inspirational spark to get the club back on its feet. Another failure and the Yanks will go down the chute with him.

A sharp form reversal on the part of the veteran slugger is called for, of course. After a week on the bench because of a nine-game hitting slump, DiMag figured to be rested and sharp. Joe was hitting only .270 when Casey Stengel was forced to quit on him a week ago tonight. He'll have to better that mark by nearly 100 points for the rest of the year to make a contender out of the Yankees.

The happiest thing would be a carbon copy of the Clipper's splurge in Boston last June, when he busted four homers in three days to sweep the Red Sox and keep the Yankees in the league lead. From that great start—it was his season debut—DiMag batted .346 and inspired the oft-injured Bombers to their pennant victory on the final day. ■

DiMag Hits 3, Yanks Blast Nats, 8-1

By Joe Trimble
September 11, 1950

Joe DiMaggio reduced the biggest ball park in the majors to a personal playpen this afternoon when he became the first batter ever to hit three homers in one game in Griffith Stadium as the Yanks took the opener, 8-1. The weather man turned it into a lake later on, causing the second game to be postponed after three and a half innings when the champs were losing, 6-2.

By winning the first and escaping the nightcap, the Yankees kept themselves in good shape in the standings.

DiMaggio had his biggest game in two years in the opener and it was the third time in his 12 years of AL play that he had pumped three out of the park in nine innings. All three drives went into the left field bleachers, clearing the wall, which is 405 feet from home plate. The park, as currently fenced, has defied the onslaughts of the AL's greatest hitters since 1920. That's when Clark Griffith erected the bleachers.

Joe's first two were solo jolts in the second and sixth innings, when tall Sid Hudson was hurling. He hit the third off reliever Mickey Harris in the ninth with a man on base. They made a total of 27 for the year. The Clipper's previous great days came in St. Louis, June 13, 1937, and in Cleveland, May 23, 1948. His four RBIs today raised his figure to 101—making this the ninth year he has knocked in more than 100. ■

AP/Wide World Photos

Joe DiMaggio shows the world that he hit three homers against the Senators to become the first player ever to accomplish that feat in a single game at Washington's Griffith Park.

DiMaggio's Homer Edges Phillies, 2-1, in 10th

By Dick Young
October 6, 1950

Maybe they're right. Maybe Joe has degenerated to the point where he's merely a terrific player. He may not do it as often as he used to, but when he gets the fat part of that bat on the ball, he rides it as far as any of the kids, and farther than most. Ask the first-row fan who made a fine catch of Joe's decisive smash. Or ask Robin Roberts, the fine Philly flinger who made DiMag look like a has-been until the big challenge arose. Ask any of Joe's mates or his competitors and they'll tell you that class will tell.

Better still, ask the Phils how they'd like to have him, even though his age might not exactly qualify him as a "Whiz Kid." They've reached the point where they'll grab anybody who can hit a single when it counts. They've got a hydramatic attack—no clutch. ■

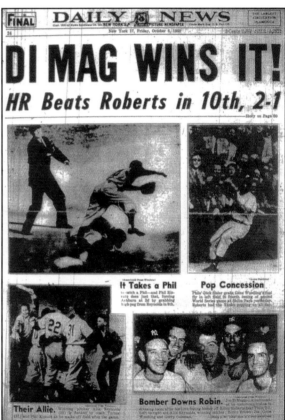

DiMaggio's smooth stroke has powered the Yankees to many World Series highlights.

Joe D. "Challenged," Accepts

By Joe Trimble
October 6, 1950

Robin Roberts, a bright young man with a college education, should have known better than to challenge Joe DiMaggio with a fast ball. That's what the 24-year-old Phil righthander did in the 10th inning today and the club pro sunk it for a hole-in-one.

"It was low and inside," DiMag said. "It certainly wasn't a careless pitch. He just didn't get it exactly where he intended, I guess."

DiMag thought the pitch was a slider but Roberts insists it was a fastball. "I was behind him, two balls and one strike, so I had to challenge him," the Whiz Kid said afterwards.

If he ever gets the chance, the red-cheeked Robin will not issue any more challenges of that nature.

Since 1936, the Clipper has left a trail of broken pitchers in the AL who made the same mistake.

The blast into the upper stands was Joe's seventh, and the first which actually won a Series game. He recalled that he had hit one off Rex Barney of the Brooks early in one of the games in 1947 and that the Yanks had eventually won by a run.

The Yankee dressing room was a bit noisier than after yesterday's victory but still there was no hilarity. Rather, there was some groaning about the bad-hop single by Eddie Waitkus—the blow that deprived Allie Reynolds of a shutout. Had the ball acted naturally, the game would have been won, 1-0, in nine innings and DiMag wouldn't have had to win it all over again in the 10th. ∎

Joe DiMaggio celebrates his home run in Game Two of the 1950 World Series with teammates (l to r) Allie Reynolds, Bobby Brown, Gene Woodling and Jerry Coleman.

AP/Wide World Photos

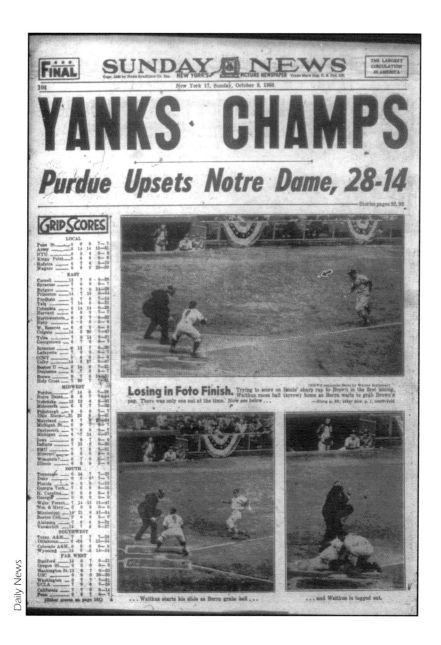

Daily News, October 8, 1950: The Yankees' four-game sweep of the Philadelphia Athletics gave the franchise its 13th World Series championship—and its second in a row. While the rest of the Yank hitters averaged a paltry .222, DiMaggio batted .308 as he, Bobby Brown and Jerry Coleman were the key figures in the team's attack. But the real stars of the Series were the Yankees' pitchers—Allie Reynolds, Vic Raschi, Whitey Ford, Ed Lopat and Tom Ferrick—who finished up with an eye-popping combined ERA of 0.73 for the Series.

Joe's Quitting Indefinite—Hinges on '51 Season

By Joe Trimble
March 4, 1951

Joe DiMaggio admitted today that he was seriously considering retirement at the end of the season, but cautioned that there was nothing definite about it. "I'll see what kind of a year I have and announce a decision at the end of the schedule," the aging star said. "I do not desire a future in baseball as a coach or manager, and would like to hang up my spikes while still on top."

Joe, who was 36 last November 25 and who has been a Yankee since 1936, seemed pessimistic, even fidgety this morning. He appeared to be a man whose mind is beset with worry—a very likely possibility in view of the serious illness of his mother, who is in San Francisco. Chances are that, if he had his way, DiMag would be at her bedside instead of here. He won't admit it, but he doesn't seem to care much about baseball at this time.

Club officials, knowing Joe's moods, were inclined to be indulgent, even indifferent, at the slugger's thoughts of retirement. Both George Weiss, the general manager, and field boss Casey Stengel indicated their belief that DiMag would be back next year if he still is a good ballplayer.

> "I'll see what kind of year I have and announce a decision at the end of the schedule."
>
> —Joe DiMaggio

Said Weiss, "Joe DiMaggio has not discussed this angle (possible retirement) with any club officials. We regret to hear anything like this and we hope he will have the sort of season which will cause him to change his mind."

Stengel, sitting at breakfast one table removed from where DiMag was having his ham and eggs, was asked his reactions and barked, "I can't help it. What do you want me to do, get a gun and make him play next year? When you get right down to it, I don't own him.

"All I know is that I ain't looking for a center fielder at this time."

This last remark by Casey reflected something which is obvious to DiMag and the rest of the players—the fact that 19-year-old Mickey Mantle is being groomed as an outfielder, under the professional tutelage of Tommy Henrich. Mantle may not be good enough to stick with the Yanks at the start of the season, but the manager would like to have him playing center field for Kansas City and readily available in the event that DiMag should hit the skids suddenly. Ol' Case may not be looking for a center fielder, but he sure is getting one ready—just in case. ∎

Charlie Hoff, Daily News

Joe DiMaggio poses with Mickey Mantle, the man who would succeed him as the Bombers' center fielder and fan favorite of the New York Yankees.

Clipper Shrewd Quitting While He's Still on Top

By Joe Trimble
March 25, 1951

Joe DiMaggio's recent decision to retire at the end of this season is admirable. Great pride in himself and his accomplishments is reflected in his desire to "quit while I'm on top." DiMag wants people to remember him as a fine ballplayer rather than have fans, particularly latter-day ones, recall him as a washed-up "old man" who tried to play too long.

> ## DiMag to Retire at Season's End
>
> Despite his earlier intention to postpone a retirement decision until the end of the season, Joe DiMaggio abruptly announced Saturday night that 1951 would be his final season. As evidenced by the 1950 MVP voting—which placed three other Yanks (Rizzuto, Berra and Raschi) ahead of DiMaggio—the Clipper's ability to lead the Yanks has been seriously eroded by his persistent injury problems.

DiMag intends to avoid the sad endings even great ballplayers such as Ty Cobb, Babe Ruth and Tris Speaker experienced. All three refusing to believe the facts, tried to go on and on. Though worn out and physically inept, they attempted to hit big league pitching and to field in major league style. They couldn't, and some fans, forgetting the immortality of these men, booed them, in their last active moments.

Joe, like every other big league star, yearns for just one more good year. He hopes this will be it so he can step aside and be remembered at his best. He has another purpose, too. The name DiMaggio has commercial value, and he doesn't want to cheapen it. The big Yank would like to carve a career in radio and television when he's through as a player. He'll hurt his chances if he hangs on until he's a joke afield and at bat. He will be 37 next November and will have been a pro ballplayer 20 years.

Baseball has been very good to him. The son of a poor San Francisco fisherman, he became the most famous player of his time and one of the all-time greats of the national game. His has a rags-to-riches story, and he's smart for not wanting any rags tied to the riches part of it. He has salted away enough to live comfortably the rest of his life and leave a fine legacy to Joe Jr., now nine.

Joe can look back on tremendous achievements. He has been Most Valuable Player in the AL three times. He has been named to the league All-Star team every one of his 12 active seasons. He played center field in the dream game his first year, 1936, and each succeeding one through 1942. He served in the Army the following three years and came back for the '46 season. An injury prevented his participation in the All-Star game that season, but he was honored with a selection. He has been in all others since.

DiMag is the highest salaried player in Yankee history and, unless Ted Williams drew more from the Red Sox in 1950, his pay was higher than any other man who ever played the game. Joe's $100,000 per year began with the '49 season and will continue through this one. He is one of the most famous Americans of the past 20 years—his name being a headline feature long before such names as Eisenhower, Truman, Taft or Wilkie.

To retire while still respected is a smart move. No one has ever accused the Yankee Clipper of being a dummy, and you can be sure he won't renege on his decision. It takes a really great athlete to quit when he still has some proficiency left. Gene Tunney did it, and Joe DiMaggio will do it too. ■

BoSox Blast Yankees, 10-4; Casey Benches Joe, Phil

By Joe Trimble
July 8, 1951

The dissolution of the Yankee empire may have begun this afternoon in the course of the champ's seventh straight walloping in Fenway Park. After one bewildering inning in which the Red Sox grabbed six runs and the makings of a 10-4 victory, Casey Stengel summarily dismissed four of his regular players from the game. Joe DiMaggio, Phil Rizzuto, Gerry Coleman and Allie Reynolds were shunted to the showers as the manager decided to try to salvage the game with youngsters.

The defeat cost the Yanks possession of first place again, pending Chicago's night action in St. Louis, and virtually locked the three top clubs at the top. A matter of but five percentage points separated the trio, with the Yanks sandwiched between the different color Sox.

The kids who were injected into action didn't help much. Actually the six-run splatter in the opening frame won it for the Sox and Ellis Kinder. The 37-year-old reliever, in his first start of the season, whiffed 10 New Yorkers and had the game in hand all the way. All four Yankee runs were due to homers by the youth brigade. Jack Jensen belted his seventh, Joe Collins his fourth (with a runner on) and Mickey Mantle got number 7.

Stengel's action in removing DiMag and the others was not a hasty one. Actually, it was premeditated. He talked about it before the game, saying, "Four or five of these players are dead tired. I'd like to take them out. Good thing they are getting a vacation next week. I hope they'll come back fresh."■

DiMaggio Bitter over Removal

By Joe Trimble
July 8, 1951

Joe DiMaggio was sullen and bitter at his removal from the field in the second inning of today's 10-4 loss to the Red Sox. The Yankee star, when questioned by reporters in the clubhouse afterward, barked, "There's nothing wrong with my legs or anything else. I was taken out and if you want to know anymore about it, see Stengel."

It may be that the lifting of the fading star is the opening wedge toward benching him again for a while. Casey astounded the baseball world by sending DiMaggio to the sidelines last August and that turned out to be a blessing for both the player and the team. Joe returned after a week's rest and played brilliantly to the end of the schedule.

DiMag Quits as Player for TV Post

By Dick Young
December 12, 1951

The magnificent playing career of Joe DiMaggio is dead—killed two years before its natural time by night baseball. In officially announcing his retirement yesterday, the immortal Yankee Clipper flatly accused the increase of arc contests, with its resultant scrambling of a ballplayer's living routine, as being responsible for the curtailment of his active career, "and that of other players."

The 37-year-old outfielder, who plans to remain with the Yankee organization as a TV broadcaster, said: "I honestly believe night ball cut short my days by about two years. You don't get to bed until two in the morning, or so, and wake up at 10. I found that wasn't enough rest to get the aches and pains out of my system. I'd go to the park for an afternoon game the next day, and sometimes I wouldn't wake up till the fifth or sixth inning.

"It should be one way or the other; either all night ball or all days, so that a player can live normally. Maybe it doesn't affect the young fellows that way, but there's no question in my mind that it does at my age."

DiMag was talking to a large assemblage of newsmen at the Yankee midtown offices. His retirement, after 13 seasons as a Yankee (with a three-year break as a GI from 1943-45), took on the appearance of a mob scene from *Quo Vadis*. Every hall and room of the Yankee suite buzzed with activity— flood lights for newsreel and TV cameras, still photogs and mere question-popping reporters.

Through it all, DiMag conducted himself with splendid poise. He was a striking figure of a man, dressed in a double-breasted gray sharkskin, and smiling pleasantly as reporters shot the questions at him.

No, he would not reconsider—ever. "I have always said, when I make the statement that I'm retiring, it will stick."

He first considered retiring last Spring, he recalled, when he said that 1951 would be his last season. "I never wavered in my decision," Joe said, adding that he would have quit even if he had hit .350 last season instead of .263.

Dan Topping, Yankee prexy, and Del Webb, vice-president, had tried to dissuade Joe when, immediately after the World Series, he notified them of his intentions. Topping asked Joe to think it over during his barnstorming trip through Korea and Japan, hopeful that DiMag would reconsider. Joe agreed, but his decision remained unchanged.

"Until yesterday," Webb told DiMag, "we had still hoped you would stay. But, since you didn't change your mind, it's a sad day, not only for the Yankees, but for all baseball as well."

What were his immediate plans?

"I have several offers—all in the same field; radio and television. I think I'm going to be around in the organization."

At this point, lest it be construed that the offer of the Yankee TV job, formerly held by Dizzy Dean, had hastened his decision to retire, Joe added: "I want to make it clear that nothing or no one influenced me in my decision to retire. It is entirely my own doing."

What was the major determining factor in his decision?

"Injuries," Joe replied quickly. "The old ones were catching up with me, and I've had some new ones. Mainly, it was my shoulders." He touched his hand first to his right collarbone, then to the left, saying: "It pained me right here, when I'd swing and when I'd throw. I've been having trouble with my right shoulder ever since 1939. In the last three years, I'd get off one or two good throws early in a game, and then I'd have nothing left. They knew it, and they were running on me. I threw a lot of them out, but a lot more of them made it."

Joe also cited trouble with his right knee. "When I'd go down for a ground ball," he said, "it would take me a trifle longer to straighten up and get the throw off, because the knee would stiffen." Asked about his heel, which developed the famous calcium spur that necessitated surgery two years ago, Joe said, "No, the heels are fine. It's the knee and shoulders that did it."

Joe added that "If I can't do it right, I don't want to play any longer."

This was the sentiment expressed in a mimeographed statement distributed to the press prior to the personal interviewing. The formal statement read: "I feel that I have reached the stage where I can no longer produce for my ball club, my manager, my teammates and my fans the sort of baseball their loyalty to me deserves."

The statement went on to say that "when baseball is no longer fun to play, it's no longer a game," and closed with:

"I would like to say that I feel I have been unusually privileged to play all my major league baseball for the Yankees. But it has been an even greater privilege to be able to play baseball at all. It has added much to my life. What I will remember most in the days to come will be the great loyalty of the fans. They have been very good to me."

During the course of discussing his future, DiMag was asked if he might "loaf for a year."

"I've thought of that, too," he said with a broad smile, "but I'm afraid I'm in no position to loaf." This from a man who has earned an estimated $700,000 in salary and World Series slices.

Joe nominated Mel Harder, former Cleveland

George Torrie, Daily News

The Yankee Clipper ponders his future after officially announcing his retirement from baseball.

hurler, as the toughest pitcher he ever faced, and said that Ted Williams is "without a doubt" the best hitter he has seen.

As for his own reminiscences, DiMag singled out three high spots as his favorites:

(1) "The day I returned to the line-up in Boston after missing the first 65 games of the season." (2) "For a long span, I'd have to go with the 56-game hitting streak." (3) "My best fielding play, I'd say,

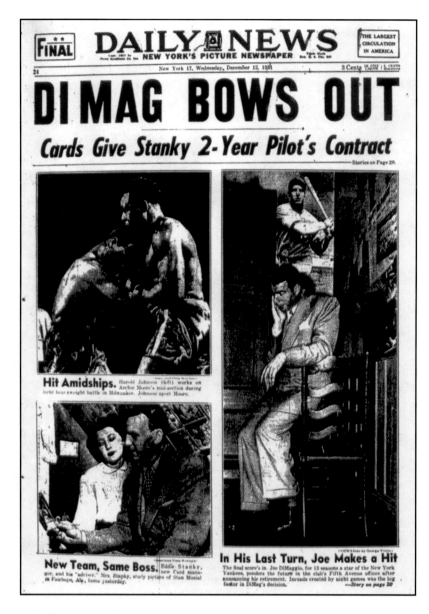

DAILY NEWS
NEW YORK'S PICTURE NEWSPAPER

THE LARGEST CIRCULATION IN AMERICA

New York 17, Wednesday, December 12, 1951

3 Cents

DI MAG BOWS OUT

Cards Give Stanky 2-Year Pilot's Contract

—Stories on Page 20.

Hit Amidships. Harold Johnson (left) works on Archie Moore's mid-section during light heavyweight battle in Milwaukee. Johnson upset Moore.

New Team, Same Boss. Eddie Stanky, new Card manager, and his "adviser," Mrs. Stanky, study picture of Stan Musial in Fairhope, Ala., home yesterday.

In His Last Turn, Joe Makes a Hit The final score's in. Joe DiMaggio, for 13 seasons a star of the New York Yankees, ponders the future in the club's Fifth Avenue offices after announcing his retirement. Inroads created by night games was the big factor in DiMag's decision. —Story on page 20

There weren't many boners spotted through the career of the great ballplayer who came up to the Yankees as a 21-year-old "gamble" in 1936. Many other big league clubs had turned down the hard-hitting kid from San Francisco because it was no secret to the industry that he had a "chronic" knee condition.

However, the Yankees, on the recommendation of two scouts, Bill Essick and Joe Devine, both of whom died recently, had DiMag examined by a Coast physician, who pronounced him sound. Prexy Ed Barrow then paid $75,000 and five ballplayers that never amounted to anything, and the Yankee destiny for the next generation was set.

Joe's tremendous influence on the Yanks is reflected by the fact that, during his 13 seasons with them, the club won 10 pennants. He was named the AL's Most Valuable Player three times—1939, '41 and '47, and was picked for every All-Star Game during his career, although he did not play in the '46 and '51 games due to injury.

His batting achievements include a lifetime average of .325 and 361 homers, but figures alone cannot reflect the true worth of DiMag as a ballplayer. There have been few men in the history of the game who possessed the rhythmic grace and sure hands of DiMag in pursuit of a fly ball. And, despite the fact that he stole few bases, Joe is rated among the finest baserunners the game has known.

Perhaps Casey Stengel said it best yesterday when in tribute to DiMag's greatness, he called Joe a "silent leader." Stengel managed DiMag the past three years only, years in which the tremendous talents of the man were fading steadily, but Casey still called him "the greatest ballplayer I've ever managed."

Stengel, under questioning, revealed that Mickey Mantle will get "first crack" at the center field job in Spring Training.

"Whether the kid can do it or not, I don't

was the catch I made on Hank Greenberg at Yankee Stadium; it was either in 1938 or '39. There was a man on first, Averill. Greenberg hit to the flagpole, and as I took off for the ball, all I had in mind was to chase it down and try to hold him to a triple. I ran to the flagpole, a few steps in front of the sign that says 461 feet, threw up my hand, and there it was.

"I was so stunned, I though there were three outs, but there were only two. I ran toward the dugout, and was halfway to second base when I woke up. By that time, Averill, who had gone halfway to third base, got back to first." Joe grinned and added, "So, the best catch I ever made, also turned out to be a beaut of a boner."

know," said Casey. "He has speed, a good throwing arm and he hits both ways, so he can be in there every day. But he's very green. Remember, he has played only one year in the outfield."

The name of Ted Williams was brought up, not as a potential center fielder, but as a possible trading target to supply the Yankees with the drawing card they lose in DiMag.

"I certainly won't break up this club to get any player," Stengel said. "Boston never offered me Williams, and I can't go around talking about another club's ballplayers, but I know that in order to get a man like that you'd have to give up five or six of your own players. I'd weaken my team too much, so I'm not interested in that kind of deal."

Stengel was asked about the rumor that he might be interested in Dom DiMaggio. There's only one DiMaggio, Stengel observed, and that's one he was losing. ∎

The Yanks' 1951 defeat of their crosstown rival, the New York Giants, in six games gave DiMaggio his ninth World Series triumph and allowed him to retire from baseball the way he always wanted—as a champion at the top of the game.

"The last chapter has been written.
I can now close the book."
—Joe DiMaggio, at his Hall of Fame
induction ceremony on July 25, 1955

Chapter 10

1952-55

On to Cooperstown

*I*t took three tries and a special exemption, but Joe DiMaggio was named to the Baseball Hall of Fame in 1955.

After retiring in 1951, DiMaggio was required by Hall of Fame rules to wait one year before being placed on the Cooperstown ballot. Despite being eligible in 1953, the Yankee Clipper joined a long and illustrious list of ballplayers who failed to be selected to the Hall of Fame in their first year of eligibility. DiMaggio was eighth in the 1953 vote, with 117 votes of a possible 264.

DiMaggio's 117 votes in 1953, while far short of the number needed for induction, were enough to keep him on the ballot in 1954 when the Baseball Writers' Association of America changed the eligibility requirements for selection. Instead of being retired for just one year, a player would now have to be away from the game for five years before becoming eligible for selection to the Hall of Fame. However, players who had garnered over 100 votes the previous year were allowed to stay on the ballot in 1954.

Even with the exemption, DiMag missed the cut again in 1954—this time by just 14 votes, before making it in 1955.

DiMaggio topped the balloting in 1955 with 223 of a possible 251 votes, easily exceeding the minimum of 75 percent required for admission to Cooperstown. He was the last player named under the exemption and at that time was the second youngest (at age 40) to be named to the Hall of Fame. Only Lou Gehrig, who was named at the age of 36, had been enshrined at an earlier age. ∎

HALL OF FAME CAREER STATISTICS

G	AB	R	H	2B	3B	HR	RBI	BB	SB	AVG.	SLG.
1736	6821	1390	2214	389	131	361	1537	790	30	.325	.579

DiMag, Terry Favored on Hall of Fame Ballot

By Joe Trimble
January 18, 1953

Ballots for the annual Hall of Fame election have been mailed out and, in a few days, the ballplayers to be honored as all-time greats will be known: Joe DiMaggio seems a cinch to be selected by veteran baseball writers and, chances are, Bill Terry will make the grade, too.

Voting is handled through the Baseball Writers' Association. All active writers, who have covered major league games for a period of 10 years or longer, are asked to vote. Ken Smith, secretary, recently sent out 300 ballots to eligible voters, of whom about 250 will respond. A player must be named on 75% of the ballots to gain admittance to baseball's shrine at Cooperstown, N.Y.

Last year, of 234 ballots cast, only two gained enough votes for admission. Harry Heilman, great Tiger slugger who had died a few months before, was chosen by 203 selectors, and Paul Waner, Pirates' long-time batting stylist, by 195.

Terry finished third with 155, and it's on that performance that he rules favorite this time. The former manager and first baseman of the Giants was the last National Leaguer to hit .400.

DiMaggio, greatest player of his era (1936-1951), wasn't eligible until this year, rules demanding one must be retired a full season before a name can be placed in nomination.

DiMag's eligibility, of course, is a blow to the chances of others. Joe is deserving, but so are many who retired earlier and are more or less forgotten. Al Simmons, a better hitter than DiMaggio; Bill Dickey, the Yanks' all-time catcher; and Red Ruffing, the best right-handed pitcher they ever had, are three who may be lost in the shuffle. ■

AP/Wide World Photos

DiMaggio's uniform made it to the Hall of Fame several years before he did. Shown here at opening day ceremonies at Yankee Stadium on April 18, 1952, DiMaggio presents his uniform to Rowan Spraker, vice president of the Hall of Fame.

Diz Dean, Simmons Enter Hall of Fame

By Hy Turkin
January 22, 1953

Jay Hanna (Dizzy) Dean, freshest and fastest pitcher of his day, and "Bucketfoot Al" Simmons, who terrorized big league hurlers for 20 years despite his vulnerable stance at the plate, yesterday became the 63rd and 64th men to enter baseball's Hall of Fame.

Dean and Simmons were named on at least 75 percent of the ballots sent in by 10-year members of the Baseball Writers' Association. However, the passport to diamond immortality was again denied to Bill Terry, former Giant first baseman and manager, by the slim margin of seven votes.

Yankee catcher Bill Dickey was fourth, while Joe DiMaggio, who quit the Yanks in 1951, finished eighth.

DiMaggio took his failure philosophically. "A lot of great players have made it in the past," he told a newsman, "and great ones were named today. If it isn't my turn now, there are other years coming up."

Auto dealer Bill Terry said tonight he was "not at all disappointed and not too much interested" in barely falling short of the Hall of Fame for the second straight year. With typical candor, he added, "DiMaggio should have had it before either Dean or Simmons. Dickey should have been up there, too." ∎

The Powerhouse

By Jimmy Powers
January 23, 1953

Sorry to see Joe DiMaggio "strike out" in his first whack at the Hall of Fame. But, as in the game of baseball, there is always another inning...another game...another season. He's sure to make it eventually. After all, he's only a rookie in this Hall of Fame balloting.

Also, the Powerhouse is powerfully sorry to see Bill Terry lead the also-rans for the second straight year. Though his disposition was never such as to remind you of the flower, Sweet William, this veritable giant was as fierce a line-drive hitter as I've ever seen, and could work more wonders with that old-fashioned, motorman-gloved first baseman's mitt than today's players can snare with their modified jai-alai baskets. Like DiMag, Terry is a triple-plated cinch to make his place in Cooperstown's hallowed gallery.

Though the present system of selection seems slow and begrudging to crown-worthy candidates, it's better this way. Any club that's easy getting into isn't worth getting into. No first flush of enthusiasm, local pride or blatant campaigning can slip a player into the Hall of Fame. It's a tough haul, as DiMag and Terry are finding out.

Dickey, Rabbit, Terry Gain Hall of Fame

By Joe Trimble
January 21, 1954

The door to the Hall of Fame at Cooperstown swung wide yesterday as three more of baseball's greats were admitted. Rabbit Maranville, the great little shortstop who died two weeks ago, Bill Terry and Bill Dickey were elected to the shrine of the national game in the annual poll of veteran members of the Baseball Writers' Association of America.

This trio of former greats were the only ones to gain mention by 75 percent of the 252 voters. A minimum of 189 votes was needed for selection. The Happy Rabbit led the list with 209, Dickey pulled 202 and Terry 195. In all, 53 former players were named.

Something of a surprise was the failure of Joe DiMaggio to make it for the second year in a row. The Yankee Clipper fell 14 short with 175 votes. This placed him fourth in the listing.

Ted Lyons, long-time White Sox pitching star and newly-appointed mound coach of the Dodgers, ran fifth with 170. Only others over 100 were Dazzy Vance, 158, and Gabby Hartnett, 151.

Due to a new set of voting rules, the field of candidates eligible for election by the writers was curtailed. A man must have been out of baseball as a player, coach, manager or umpire for five years, with the exception of those who received 100 or more votes last year. Dickey, DiMaggio and Lyons were the exceptions. Also, a player's career had to cover the period between 1928 and 1948. Only writers of 10 or more years' experience voted. ■

The Powerhouse

By Jimmy Powers
January 22, 1954

Joe DiMaggio fans are quite naturally disappointed. Their hero failed by 14 votes to make the Hall of Fame. I have no way of breaking down the ballots into geographic locations, but I will wager the area outside New York was slightly reluctant to give Joe the honor at this time. He will eventually make it, and there no doubt are worthier men his senior, all in line ahead of him.

The Hall of Fame balloting is in danger of becoming a popularity contest. I say this despite the fact that Bill Terry made it. Bill was once unpopular. But, in recent years, he made himself agreeable in the World Series press rooms. I think it is fair to say that Terry today is popular.

Western critics, over a period of time, have taken cracks, not at Joe DiMaggio, but at his overly enthusiastic supporters in cafe society, in the Toots Shor and Lindy belts, where he was regularly on display night after night. Joe's clippings will show an unusually large origination in columns dealing with Broadway chorines, Wall Street spenders and international playboys. Joe, of course, is an innocent victim but this, I maintain, partially explains his weakness in the polls, despite the heavy drumfire of local ballyhoo. We had instances of weird balloting recently in the MVP elections and talk of "Big City ballyhoo."

Daily News

New York writers speculated that DiMaggio's surprise wait for Hall of Fame honors may have been fueled by writers outside New York who were put off by Joe's popularity with the "cafe society" of Broadway stars, Wall Street spenders and international personalities. Here, DiMaggio shares dinner with author James Michener and fashion designer Molly Parnis.

First-Year Induction Loses Luster

By Phil Pepe
January 8, 1989

Joe DiMaggio, voted baseball's greatest living player in 1969, failed to be elected to the Hall of Fame in his first year of eligibility, but Willie Stargell made it in his first year.

Bill Terry, the National League's last .400 hitter, waited 12 years before being elected. Mel Ott waited three. Whitey Ford, Yogi Berra and Carl Hubbell were not elected in their first years of eligibility, but Lou Brock, Ernie Banks, Willie McCovey, Al Kaline and Brooks Robinson were.

Before 1962, only two players were elected in their first year of eligibility. Since then, there's been 15, and that number is almost certain to increase by two tomorrow night with the announcement that Johnny Bench and Carl Yastrzemski—both on the ballot for the first time—have been selected.

Does that mean the modern player is better than his old-time counterpart? Hardly. What it means is that the system has finally caught up with itself; first-year election is not as meaningful as it was.

The Hall of Fame opened its doors in 1936 with the induction of five charter members as voted by baseball writers. The Charter Five were Babe Ruth, Ty Cobb, Honus Wagner, Walter Johnson and Christy Mathewson—and none was a unanimous selection. In fact, there never has been a unanimous selection—Cobb missed by four votes, Hank Aaron by nine, Willie Mays and Stan Musial each by 23, and Mickey Mantle 43. And there will probably never be a unanimous selection for reasons including: 1) human error; 2) personal dislike for the candidate; 3) an antiquated theory held by some voters that no player deserves to be elected in his first year.

Why players such as DiMaggio, Ott, Hubbell, Berra, Ford and Terry were denied admittance in their first year—while Stargell, Kaline, Brock and McCovey made it in their first crack—is simply explained. In the first election of 1936, voters were judging thousands of players—dozens of whom were worthy of enshrinement—who had played in the 60 years before the Hall of Fame.

It took until the early '60s to catch up with the greats of the past. When all the worthy recipients were inducted, many of them years after retiring, the road was clear for first-year induction, as it is now. ∎

AP/Wide World Photos

Baseball Commissioner Ford Frick welcomes three Hall of Famers to Old Timers' Day in Boston: (L-R) Jimmie Foxx, Frick, DiMaggio and Home Run Baker.

DiMaggio, Vance, Hartnett, Lyons in Hall of Fame

By Joe Trimble
January 27, 1955

The massive doors of baseball's Hall of Fame swung open yesterday, admitting four more of the game's great players. Stepping proudly through to enshrinement among the immortals were Joe DiMaggio, Ted Lyons, Dazzy Vance and Gabby Hartnett, all named on at least 75 percent of the 251 ballots cast by veteran members of the Baseball Writers' Association of America.

The quartet will be installed in the national game's shrine at Cooperstown, N.Y., in a picturesque ceremony the morning of July 25. That afternoon the annual Hall of Fame game will be played between the Braves and the Red Sox.

A total of 189 votes was necessary for election. DiMaggio received 223, Lyons 217, Vance 205 and Hartnett 195. The quartet topped the also-rans a year ago when Bill Terry, Bill Dickey and the late Rabbit Maranville were elected.

Yesterday's selectees comprised the largest number to be named in one year since 1947, when Frank Frisch, Mickey Cochrane, Carl Hubbell and Lefty Grove made it. The shrine now contains 77 honored greats. DiMaggio incidentally, will be the last one to gain the Hall of Fame so soon after retirement.

The Yankee Clipper, who ended his active career after the 1951 season, was made eligible this year by a special ruling because he had drawn over 100 votes in the 1953 election. Subsequently, a rule was passed requiring a lapse of five years from retirement before a man becomes eligible.

DiMag had a lifetime batting average of .325, hit 361 homers, was the AL's Most Valuable Player three times (1939, '44 and '47) and holds the all-time consecutive game hitting record of 56, which he set in 1941. Joe played in more World Series games than any other man, 51, and was in 10 of the classics, nine of which the Yankees won.

Joe was one of the highest-paid players of all-time, with earnings of approximately $645,000 in regular salaries for 13 seasons and $58,519.71 in World Series cuts. He also earned many thousands of dollars in testimonials, endorsements and personal appearances.

DiMaggio is one of the youngest members of the shrine, being just 40. Lyons and Harnett are each 54 and Vance is 62. ∎

DiMag, Daz among 6 Feted at Hall of Fame

July 26, 1955

Baseball's immortal Hall of Fame increased its membership to 80 when it opened its gates to six newcomers, ranging from 69-year-old Frank (Home Run) Baker to 40-year-old Joltin' Joe DiMaggio.

The select six, which also included former major league greats Leo (Gabby) Hartnett, Arthur (Dazzy) Vance, Ted Lyons and Ray Schalk, were honored in a special 45-minute ceremony presided over by Baseball Commissioner Ford Frick.

DiMaggio, perhaps the best remembered because of his comparative youth, received the biggest applause. There were loud whistles from youngsters sitting in trees across the street from the red brick Hall of Fame museum.

The last of the sextet to be presented, DiMaggio glowed with pride as Frick recounted his diamond exploits, including his amazing 56-game streak, his participation on nine world championship Yankee clubs, his three MVP awards, his 11 All-Star team nominations and his .325 batting average and 361 home runs through 13 seasons.

"This is a happy day for me," Joe said feelingly. "It's a long step since that day 20 years ago when I was riding to St. Petersburg with Tony Lazzeri and Frank Crosetti for my first spring training trip with the Yankees.

"They asked me to drive the last 200 miles and I said sheepishly, 'I don't drive.' I thought that was the end of my career."

DiMaggio told the crowd he had tried to pattern himself after the late Lou Gehrig.

"I watched every move Lou made on and off the field," Joe said. "Also, I'd like to thank Joe McCarthy, my first major league manager, for the early training he gave me."

The former Yankee Clipper closed by saying: "The last chapter has been written. I can now close the book."

DiMaggio, Hartnett, Lyons and Vance were elected to the Hall of Fame last January by members of the Baseball Writers' Assn. of America. Baker and Schalk were chosen by the Hall of Fame committee.■

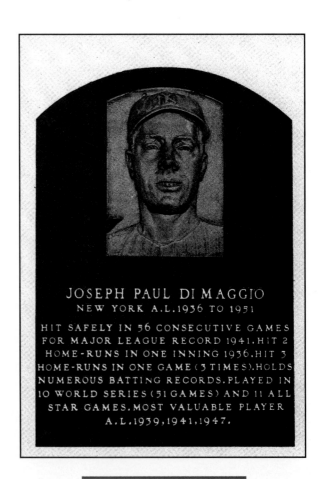

The plaque dedicated to Joe DiMaggio as seen in the Baseball Hall of Fame.

The Powerhouse

By Jimmy Powers
July 27, 1955

E very baseball fan—and that includes you and me—has a favorite ball player. If you've been a fan for a quarter century or more, your all-time favorite might well be Ty Cobb or Tris Speaker, peerless outfielders, but if your enthusiasm goes back only a few years, you might prefer Joe DiMaggio, or Gabby Hartnett, or Bill Terry.

Regardless of what great star you've followed through the years, the chances are he'll be at Yankee Stadium next Saturday afternoon, when the Yankees again play hosts to baseball's great and near-great in the annual Old Timers' Day celebration.

Of the 31 living members of the Hall of Fame, 24 have accepted invitations to attend Saturday's day of nostalgia at the Stadium. In addition to the greats who have been enshrined in Cooperstown's pantheon, a host of DiMaggio's former Yankee teammates also will be on hand as we all join in paying tribute to the newest inductees. Last Monday, in appropriate ceremonies at Cooperstown, DiMag, Home Run Baker, Dazzy Vance, Gabby Hartnett, Ted Lyons and Ray Schalk were formally inducted into baseball's shrine.

This year's Yankee Stadium tribute to the old-time stars is especially dedicated to the Yankee Clipper and to Baker, the latest two former Yanks to be honored with selection. However, all six will be on hand Saturday.

The Hall of Fame in baseball is quite different from any other such museum for famous personages. In baseball, fortunately, you can take your living hero down from the museum shelf, and briefly—all too briefly—return him to his field of glory. In this way, the younger fans of today who know the Cobbs, Speakers, Youngs, Cochranes, Dickeys and other stars only as records in a book, may get one glance at these "greats" of the game. To be sure, they can't step out and hit .350 or post 20-game winning season, but can appear in their old clubs' uniforms, take a bow...and even take a few cuts at the plate in something resembling their greatness of yesterday.

> Of the 31 living members of the Hall of Fame, 24 have accepted invitations to attend Saturday's day of nostalgia at the Stadium.

There are all too few such opportunities in sports. A day of tribute to the living Hall of Famers, and to our other diamond favorites, is a tradition I think should be preserved, and I'm glad to know that so many of yesterday's heroes have accepted the Yanks' invitation to return Saturday.

For the DiMaggio era team, the Yankees have received acceptances from such former favorites as Charley Keller and Tommy Henrich with DiMag (reuniting one of the greatest outfields ever to grace our fair city), Allie Reynolds, the recently retired Chief, irrepressible Lefty Gomez, Buddy Hassett, Hank Borowy, Spud Chandler, Joe Page, Marius Russo, Red Rolfe, Red Ruffing, Johnny Lindell, Johnny Mize and Rollie Hemsley. ∎

2nd Youngest

Practically a kid as Hall of Famers go, Joe DiMaggio stated yesterday that it is a great honor to be on the same team with all those oldtimers.

DiMag, 40, is the second-youngest man to be elected to Cooperstown. Only the late Lou Gehrig, 36 when chosen, was younger.

Joe told of how he learned of his election from an unknown truck driver. "I was driving down from Boston when this guy leans out of his cab and shouts: 'Congratulations, Joe.' I turned on my radio and heard the good news."

"She's a plain kid. She'd give up the business if I asked her.
She'd quit the movies in a minute."
—Joe DiMaggio on Marilyn Monroe

Chapter 11

Joltin' Joe and Miss Monroe

Hollywood created a superstar and pain was the price you paid." The relationship between bombshell pinup girl Marilyn Monroe and baseball hero Joe DiMaggio is embodied in these lyrics from Elton John's "Candle in the Wind." Their stardom was what brought them together and, in the end, kept them apart.

Marilyn Monroe and Joe DiMaggio were married on January 15, 1954, in San Francisco. The superstar relationship was highly publicized, and it was followed by fans and the press almost daily. Life in the spotlight was arduous for the couple, but there was no escape.

Later that year, Marilyn starred in The Seven Year Itch, *and filmed a scene that America would never forget. With her skirt blowing up to reveal more than Joe thought necessary, Marilyn stood above a wind machine on a busy New York street in front of 1,500 onlookers. This scene was linked by many to the breakup of Monroe and DiMaggio.*

The difficulty of a relationship that could never be private was too much for the couple, and in October of 1954, Marilyn filed for divorce.

The fire never burned out, though, and years later the two would rekindle their relationship. But at the height of their renewed happiness, tragedy struck. Marilyn was found dead in her apartment in 1962. Shock swept the nation, but no one was more devastated than Joe DiMaggio at the loss of the nation's glamour girl.

AP/Wide World Photos

Marilyn Weds Joe DiMaggio

January 15, 1954

Marilyn Monroe and Joe DiMaggio were married by a Municipal Court judge yesterday.

The calendar girl actress and the former Yankee outfielder said their vows in private in the judge's chamber at City Hall. The wedding had been rumored for weeks.

Municipal Judge Charles H. Perry performed the single-ring rites while about 100 reporters, photographers and well-wishers waited in the corridors. Hundreds waited outside the building for a glimpse of the couple.

Bride and groom appeared nervous and excited but happy. Marilyn was hatless and wore a sleek-fitting chocolate brown suit with a white collar. DiMaggio wore a blue suit and a polka-dot tie.

On the license Marilyn gave her age as 25. Joe said he was 39.

DiMaggio, usually reticent, beamed as he told reporters he and Marilyn had planned the wedding for some time.

"We decided to go through with it about two days ago," he said.

"It isn't snap judgment, you know. It's been talked about for some time."

He said they planned a short honeymoon—about 10 days—before business takes him to New York.

"We are going to climb into the car and take off," he said. "The car's all packed, jammed full of stuff."

> "It's got to be better than rooming with Joe Page."
> — DiMaggio's response to being asked whether his marriage to Marilyn Monroe was going to be good for him.

Marilyn, after smearing her lipstick with a long kiss for the benefit of photographers, said she "couldn't be happier."

"I'm terribly excited," Monroe gushed.

She said she intended to keep working in the movies but "I'm looking forward to being a housewife, too."

Asked if they intended to have a family, both blushed in some confusion and DiMaggio murmured: "Sure there's going to be a family."

The pair had waited in a corridor for the judge, and on a signal from his chambers, Joe jumped up and exclaimed: "Okay, let's get this marriage going."

The crowd attempted to jam into the chambers but was shunted aside and only the wedding party was admitted. A few of the curious got a glimpse through a small window and one man peeked through the transom.

The wedding party included Joe's brother, Tom, and his wife, Lee; the groom's sister, Mrs. Betty Barsocchini, and brother-in-law, Reno Barsocchini, and Joe's old boss, Lefty O'Doul, ex-manager of the San Francisco Seals.

DiMaggio's first wife was actress Dorothy Arnold. Divorced 10 years ago, they have a 12-year-old son, Joe DiMaggio III.

Marilyn, too, was married once before at 16 to James Dougherty, now a policeman in Van Nuys, California. ■

Joe and Marilyn Spent First Night in $4 Motel

January 16, 1954

Marilyn Monroe and Joe DiMaggio spent their wedding night in a $4 motel room and then drove off in Joe's Cadillac this afternoon without breakfast.

When the newlyweds drove up to the Clifton Motel about 8 o' clock that night, proprietor Ernest Shape was the most surprised man in California. He recognized them, of course.

"I just heard on the radio they'd been married or I would have given them the cold shoulder," he said today.

When Joe asked for a room with a TV, Sharpe asked Joe:

"I don't suppose you want twin beds?"

"Oh boy, I'll say not," said Joe.

Marilyn and Joe had stopped for lunch in Monterey where crowds besieged the hotel in the mistaken belief that the couple would honeymoon there.

But somehow, the actress and the former Yankee slugger sneaked away unseen and didn't stop till they reached Paso Robles, 175 miles south of San Francisco.

At 1 p.m. yesterday—15 hours after they had hung out a "Do Not Disturb" sign—Joe and Marilyn squared their bill with the motel man, politely turned down a proffered cup of coffee, saying they would have breakfast down the road, and drove away.

Just where they would continue their honeymoon, no one knew. Some said they might be heading for Mexico. Others thought they'd be in Hollywood by Monday so Marilyn could report for work at her studio.■

FINAL **DAILY NEWS** 5¢
NEW YORK'S PICTURE NEWSPAPER

Vol. 35. No. 175   New York 17, N.Y., Friday, January 15, 1954

MARILYN WEDS JOE IN FRISCO

Story on Page 3

Raid $6,000,000 Horse Room

Story on Page 2

DiMaggio Signs With a New Manager. Joe DiMaggio and blonde Marilyn Monroe wear cheek-to-cheek smiles as they leave San Francisco City Hall where they were married yesterday. Simple wedding of former Yankee star and movie actress drew nearly 500 spectators. —Story on page 3

Two Scratch Hits

September 13, 1954

Recovered from an attack of hives which kept him in California, Joe DiMaggio, the ex-Yankee great, flew into New York yesterday and joined the missus, Marilyn Monroe, who is in town to make a film, *The Seven Year Itch*. DiMaggio said he will stay here until Marilyn completes the local sequences of her movie, then return with her to their West Coast home. ∎

Marilyn Monroe talks to reporters on the set of *The Seven Year Itch*.

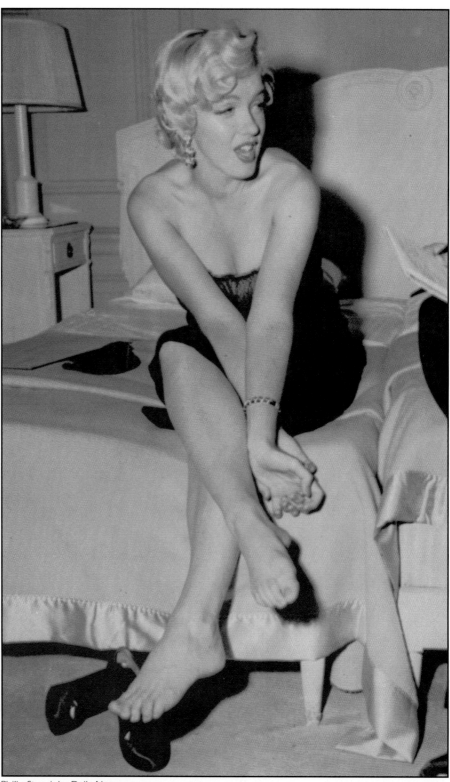

Philip Stanziola, Daily News

Back to the Hollywood Mines

September 17, 1954

Marilyn Monroe flew in from New York yesterday and said she had a "wonderful time" doing a sidewalk movie scene in which a blower lifted her skirt 15 times as 1,500 fans cheered. "But I'm sleepy," she said, stifling a yawn, as she stepped from a plane with husband Joe DiMaggio. "I've been reading this (movie) script all night." She will continue work here in less spectacular scenes. DiMaggio said he is returning to New York for the World Series. ∎

Joe DiMaggio and Marilyn Monroe as they board the plane heading back to Hollywood after their stay in New York.

Jack Clarity, Daily News

Marilyn, Joe Break Up over Sexy Pictures

Florabel Muir
October 5, 1954

The incomparable Marilyn Monroe is divorcing baseball hero Joe DiMaggio because of a long-smoldering quarrel about the sexy cheesecake pictures that made her famous, it was disclosed yesterday.

The blonde star, who once said "you can't curl up with a career on a cold night," blamed "incompatibility" and "conflicting career demands" for the shattering of their eight-month marriage.

The DiMaggios remained in seclusion at their Beverly Hills home—with twin black Cadillacs parked outside—after Marilyn telephoned 20th Century Fox in the morning and the studio announced the breakup.

Then late yesterday Marilyn's lawyer, Jerry Giesler, went to the DiMaggio home. Together Giesler and Joe went upstairs where Marilyn lay in bed, not feeling well.

They had a long talk. Then Giesler announced that Marilyn would file for divorce tomorrow morning in the Santa Monica branch of the Supreme Court. Joe said he would return to his family—and restaurant—in San Francisco tonight.

Friends said DiMaggio, one-time New York Yankee outfield star, had long been upset about his wife's being ogled across the country in various stages of undress.

"Being married to Marilyn is like being married to an institution," one friend quoted him as saying.

The last straw was believed to have been a scene in New York September 15, when a wind machine in a subway grating blew Marilyn's skirt around her neck 15 times in two hours of filming for *The Seven Year Itch*.

The cameras ground, some 2,000 fans behind police barriers cheered lustily for each windblast—and Joe stood by gloomily. "No comment," was all he would say to them.

Joe and Marilyn continued heatedly to deny recurrent rumors that they were having troubles and had no interests in common. But Marilyn was always busy with her career, and Joe hated the spotlight. She went to parties alone. He liked to play poker with the boys.

Six weeks ago he made his first studio visit to watch her filming *There's No Business Like Show Business*. One official said he refused to pose for a picture with her because she was "too scantily dressed."

The set was crowded with other onlookers besides Joe. The star's midriff was bare. She wore only a fragile bra, shoulder cloak and slacks for the dubbing of the movie's top song, "Heat Wave."

The secret troubles apparently reached their peak during and just after the eight-day trip to New York last month. By the time Joe flew back to New York to cover the World Series for a syndicate, they had just about reached the end, friends said.

Joe flew in from Cleveland Saturday night. There were apparently more discussions, and Marilyn told the studio about 9 a.m. the next day.

"His career and mine don't mix," she told studio publicity chief Harry Brand.

Giesler indicated he had been called in sometime before the announcement. "I've talked to both and come to the conclusion they cannot get together," he said.

"They talked it over and reached a pleasant understanding," he said. "We're going ahead with the divorce."

The breakup rocked the film colony, where many marriages come and go but even the biggest cynics figured Joe and Marilyn's union would last.

They had met three years ago on a blind date arranged by a mutual friend, press agent David March. Marilyn hadn't wanted to go. She telephoned

March that she was "very tired," but he talked her into it.

"I'd heard of Joe DiMaggio," she recalled later, "but I didn't know much about him. When I met him that first night, my first thought was: he's different."

Both had been stung by unhappy marriages.

Joe had married actress Dorothy Arnold in 1939, divorced in 1944. They have a 12-year-old son, Joseph Paul DiMaggio III.

Marilyn, born Norma Jean Baker, had grown up in a Los Angeles orphanage—her father dead, her mother sickly. At 16, after 11 foster homes, she married Jim Dougherty, now a policeman.

They were divorced in 1944 as Marilyn started her rise to fame.

Joe and Marilyn went steady for two years. They liked cooking meals together—especially steaks—and they liked each other's company. It was a quiet romance.

On January 14, 1954, Marilyn, 27, skipped out on her studio and eloped with Joe, 39. The "secret" civil wedding in San Francisco was cheered by some 500 fans, and the bridal couple disappeared for a short honeymoon.

It was after the honeymoon that Marilyn said she wanted six children.

The month after the marriage, Joe and Marilyn went to Japan to help launch an exhibition baseball tour. The riotous welcome for Marilyn may have been the first storm cloud.

Some 4,000 Japanese went wild when they arrived, and one town was reported to have made Marilyn a local deity. In Korea, 60,000 girls yelled themselves hoarse when Marilyn appeared in a skintight purple dress. Joe stayed in Japan.

"I don't mind playing second fiddle to Marilyn," he said.

When Marilyn flew to New York on September 9, hundreds of fans shrieked their welcome. A couple of days later traffic was jammed for four hours around 61st and Lexington Ave. Marilyn was being filmed in a white bathrobe.

Joe came to New York to join his wife and watched the skirt-blowing. Marilyn's white backless dress flew high, revealing white panties and bare legs. Joe didn't like it.

Just before marrying DiMaggio, she said, "When and if I marry again it will be for life, because I'm a one-man woman."

Marilyn reported herself sick today but promised to be back at the career tomorrow. ■

Marilyn Monroe, during the filming of the world-famous scene from her movie *The Seven Year Itch*.

20th Century Fox

I'll Never Be Back, Joe Vows

By Florabel Muir
October 6, 1954

At 10:30 this morning, Joe DiMaggio's friend Reno Barsoccini, came out of the house carrying two big suitcases and a set of golf clubs. He put them in the trunk of Joe's baby-blue Cadillac convertible, parked in the driveway.

He went in again, and came out with another bag—and Joe.

The Yankee Clipper looked glum. His eyebrows curved into a frown, his lips were pressed tight.

Then he saw all the reporters, "Hiya, fellows," he said.

"Where are you going?" a reporter asked.

"I'm driving to San Francisco right now."

"Is that going to be your home?"

"That is my home and always has been."

"Are you coming back?"

"I'll never be back."

Then Joe slid under the wheel, took a glance at the black Cadillac convertible with white leather upholstery parked nearby—Marilyn's car—and drove off. ■

DAILY NEWS FINAL 4¢
NEW YORK'S PICTURE NEWSPAPER ®
Vol. 36. No. 89 New York 17, N.Y. Thursday, October 7, 1954

I'LL NEVER BE BACK: JOE

→Story on Page 3

Tearful Parting

A glum Joe DiMaggio walks toward his car after he left honeymoon house he shared with Marilyn Monroe. Said Joe: "I'll never come back to this house." An hour later, Marilyn made her appearance en route to studio. Apparently on the verge of collapse, she faced reporters and photographers. All she would say was, "I'm sorry!" Studio officials sent her home because her movie is comedy and "she couldn't see any comedy in life today." *Story page 3*

Famous Last Words

October 6, 1954
—Spoken during the eight months of their marriage

MARILYN

January 15, 1954, the wedding day: "I couldn't be happier. I'm looking forward to being a housewife, too….I want six babies."

March 6, 1954: "He's the head of our household and I'll live wherever he decides."

April 15, 1954: "I'm really a very happy wife. I even like the cooking part of it."

June 6, 1954: "The husband should be the head man and the wife should always remember that she's a woman. I am certainly no authority on the subject, but when someone asks me how to hold a husband, I tell them this: Be yourself, but don't let down."

September 10, 1954: "I'll call him Joe and Giuseppe and some pet names I want to keep secret, but when I refer to him, I say…my husband."

JOE

January 15, 1954, the wedding day: "We decided to go through with it about two days ago. It isn't snap judgment, you know. It's been talked about for some time. Sure, there is going to be a family. Well, at least one."

February 2, 1954, in Tokyo: "I don't mind playing second fiddle to Marilyn. She's my wife."

March 6, 1954: No comment.

June 6, 1954: No comment.

September, 1954: Asked to pose with Marilyn on her movie set—"No, I'm not dressed properly."

September 13, 1954: Watching Marilyn's skirt blowing over her head in New York for a movie, Joe said, according to bystanders: "What the hell is going on here?"

September 16, 1954: No comment.

AP/Wide World Photos

Joe DiMaggio closes, for the last time, the door of the honeymoon home he's shared with Marilyn Monroe. The former baseball star packed up and left for San Francisco an hour before his wife, who instituted divorce proceedings the previous day, emerged and headed for her studio.

Marilyn Is Free; Love Caught Cold from Joe

By Florabel Muir
October 28, 1954

Marilyn Monroe won an uncontested divorce from Joe DiMaggio today after sobbing that Joe was "cold."

He was "indifferent" and terribly "moody" too, Marilyn testified, when all she wanted was love.

Once he wouldn't talk with her for 10 long days, she said, and "when I tried to find out what was the matter with him he would say 'Leave me alone!' and 'Stop nagging me!'"

A man sitting next to me said out loud: "That guy must be nuts." A woman on the other side remarked: "She isn't telling the whole story."

Marilyn's five-minute testimony was packed with emotion. She sighed. Her voice broke twice. Once it was in a sob. She brought a handkerchief toward her face, but there weren't any tears to wipe away.

She tilted her head slightly forward and erupted her little words to Judge Orlando H. Rhodes. The judge seemed quite interested when Marilyn said Joe was indifferent to her.

A two-piece black silk faille suit with half-plunging shawl collar, black straw hat tilted back on her head, and white gloves—she was asked right off what her name was.

"Marilyn DiMaggio," she told her attorney, Jerry Giesler.

"You mean Norma Jean, don't you?"

"Oh, yes," she said.

Then she plunged into her story of how Joe had spurned her charms during their eight and a half months of marriage.

> Marilyn's five-minute testimony was packed with emotion. She sighed. Her voice broke twice. Once it was in a sob.

"I expected to find love, warmth, affection, and understanding in my marriage," she said. "Instead I found complete indifference and coldness."

Marilyn said she even offered to give up her acting career, "but he was indifferent to that offer, too."

Not once did she refer to Joe by name.

"My husband," she went on, "would get into moods where he wouldn't talk to me for seven or eight—one time it was 10 days. When I tried to find out what was the matter with him he would say 'Leave me alone' and 'Stop nagging me.'"

"I was not permitted to have any visitors in the house without an argument. I don't think we had visitors more than three times during our marriage."

Once, Marilyn said, Joe permitted someone to come into their big house "when I was sick, but all during the visit there was great strain." She didn't say who the visitor was.

Marilyn said Joe's coldness and indifference affected her health and "I was under the care of my doctor quite a bit of the time."

Marilyn's business manager, Mrs. Inez Melson, corroborated her story. She said when Marilyn tried to give Joe warmth he would push her away and say "Don't bother me." She swore that before Joe and Marilyn broke up in late September—they lived under the same roof for a week, he downstairs and she upstairs—Joe told her: "I know I am wrong in my approach of coldness and indifference. I regret it but I cannot help it." ■

Joe approved of this recent night club picture—but not of cheesecake!—Story page 3.

Joe's Dating Marilyn— Last Night Anyway

June 2, 1955

Marilyn Monroe and Joe DiMaggio showed the world last night that they were buddy-buddy again, but it does not mean they plan to remarry.

In the glare of klieg lights with thousands of enthusiastic onlookers held back by police lines—and in the shadow of a 52-foot-high replica of the movie's famous skirt-blowing scene from "Seven Year Itch" which led to divorce—Marilyn and Joe attended a preview of the film in Loew's State Theatre, Times Square.

Later Joe threw a party for his former wife, but he made clear it was only a friendly gesture.

The fans loved the reunion, for whatever it was worth. Before the preview, when the couple appeared, a woman sighed: "They look like lovebirds."

Young girls screamed with delight as the pair walked into the movie, crammed with hundreds of celebrities.

Earlier arrivals had included songwriter Harold Arlen and singer Margaret Truman, who happens to be the daughter of former President Harry S. Truman, actress Grace Kelly, singer Eddie Fisher and many another big names.

Those in the know said that Joe's appearance at the theatre last night was a major concession on his part.

The divorce of the DiMaggios in Hollywood last October 27 after 10 months of marriage was blamed in large measure on a scene made last September for "Itch." With 1,500 entranced onlookers on hand, Marilyn stood over a Lexington Ave. grating and had her skirt blown high into the air 15 times.

One man was openly unhappy about the exhibition. That was Joe. He let friends know later he didn't like that sort of thing.

However DiMaggio felt, 20th Century-Fox thought the shot was grand, and the huge replica of the controversial scene stands atop the theatre marquee.

After the preview, Joe was host at a surprise birthday party for Marilyn—she's 27, he said—in Toots Shor's restaurant. More than 50 pals in the theatrical and sports worlds attended. DiMaggio denied that the party was more than a friendly gesture. "We're just good friends," he said. "We do not plan to remarry. That's all I care to say."■

(at right) Former baseball star Joe DiMaggio and actress Marilyn Monroe walk hand in hand as they arrive for the preview of Marilyn's new picture, "The Seven Year Itch," at a Broadway movie house in New York City, June 1, 1955.

197

MM's Operation a Success, Hospital Reports

By Henry Machirella
June 30, 1961

After two hours and 15 minutes in the operating room at Polyclinic Hospital, Marilyn Monroe emerged at 9:05 last night minus her gall bladder but otherwise in satisfactory condition.

She was wheeled into her private room under sedation, to be greeted there by a private nurse and her ex-husband, Joe DiMaggio, who had been standing by all day at the hospital.

The official bulletin issued by the hospital said: "Everything at the present time is uneventful. Things are going normally with Marilyn, and there is no reason at this point to expect complications. It was a successful operation."

The gall bladder surgery was scheduled after X-rays and lab tests earlier in the day had pinpointed an impacted stone as the source of Miss Monroe's disorder.

> DiMaggio was her only visitor. The one-time Yankee star, who was Marilyn's second husband, has been seeing her frequently since her divorce from her third spouse, playwright Arthur Miller, early this year.

She had entered the hospital by ambulance, with DiMaggio at her side, at noon Wednesday following 48 hours of abdominal pain.

There were seven doctors in attendance during the operation, including Marilyn's personal physician who had flown in from California. The name of the chief surgeon was not revealed by Polyclinic.

A hospital spokesman said gall bladder surgery normally requires 10 to 12 days of convalescence in the hospital.

DiMaggio was her only visitor. The one-time Yankee star, who was Marilyn's second husband, has been seeing her frequently since her divorce from her third spouse, playwright Arthur Miller, early this year.

This was Miss Monroe's fourth hospital confinement in the last five months. ∎

An Ex-husband Can Be a Girl's Best Friend

By Henry Lee
January 22, 1961

With St. Valentine's Day just around the corner, it is a pleasure to report that several celebrated couples, sadly sundered by divorce or separation, are showing renewed interest in each other.

Possible candidates for reconciliations include Marilyn Monroe and Husband No. 2, Joe DiMaggio. She and DiMaggio were married in January 1954, and divorced nine months later.

Since then, Joe has been a successful but lonely guy, his intimates say. He lives in a two-room suite in a midtown hotel near his office. He gets $100,000-plus yearly as executive vice president of V. H. Monette Co., representatives for food and grocery concerns.

Joe's job takes him to U.S. bases all over the world, as Monette does some $100 million yearly in government business, but it is a suitcase-and-hotel-room kind of life.

Only once since his divorce from Marilyn has big Joe been even tentatively linked with a girl. That was two years ago when a 21-year-old blonde beauty queen from South Carolina, Marian McKnight, endorsed Joe as "a very charming and a very wonderful man," but positively dismissed any talk of matrimony.

Suddenly, all within the past few weeks, lonely Joe and Marilyn have been going out together again. They caught the last performance of Brendan Behan's "The Hostage" and dined together at Le Pavillon (chaperoned by young Susan Strasberg and George Solotaire, an old friend of Joe). There have been "several" such dates, and reaction along Broadway is mixed.

Some friends think maybe there is a chance of a reconciliation; others say their brief, tempestuous marriage proved to both that they couldn't make a go of it together. But that was seven years ago...

"He's just a good friend," Marilyn insists. ∎

Beauty and Brains End Their Idyll

January 22, 1961

Marilyn Monroe filed suit for divorce from playwright Arthur Miller here last night, ending their four-year "beauty and brains" marriage.

The pinup girl of the century was understood to be returning to New York, where she has renewed her friendship with her second husband, retired baseball star Joe DiMaggio.

AP/Wide World Photos

Actress Marilyn Monroe and ex-husband Joe DiMaggio happily walk the shores of the Gulf of Mexico as they enjoy a day together at Bellaire, Florida, March 29, 1961.

MM's Operation a Success, Hospital Reports

By Henry Machirella
June 30, 1961

After two hours and 15 minutes in the operating room at Polyclinic Hospital, Marilyn Monroe emerged at 9:05 last night minus her gall bladder but otherwise in satisfactory condition.

She was wheeled into her private room under sedation, to be greeted there by a private nurse and her ex-husband, Joe DiMaggio, who had been standing by all day at the hospital.

The official bulletin issued by the hospital said: "Everything at the present time is uneventful. Things are going normally with Marilyn, and there is no reason at this point to expect complications. It was a successful operation."

The gall bladder surgery was scheduled after X-rays and lab tests earlier in the day had pinpointed an impacted stone as the source of Miss Monroe's disorder.

> DiMaggio was her only visitor. The one-time Yankee star, who was Marilyn's second husband, has been seeing her frequently since her divorce from her third spouse, playwright Arthur Miller, early this year.

She had entered the hospital by ambulance, with DiMaggio at her side, at noon Wednesday following 48 hours of abdominal pain.

There were seven doctors in attendance during the operation, including Marilyn's personal physician who had flown in from California. The name of the chief surgeon was not revealed by Polyclinic.

A hospital spokesman said gall bladder surgery normally requires 10 to 12 days of convalescence in the hospital.

DiMaggio was her only visitor. The one-time Yankee star, who was Marilyn's second husband, has been seeing her frequently since her divorce from her third spouse, playwright Arthur Miller, early this year.

This was Miss Monroe's fourth hospital confinement in the last five months. ∎

Joe Won't Say It's So

By Daniel O'Malley
June 30, 1961

Will Marilyn wed Joe again? Has the flame of love been rekindled between the blonde film goddess and the former Yankee Clipper?

The answer last night from the party of the second part—Joe DiMaggio—was a broad, enigmatic grin.

Emerging from Polyclinic Hospital after an all-day vigil that ended with the successful gall bladder surgery on Miss Monroe, DiMag was buttonholed and pointedly queried on the prospect of a remarriage with Marilyn.

He grinned and said nothing.

The question was pressed, a reporter noting that DiMaggio was the only one of Marilyn's three ex-spouses to show up at the hospital.

"What can I say?" DiMag responded. "The girl is up there after a major operation. What can I tell you?"

He was advised that he could announce whether he planned to marry Miss Monroe again.

Once more DiMag broke into a broad smile.

A cab rolled up and the one-time Yankee star jumped in. ■

Hy Rothman, Daily News

Joe DiMaggio with ex-wife Marilyn Monroe at the St. Regis Hotel.

Marilyn Monroe Found Dead

Sleeping Pill Bottle at Bedside, Her Hand Touching Phone

By Florabel Buir
August 6, 1962

Marilyn Monroe, America's symbol of sex and glamour, was found dead today, sprawled in her queen-size bed, her hand near a telephone that was off the hook.

The 36-year-old star, who had been depressed over her skidding movie career, apparently died of an overdose of sleeping pills. No notes were found.

It could have been an accident, or it could have been suicide, a coroner said.

A bottle of Nembutal which had contained 40 to 50 pills was found empty among a mass of medicine bottles on her bedside table.

She was found nude, lying face down, a sheet pulled up over her. A champagne coverlet was at the foot of her bed. ■

AP/Wide World Photos

Joe DiMaggio enters the offices of the Westwood Village Mortuary in West Los Angeles on August 6, 1962, to assist in making final arrangements for Miss Monroe's funeral.

DiMag Says It With Roses

October 21, 1962

Six red roses—"twice a week, forever"—at the crypt of Marilyn Monroe. This was the order a grieving Joe DiMaggio gave for a constant remembrance at his ex-wife's grave, Guy Hockett, chief mortician at Westwood Memorial Park, disclosed today.

He said Joe's request was simply: "twice a week, forever."

And since the blonde star's entombment on August 6, fresh roses fill a black vase near the crypt, just as Joe asked. ■

Six red roses occupy a black metal vase at the grave of Marilyn Monroe. Joe DiMaggio ordered the roses to be placed there—twice a week, forever.

AP/Wide World Photos

Dan Farrell, Daily News

"He became Amercian royalty from the day he stopped playing."
—Reggie Jackson

Chapter 12

Bigger Than Baseball

*E*ven though he retired as a player, Joe DiMaggio's legend continued to grow as he attended numerous oldtimers' events and, during baseball's centennial celebration in 1969 was named "baseball's greatest living player." When he appeared at oldtimers' games with some of the most legendary names in baseball history—Mickey Mantle, Roger Maris, Yogi Berra, Whitey Ford, Casey Stengel, Phil Rizzuto, Duke Snider, Willie Mays, and many more—his time was often spent signing autographs for his fellow players or regaling them with baseball stories.

After retirement, DiMaggio served as a Yankee announcer and batting coach, as well as an executive for Charley Finley's Oakland Athletics. Joe also became well known to younger generations as the spokesman for Mr. Coffee and Bowery Bank. In 1967, he was enshrined in pop culture forever when Paul Simon's song from the hit movie The Graduate asked the eternal question, "Where have you gone, Joe DiMaggio?" ■

Daily News

Two of America's brightest stars, Joe DiMaggio and Frank Sinatra, share the spotlight in the Yankee Stadium dugout.

The Powerhouse

By Jimmy Powers
March 25, 1952

When the umpire snaps "Play ball!" at Yankee Stadium on Friday, April 18, a familiar face and number will be missing from the home team lineup. Joe DiMaggio will no longer stand in that flawless upright stance at the plate, arms and bat high, staring intently at the pitcher. From now on, baseball-wise Joe will be just another agate line in the record books.

Joe, however, will not be missing from the park, because on opening day he will make his debut as a television commentator.

Millions of fans, those within pick-up range of the WPIX signal, and those across the country, are asking the same questions.

"How good will Joe be?...Has he a sense of humor?...Will he second-guess the stars?...What's his voice like?...Can he do a first-class job?"

These questions cannot be answered in a day, a week or a month. It takes time. But I'm certain of one thing. Joe DiMaggio will be a definite hit.

In his new Stadium assignment, Joe will have the assistance of two of the most able and experienced men in sports televising: Jack Murphy and Arthur Susskind, Jr. These WPIX sports directors, together with Jackie Farrell of the Yankee organization, will make Joe's pre-game presentation one of the best in any ball park.

I predict Joe will bring to millions of television screens the poise of a true champion. He definitely knows baseball. He will have a lot of material to draw on that will help make an educational and entertaining show.

Some years back I appeared on a radio show with Joe. When it was over everyone within reach of the Clipper rushed to his side to congratulate him on a job well done. He has a pleasing, well-modulated voice with surprising warmth.

DiMag Inks 30G-Plus TV Pact with Yanks
December 14, 1951

Joe DiMaggio won't lift a bat or catch a ball at the Stadium next year, but he'll still draw more money from the Yanks than most players. The freshly retired Yankee Clipper signed a contract yesterday for an estimated $30,000-plus to conduct pre-game and postgame shows (interviews and commentary) of all Yankee home games over WPIX, Channel 11.

Joe told me he would rather face Bob Feller, Lefty Grove, Walter Johnson or Dizzy Dean on one afternoon than pick up a TV mike and start talking. Thinking of it makes him perspire the way the thought of playing the strange position of first base did when Casey Stengel was desperately casting about for ways of prolonging Joe's baseball career.

I am sure you will be delighted with Joe's work. It is comforting to know that, unlike other idols of the past, Joe DiMaggio will still be with us, chatting pleasantly through warm summer days and nights. He will greet old friends affectionately, counsel young rookies, reminisce with veteran umpires, scouts and managers. It could, and it should add up to a tip-top TV sports show. Good luck, Joe! ∎

Oldtimers' Day brings back one of the top outfields of all time: (left to right) Charlie Keller, Joe DiMaggio and Tommy Henrich.

Daily News

AP/Wide World Photos

The DiMaggio brothers, Vince, Joe and Dom, left to right, played the outfield as San Francisco heroes of yesteryear as they edged the Los Angeles Oldtimers, 3-2, in a three-inning exhibition game prior to a Pacific Coast League game between the two cities.

DiMaggio Leads Helms' PCL Nine

August 14, 1957

Joe DiMaggio today headed a cast of six former San Francisco players named to the Helms Athletic Foundation's all-time Pacific Coast League baseball team.

DiMaggio edged out Arnold Statz of Los Angeles for the centerfield berth in the selections. San Francisco provided six of the 14 players named to the team.

DiMag's Job

August 26, 1958

Joe DiMaggio, former Yankee slugger, said today he was tired of doing "nothing" during his seven years of baseball retirement and has taken a job.

DiMaggio has become an executive vice president of V. H. Monette & Co., Smithfield, Virginia. He said his assignment would be to create goodwill for the firm, which distributes food products to the armed forces.

"I love to travel," he said. "This is what induced me."

DiMaggio, who said he has been living on investments, said he would travel all over the world in his new capacity.

DiMag's No. 1

October 16, 1958

In reviewing his 10 years as Yankee manager, Casey Stengel yesterday named Joe DiMaggio, Yogi Berra and Hank Bauer as his three greatest players, in that order. He reserved opinion on Mickey Mantle "until he does big things for five straight years. He may be the best of all but he has to do it. The ability is there.

It is up to Mantle. I hope he does it tomorrow—if the season was starting tomorrow, I mean. Mantle is good and bad, but I'm glad I own him. It wouldn't be funny to me if I saw him hit 50 homers. He has the points to lead the league in everything. After he's here 10 years, I'll tell you how he rates with DiMaggio."

Daily News

Among DiMaggio's many post-baseball interests was his service as an Honorary Committee member for the Long Island Opera Co. Here, he listens to Opera impresario Guido Salmaggi.

Margaret Truman and Joe DiMaggio pose together at Yankee Stadium, prior to a benefit game between the Yankees and the New York Giants. In a pre-benefit game, DiMaggio played for the Toots Shor Crumbums as they defeated the 21 Club Gentlemen, 1-0.

AP/Wide World Photos

Daily News

"Scuse me, somebody important just came in."

—Toots Shor reportedly told Sir Alexander Fleming, discoverer of penicillin, upon seeing Hall of Famer Mel Ott enter his restaurant.

Yankee Clipper Dons Famed No. 5 Uniform

DiMag Will Tutor Young Yanks

March 9, 1961

Joe DiMaggio returns to spring training with the Yankees tomorrow, marking the first time in 10 years he has put on pinstripes except for annual appearances in the Stadium Old Timers' game each summer.

The Yankee Clipper will work as a special batting coach for two weeks, imparting his knowledge and instruction to young hitters.

He'll wear his famed No. 5 uniform, which has been retired and is in the Hall of Fame at Cooperstown. That is, this is a facsimile. Actually, it is a size 44 Spalding blouse which was No. 6 and was worn by Andy Carey before he was traded to Kansas City last summer.

"I had it made up for the Old Timers' game," clubhouse custodian Pete Sheehy explained today, "When I heard he was coming here, I got it out. I keep it in a separate place so it doesn't accidentally get mixed up with others and given out to some other player."

Sheehy will get the Clipper new spikes too. A sporting goods equipment man will be present at 11 a.m. to fit Joe. Newsreel, TV and press men also will be on hand.

The Hillerich and Bradsby bat manufacturers sent half a dozen of Joe's model so he can take batting practice if he cares to do so.

Manager Ralph Houk has not mapped out any specific assignment for DiMag. In fact, Houk hasn't selected any players for particular instruction.

"I figure Joe will look around and decide where he can help," Ralph said. "Each player knows his own problem, his weakness. When Joe talks to him after a few days of observation, they may be able to work together and make some improvement." ■

Joe DiMaggio, Red Rolfe, George Selkirk, Bill Dickey, John Murphy and Lefty Gomez share a laugh at the 1964 Old Timers' game.

Charles Hoff, Daily News

NL Old Timers Blast AL, 4-2; DiMag Homers

By Joe Trimble
August 1, 1965

Yogi Berra received the biggest ovation, and Johnny Keane, the man who succeeded him as Yankees manager, drew the loudest boos yesterday in the 19th annual Old Timers' Day game at the Stadium. Joe DiMaggio supplied the familiar touch—a homer—but it wasn't enough to prevent a two-inning, 4-2 victory by the NL over the AL greats.

The first inning was scoreless. The NL banged out six hits in the second for its runs. The Yankee Clipper led off the AL second and was given three chances to bat. In the free-and-easy fashion of this game, Joltin' Joe was permitted to stay up until he hit a fair ball.

Batting against Bucky Walters, former Cincy great, Joe popped foul to Jim Hegan, NL catcher, who caught it and dropped it on purpose. DiMag then hit another which Monte Irvin, former Giant, caught backhanded from his third base post in foul territory. Monte went along with the gag and dropped it, too.

So Joe, who never needed that kind of help, gave the fans what they wanted—a long drive into the lower deck in left field. The crowd rose to its feet as Joe rounded the bases. He doffed his cap after crossing the plate, and the crowd went wild.■

Charles Hoff, Daily News

John Keane (left) with Joe DiMaggio, Yogi Berra and Charlie Keller.

DiMag Back to Groom Yanks

By Joe Trimble
January 10, 1967

Joe DiMaggio will be back with the Yankees again as a special instructor at their training camp at Fort Lauderdale. This will be the Yankee Clipper's seventh successive spring as a good will man and batting tutor . . . and never did the battered Bombers need him more.

As the star of stars, DiMaggio was always surrounded by a crowd at the annual Old Timers' games. Here, he swaps tales with former teammate Charlie Keller (left) and Hall of Famer Joe Medwick (center).

"I don't claim I can teach anybody to bat," Joe said yesterday at a luncheon at the Sporting Goods Fair at the *New Yorker*. "But I can teach a kid to field and run bases. I'm happy to be back and I hope I can help the club get going again. I enjoy working with the young players. I realize there is a lot to be done."

Joe works without compensation, other than his board and room. "Actually it costs me money," he said. "But I do have a good time and it is worth it."

Joe, suntanned, has just returned from a Florida vacation. He is leaving Thursday for his home in San Francisco and will report to Lauderdale February 20.

"I'll go down around the 20th and spend a few days playing golf," Joe said. "I had a date to play with Jackie Gleason when I was down there last week but I had to call it off as I had to go to Lucaya, in the Bahamas." ■

Dan Farrell, Daily News

DiMag Flips 1st Pitch, A's Flip Yankees, 4-1

By Joe Trimble
March 14, 1968

J oe DiMaggio, wearing uniform No. 5, threw out the first ball today before the Oakland Athletics stepped on the Yankees, 4-1. The victory was the fourth in five games for the new Oakland club.

DiMag looked strange in the garish green and gold playsuit the A's wear, with vests instead of blouses. The No. 5 uniform was made especially for him.

Joe Pepitone came over and said, "You don't look right. You should never wear anything but pin-stripes."

Former Yank Joe DiMaggio, now in an Oakland uniform, signs the cast of Joe Pepitone prior to a game between the Yanks and Oakland.

Oakland's new veep laughed and admitted the garb did feel strange.

"But I'm happy," he said. "The Oakland A's are coming. They will never finish last again. There are too many good young ballplayers here. Some may be great, particularly the young pitchers."

DiMag intends to travel with the team all season. "I'll sit on the bench if the league will let me," he said. "If not, I'll be in a box near the dugout."

Asked if he would be willing to wear the white kangaroo shoes that owner Charley Finley made the A's don last year, the Yankee Clipper smiled and replied: "I sure will. I don't have mine yet. But three pair have been ordered for everyone and I'll use them."

The gray-haired Hall of Famer obviously is glad to be back on the ball field.

"They've even got me riding the buses with the team," he grinned. "And I like it."

Joe said the enthusiasm in Oakland for the team is high. "We have sold 4,000 season subscriptions," he said. "And the entire park, which seats 50,000, was sold out for the opening game about a week before March first." ∎

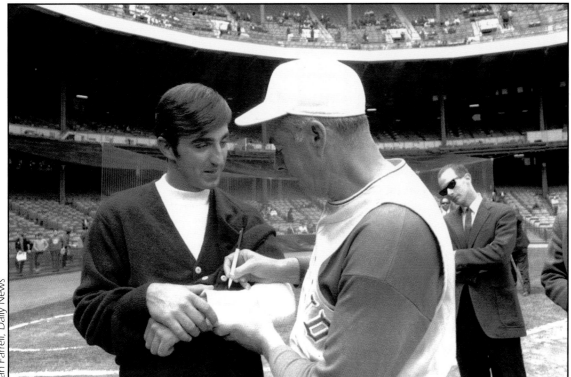

Dan Farrell, Daily News

Most Popular Oldtimer DiMag in 17th Game

By Joe Trimble
August 10, 1968

When he strides majestically out onto the Stadium stage this afternoon and doffs his blue cap, revealing almost white hair and that familiar profile, Joe DiMaggio will receive the largest ovation of Old Timers' Day—as usual.

"I've never missed one since I quit playing," he said proudly yesterday. "This will be my 17th here. And it makes 50 altogether. Hey, that's about one-third of a season. I hit a homer in my first one but it is harder now."

The 53-year-old Hall of Famer spent the day in town while the Athletics got along without his coaching for 24 hours. They were in Washington for a two-nighter last night, after knocking off the Yanks, 6-4, Thursday night to win the set of three.

"I've been to the Old Timers' thing already at Shea Stadium," Joe said. "And I have two more after this one. I promised to go to Houston's and we are having one of our own a week from Sunday when the Yanks are in Oakland. My brothers (Dom and Vince) will be there and so will Casey Stengel and Lefty O'Doul. They are honoring Coast League oldtimers."

This will be DiMag's last year in uniform. But he will remain on the A's payroll as a vice president. "Oh, I'm going to spring training and will be coaching there," he said.

"We'll be in Arizona next year (at Mesa) and that will be closer to home. I liked it when we trained at Phoenix in my last year with the Yankees in 1951."

Joe made a smart move in returning to uniform as a coach this year. It makes him eligible for the increased payments and benefits under the improved pension plan. ∎

Joe to Coach

April 6, 1968

Oakland Athletics owner Charles O. Finley announced today that Joe DiMaggio, executive vice president of the club, will become a full-time coach on the staff of manager Bob Kennedy.

Kennedy said that DiMaggio, a former Yankee great, would be with him on the bench, not on the coaching lines, and would continue to instruct A's players in hitting.

"So many people upstairs today. They wanted some baseball stories. I told them I had at least a few to tell."

—Joe DiMaggio, apologizing for being a few minutes late to throw out the first pitch at Yankee Stadium on opening day 1998.

Joe DiMaggio visits with an old friend and another baseball legend, Roy Campanella.

When not gracing the ballparks, DiMaggio offered his help in more serious matters. In late 1969, DiMaggio joined other baseball stars and Commissioner Bowie Kuhn on a tour of the troops in Vietnam.

Yankees Honor Living Legends

By Joe Trimble
October 11, 1970

Wasn't it Jimmy Walker who, with reference to memorials honoring the deceased, quipped: "I would rather smell the roses?" The Yankees prefer that philosophy and tomorrow at the Stadium will unveil plaques to Joe DiMaggio and Mickey Mantle.

Both greats of the recent past will be on hand for the ceremony between games of the twin bill with the Indians.

This will be the first time the Yankees are honoring a living person in this manner. It will bring the number of memorials to eight out in distant centerfield.

There are three granite headstones dedicated to the memories of Lou Gehrig, Miller Huggins and Babe Ruth. On the centerfield wall behind the tablets are plaques in memory of former Yankee owner Jake Ruppert and Ed Barrow, the general manager who built baseball's dynasty.

The sixth plaque honors Pope Paul's Mass in the Stadium October 4, 1965. That one is in memory of the occasion more than the Pontiff, himself.

The 60-pound DiMag and Mantle plaques are on the bleacher facing in right-center...at least, to the right of the other memorials.

The face of each of the two superstars stands out in base relief.

A couple of feet to the right of the Mantle plaque, on equal level, is DiMag's and it reads:

Joe DiMaggio, N.Y. Yankees 1936-1951.
The Yankee Clipper
Hit in 56 straight games
"Greatest Living Player" in Baseball's Centennial Year.

In recognition of his singular excellence and for his legacy of greatness.

This plaque presented to Joe DiMaggio by Mickey Mantle in a ceremony at Yankee Stadium on June 8, 1969.

Replicas of the plaques were presented, one to the other, during Mickey's retirement ceremony on that date last year. ■

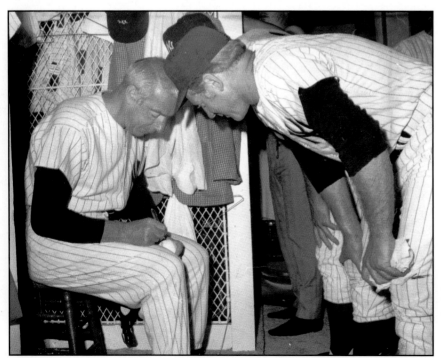

Joe DiMaggio autographs a baseball for Whitey Ford at an Old Timers' Day game.

Hal Mathewson, Daily News

Yankee legends (from left) Mickey Mantle, Yogi Berra,
Whitey Ford, Joe DiMaggio and Casey Stengel pose before
an Old Timers' game in 1974.

Even as an "Old
Timer," Joe's smooth
swing still keeps the
fans on the edges of
their seats whenever
he comes to bat.

Joltin' Joe is Still an Icon

By Art Spander
June 6, 1989

Joe DiMaggio sat there in the cluttered office, properly mysterious and tantalizingly private, a lonely reminder of innocence lost and pennants won.

He is an enduring symbol of elegance, whose fame bridges generations and whose presence evokes memories, a hero untainted, a myth unconquered, an idol esteemed.

This was Equitable Oldtimers Day at Oakland Coliseum, and DiMaggio, "the great DiMaggio," as Hemingway called him, had come back from the past. But he would not dress in uniform. He would not play. He would simply acknowledge the throaty roar of the crowd with a two-armed wave and then return to the dugout.

Now as then, Joe DiMaggio remains a man apart, separated from others on the diamond by his skills, and from others off the field by his choosing.

When Paul Simon wrote, "Where have you gone, Joe DiMaggio?" he did it, Simon explained, because of the rhythm of the words rather than the

> We always seem to be asking where Joltin' Joe has gone, which is the way DiMaggio likes it. We may grow weary of others, but Joe is always welcome—perhaps because he's always evasive.

content. And yet, Simon's plea is not inappropriate.

We always seem to be asking where Joltin' Joe has gone, which is the way DiMaggio likes it. We may grow weary of others, but Joe is always welcome—perhaps because he's always evasive.

Two hours before the old-timers' game, DiMaggio had moved away from the mainstream and into the office of A's equipment man Frank Cienscyzk, an old pal from the days in the late 1960s when Joe was an Oakland coach.

The place was hardly a refuge. Dave Parker would shuffle across the hallway from the A's clubhouse to

Dan Farrell, Daily News

extend a hand to "Mr. DiMaggio," as Dave addressed him.

Some outsider would slip in to try to persuade Joe—fruitlessly—he should market a videotape interview.

Always, the country has tried to intrude into DiMaggio's life. Always he has attempted to avoid the intrusion.

"It has its good moments," DiMaggio would say of the adulation, "and its bad moments. I feel very flattered. But I can get irritable."

DiMaggio is 74 now, weighs maybe 190 pounds and looks in fine health after a heart problem. He golfs, travels and attempts to keep his thoughts to himself—while the rest of us keep trying to make them public. Without much success.

David Halberstam has written of war, of the communications industry, even of basketball. His prose is sparkling. He owns a Pulitzer Prize. All of which means little to Joe DiMaggio.

Halberstam's newest book, *Summer of '49*, details the pennant race that year between the Boston Red Sox and a Yankees team that struggled through the early part of the season without an injured Joe DiMaggio.

The author interviewed every living member of either club...except DiMaggio.

"I did talk to him briefly," DiMaggio said, "but I told him I might want to use what I knew for my book."

Said Halberstam: "He and Ted Williams are the last icons, the players before television. I can understand his feelings. He is besieged. I did everything I could to interview him. I was disappointed. But I didn't let it touch the way I wrote about him."

Not at all. Halberstam, like most American men in their 50s, venerates DiMaggio. "He was," writes Halberstam of the era, "the most famous athlete in America."

And Halberstam reminds us of a different United States, of a country that cared about its products and its people. The late sportswriter Jimmy Cannon once asked DiMaggio why he played so hard. "Because," answered DiMaggio, "there might be somebody who's never seen me play before."

"From the start of the season to the end," Joe admitted on Oldtimers' day, "I had strawberries on my legs from sliding, and I was always in pain. We'd use sliding pads, but they'd fold up under you. Then I saw George Stirnweiss wearing shorts—like they do now—instead of pads. I tried them and I never got a strawberry again."

What kind of ballplayer was Joe DiMaggio? Graceful, that's what kind. And smart. We know about that record 56-game hitting streak in 1941. But did you know that DiMaggio hit 361 home runs and only struck out 369 times? In 13 seasons? In the 1980s, sluggers strike out 369 times in three seasons. ∎

On July 10, 1991, President George Bush honored Boston's Ted Williams and the Yankees' Joe DiMaggio in a White House Rose Garden ceremony commemorating the 50th anniversary of the great 1941 season.

AP/Wide World Photos

Quake Jolts Joe DiMag

By Bob Klapisch
October 19, 1989

You looked once, then twice and still, you couldn't believe your eyes. There he was, dressed casually, standing in the middle of a Red Cross shelter in the Marina District, waiting in line.

Joe DiMaggio.

"I'm here to find somebody," the 74-year-old Yankees great said. "I don't know where he is."

DiMaggio lives in the district, which was devastated by the earthquake. And although DiMaggio didn't have to spend the night on a cot in a gymnasium, his life was altered by the disaster, along with virtually all other San Franciscans.

"My home has been pretty badly damaged," DiMaggio said, "and right now they won't let me back in. They won't allow it."

Surprisingly, few in line seemed to recognize the Yankee Clipper. Almost everyone was concerned with getting a bed, food and water.

DiMaggio was lucky enough—he escaped injury. Unlike the seven people who perished in a building not 50 feet from where DiMaggio stood in the shelter, he was at Candlestick Park when the quake hit.

"I was sitting with the American League president (Dr. Bobby Brown, a former Yankees team-

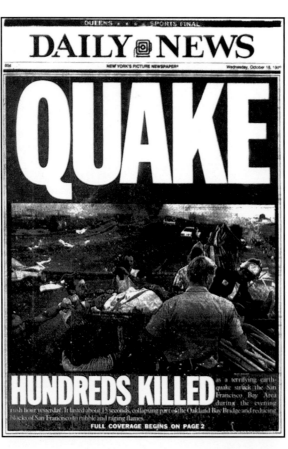

mate) and I felt something," he said. "It took a little time to distinguish it. Afterward, the fans cheered, and everybody thought things were all right. But then I heard about the fires in my neighborhood and I thought my place went along with them. That's when I left."

He said his home was only two buildings away from the great Marina District fire that raged the first night of the earthquake.

He said, "I hear they're going to have to destroy 60 homes (in the Marina District) and it could be 14 to 16 weeks before we get our water and power back.

"I have been through little ones before but his one was pretty bad, I guess," Joe said. "The scary thing is that the worst might not be over.

"We might be getting some aftershocks in the next couple of days."

Just as no one had noticed DiMaggio in the shelter, no one noticed as the handsome Yankee walked along in the anonymous darkness. He never did find the friend he was looking for in the shelter.

He kept asking when the World Series would be resuming.

"A cop told me they were going to start again on Tuesday," he said. ■

DiMaggio Gets Columbia Citation

May 20, 1990

Columbia University awarded Joe DiMaggio an honorary Doctor of Laws degree last week. The citation said what countless fans have felt about a man who has graced New York and America with his presence:

Joseph P. DiMaggio:

A true American legend, you have earned many names: the Yankee Clipper, Joltin' Joe, the Greatest Living Baseball Player. You are, unabashedly, our hero—the sports figure whose achievement inspires everyone's admiration and respect, and excites us all to excel.

We honor you today for more than your records, though they are extraordinary: your starring role in 10 World Series and, unequalled before or since, your hitting streak in 56 consecutive games.

We honor you as the earnest and gentle son of a San Francisco fisherman, as a proud and sensitive man with an enduring sense of responsibility to your millions of admirers, and as the graceful athlete whose inspiring play helped lift America out of the gloom of the Great Depression.

Baseball has never known a player who worked and practiced harder to make every home run look elegant and every spectacular running catch look easy. You are justly celebrated in the Baseball Hall of Fame and in popular music, art and literature. Your loyalty and decency as a human being are qualities to be emulated by every generation. Columbia University cheers the life of dignity and integrity you represent. ∎

Pat Carroll, Daily News

Joe DiMaggio accepts his honorary doctor of laws degree from Columbia University.

Daily News

Grand Marshalls Gina Lollobrigida and the Yankee Clipper, Joe DiMaggio, salute the crowd during the 1991 Columbus Day Parade.

Joltin' Joe Jilted

By Rosemary Metzler Lavan
April 7, 1992

Baseball legend Joe DiMaggio—spokesman for the Bowery Savings Bank over the last 18 years—will be dumped from the lineup come May.

The California bank that owns the New York institution is changing the Bowery name to Home Savings of America and replacing New York hero DiMaggio with George Fenneman—best known as second banana to Groucho Marx on the 1950s quiz show "You Bet Your Life."

Some New Yorkers think this swap tops the Nolan Ryan for Jim Fregosi trade as the worst New York deal ever.

"What a mistake!" railed Jerry Della Femina, chairman of New York advertising firm Della Femina McNamee WCRS Inc. "George Fenneman

> Some New Yorkers think this swap tops the Nolan Ryan for Jim Fregosi trade as the worst New York deal ever.

never hit in 56 consecutive games."

Della Femina called this "a case of out-of-towners screwing up a local institution. They are switching their hero for ours and theirs is just an announcer. Joe DiMaggio is a hero for all New Yorkers."

DiMaggio could not be reached for comment.

Della Femina added: "And what would their California customers think if the Home Savings of America name was changed to the Bowery?"

DiMaggio will be used in radio and print ads during a two-month transition period, said Home Savings spokeswoman Mary Trigg. And then the Yankee great will hang up his banker's pinstripes.

Outside the Bowery's main branch near Grand Central Terminal yesterday, customer reaction was mixed.

"As long as the service is the same, I don't care what they call the bank," said Brooklyn resident Marjorie Hendricks.

But Queens resident Grace McNeil said, "I think they should keep the Bowery. That's a New York name. Home Savings of America—that's so general. It sounds like every other bank."■

"If you're tired of the ups and downs of the market, The Bowery offers you a calmer investment."
—Joe DiMaggio

The Bowery's not saying "don't invest." Only that you put some of your hard-earned money into safe, insured, high-interest Bowery savings.

That investment has paid interest and dividends for 145 consecutive years – despite recessions, depressions, and stock market jitters.

It pays to bank at
THE BOWERY

Customers Go to Bat for DiMag

By Rosemary Metzler Lavan
April 8, 1992

The Bowery Savings Bank heard more than a few Bronx cheers yesterday after New Yorkers learned that their beloved Joe DiMaggio will be yanked from company ads.

Some bank employees worked extra innings yesterday fielding calls from irate New Yorkers concerned about the status of their spokesman.

The California bank that owns Bowery announced it is not only changing its name to Home Savings of America, but in a month's time is replacing Joltin' Joe with George Fenneman—who was straight man to Groucho Marx on the 1950s quiz show "You Bet Your Life."

One of four Bowery customer service representatives clustered in front of the bank's main office said: "Some of us worked overtime to cover all the calls. I saw red (telephone) lights all day. Customers were most worried about Joe DiMaggio, but they were also worried about what they should do with their passbook and checking accounts."

> "Customers told us they opened their account because of Joe, and they'll close it if he goes."
> —Bowery Bank Service Representative

Another service rep said, "Customers told us they opened their account because of Joe, and they'll close it if he goes."

Bowery competitors questioned the decision to replace DiMaggio.

Dime Savings Bank spokesman David Totaro asked a question on a lot of New Yorkers' minds: "Who is George Fenneman, anyway?"

Chemical Bank spokesman John Stefans said, "I couldn't believe the news. Do you know anyone who doesn't admire Joe DiMaggio? There is no classier act. I'm sure a lot of New York banks will jump at the chance to pursue DiMaggio as their spokesman." ∎

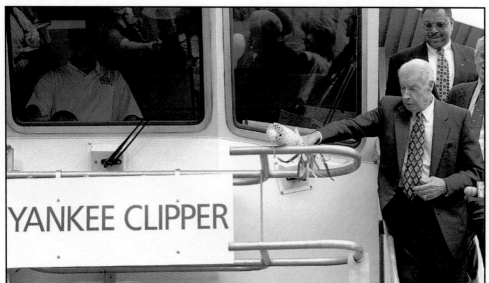

Yankee great Joe DiMaggio helps launch the new Yankee Stadium water shuttle from South Street Seaport.

Mike Albans, Daily News

Yankee Clipper Brings Back Class, Clout

April 12, 1992

At 77, there is still no one who is more of a presence than Joe DiMaggio. Happily, the Yankees had the presence of mind to recognize that by having the Yankee Clipper throw out the first ball on Opening Day. The ovation accorded DiMaggio from the packed house of 56,000-plus (most of whom probably never even saw him play) bore witness to the fact that Yankee fans are longing for a return to tradition, stability and class.

For his part, DiMaggio got so caught up in the upbeat mood enveloping The Stadium this week that he decided to stay around for the second game. It was while he was sitting in a private box, watching Thursday night's second straight come-from-behind Yankee win over the Red Sox, that DiMaggio talked about his most cherished encounter with a "presence."

"I was sitting at the head table at the Stork Club

one night," DiMaggio recalled. "At the table with me were Walter Winchell and Marlene Dietrich. All of a sudden, I became aware of the people at all the other tables stirring as someone was approaching our table from behind. I felt a tap on my shoulder and I turned around to hear this fellow say: 'Mr. DiMaggio, I have always wanted to meet you and shake hands with you. You have no idea what an honor this is.'

"Well," DiMaggio continued, "*I* was the one who was honored—to be singled out like that in *that* company. It was Charlie Chaplin." ■

(Left to right) Henry Kissinger, Joe DiMaggio and Joe Franklin

Joys of Summer Past and Present

By Mike Lupica
September 28, 1998

At the end of summer, the kind of golden summer they knew once, Joe DiMaggio and Phil Rizzuto were together again on the field at Yankee Stadium. Maybe it will be this way for Mark McGwire someday, when he is old and seems half the size he is today. Maybe he will drink in the sun and cheers and remember what it was like in September of '98, when he made us believe he could do anything he wanted with a bat in his hands, when he made us remember how and why we came to love baseball in the first place.

Maybe someday it will be this way for Bernie Williams and Derek Jeter on the kind of baseball Sunday we had yesterday in New York. Williams plays center field for the Yankees, sometimes with the grace DiMaggio did. Jeter is a Yankee shortstop who will end up being called the best to play the position for the Yankees, even better than Rizzuto. Maybe they will stand together when they are old and remember the season when they won more games than any Yankee team ever had.

But for now, at the end of the home run summer of McGwire and Sammy Sosa, on a day when McGwire would go deep twice more and get to 70 for the season, Rizzuto, 81 now, stood near home plate with DiMaggio, who will be 84 in November. Old boys from other summers.

But never a better baseball summer than this.

Before DiMaggio was on the field yesterday, making a grand tour around the ballpark in a '56 white Thunderbird convertible, he was asked if he has followed the amazing long-ball, long-distance theater of McGwire and Sosa. Once, almost 50 years ago, in 1941, people tracked DiMaggio's 56-game hitting streak this way.

"You bet I've followed them," DiMaggio said. "Hasn't everyone?"

The old man smiled. He was sitting in a white golf cart. He would be driven out to the old bullpen at the Stadium and then get into the white T-Bird. Joe Torre would present him with a proclamation from the mayor about Joe DiMaggio Day, and Rizzuto would eventually bring out replicas of all the World Series rings that DiMaggio once had stolen from him. The only one he managed to keep was the one he has always worn and wore yesterday, from the '36 Series.

"My first," he said yesterday, showing it to you.

He had just come from Chicago, being honored over three days of ceremonies. At one point, DiMaggio was asked to ring the bell at the Chicago Commodities Exchange. Of course he did this with a baseball bat. He said he swung three or four times, just to get the right sound. And just that much, DiMaggio with a bat in his hands, must have been something to see.

"They all stopped work and began to applaud," he said. "It went on for 15 minutes. I felt as if millions of dollars were being lost."

Over a different kind of American treasure. One who has lasted. Sinatra is gone. There is still DiMaggio, who was last honored this way at Yankee Stadium at the end of the 1949 season.

"It has been a while," he said when it was over.

Then he opened the box and looked at the Series rings, from the '30s and '40s, all the way to his last season, in 1951. The diamonds in the rings were quite bright, even in the shadows under the ballpark, across from the Yankee clubhouse.

"So many memories," he said quietly. "So many seasons."

He knows better than anyone: Baseball still builds the brightest memories. Now no one will forget this about baseball ever again. The home runs have been the best of it. Just not all of it. The Yankees won 114 and acted as if they could beat the world again, the way DiMaggio's Yankees could. There was David Wells' perfect game and a Little League team from Toms River, N.J., that got into everybody's heart and still won't get out. The Mets were alive for the playoffs and so even Shea Stadium came back to life, after such a long deep sleep.

Even yesterday, on the last day of the regular season, a kid for the Blue Jays named Roy Halladay came within an out of a no-hitter. And the playoffs do not begin until Tuesday night. We are still a few days from October.

"Every time you think the season can't get better, it gets better," Scooter Rizzuto said.

He carried Joe DiMaggio's rings like a best man at a wedding. Then the two of them, shortstop and center fielder, were together again at Yankee Stadium. Before Williams and Jeter and the '98 Yankees took the field to thunderous cheers of their own. Such a wonderful beginning to what was really the last day of summer. Such a wonderful season. In a little while, halfway across the country in St. Louis, McGwire would go deep again. And again. One last time, until the spring, we would watch with wonder.■

Richard Harbus, Daily News

In 1993, when Phil and Cara Rizzuto celebrated their 50th wedding anniversary, DiMaggio presented Rizzuto with a watch.

Mr. Coffee's Back

By Mark Kriegel
September 6, 1990

" Where have you gone, Joe DiMaggio?" This is what the people at Mr. Coffee Inc. have been asking for the last five years—ever since the grandest name in baseball took a hiatus as spokesman. The good news? DiMaggio, synonymous with the product, will begin to appear once more, in October, as the star of Mr. Coffee's caffeine, decaffeinated drip and automatic iced tea commercials. ■

The modern coffee-making machine, developed in 1971 by a Cleveland real estate developer, soon spawned one of Joe DiMaggio's most enduring pop images. From 1974 through 1985 and returning in 1990, DiMaggio was known to TV viewers across America as "Mr. Coffee." In fact, one Madison Avenue advertising executive commented, "A lot of young people think Joe DiMaggio was just a guy who did commercials for Mr. Coffee."

Photo courtesy of Sunbeam Corporation

DiMaggio Was Perfect Fit for My Song, Simon Says

By Mark Kriegel
November 27, 1998

As a child, Paul Simon would listen to Yankee games on his father's lap. He was maybe 7 years old when he made his first journey from Forest Hills to the big Bronx stadium.

It was the late 1940s. The Yankees were playing the Indians that day. "Joe DiMaggio hit the ball and everybody stood up," says Simon. "I was a little kid so I couldn't see anything except the backs of men. Then my father lifted me up so I could see that he just hit a home run. My father was trying to explain about Joe D, but I didn't quite understand."

It would be a while before he did. Even as Simon became a more devout fan and a player himself, DiMaggio remained the psychological property of his father's generation. Simon grew up in the '50s, meaning he was a Mickey Mantle fan. "Mantle was my guy," he says. "Mantle was about the promise of youth."

As it happened, the promise of Simon's own youth led him to acquire considerable fame as a superlative singer and songwriter, whose "Mrs. Robinson" contains what might be the best-known lyric in American popular music. It was written for a movie called "The Graduate," about a well-to-do Mrs. Robinson who seduces her daughter's fiance. That was 1967. The country was in between assassinations. There was war in Vietnam, race riots in the cities. And Mickey Mantle was still Paul Simon's guy.

It was during a commercial break on "The Dick Cavett Show" when Mantle turned to Simon and asked, "How come you wrote that song about DiMaggio? Why didn't you write it about me?"

"It's about syllables, Mick," said Simon. "It's about how many beats there are."

Mantle seemed OK with the explanation, the idea that the famous lyric was merely a matter of cadence.

Where have you gone, Mickey Ma-a-ntle, a nation turns its lonely eyes to you . . . What's that you say, Mrs. Robinson, Mi-i-ckey has left and gone away . . .

No, it wouldn't have worked. It wouldn't have worked rhythmically. But it wouldn't have worked metaphorically, either. "Mantle was similar to Elvis," says Simon. "There was that incredible burst of vitality and youth, and the eventual corruption of it. DiMaggio was never corrupted."

Of course, DiMaggio himself didn't think "Mrs. Robinson" worked. Word was, he wanted to sue Simon. He thought he was being made fun of, not an illogical assumption considering the hallucinogenic sensibilities of the '60s that reduced virtuous All-America types to corny characters.

"The first time I met DiMaggio, I guess it was the year the song came out," says Simon. " 'Mrs. Robinson' was still new and big. I was in an Italian restaurant on Central Park South. I went over and introduced myself. 'Mr. DiMaggio, I'm Paul Simon. I'm the guy who wrote 'Mrs. Robinson.' He knew. He invited me to sit down."

"What does that mean?" DiMaggio asked. "Where have you gone . . . ?"

> Mantle turned to Simon and asked, "How come you wrote that song about DiMaggio? Why didn't you write it about me?"
> "It's about syllables, Mick," said Simon. "It's about how many beats there are."

The greatest living ballplayer explained that he was doing ads for Mr. Coffee and a bank, that he had never gone anywhere.

"Hey, it was still the hippie days and he was wondering whether I was making fun of him," says Simon. "And I told him I wasn't making fun of him. I said the song was about heroes, a certain type of hero."

That was the truth. But 31 years later, with Joe DiMaggio gravely ill in a Florida hospital, there is still another truth.

"I still don't know exactly why or how I wrote that line," says Simon.

He had been playing with the beats and the words, writing a melody off the chorus he was constructing as, Here's to you, Mrs. Roosevelt. Then Roosevelt became Robinson. Then . . . DiMaggio.

"I wasn't looking for a baseball image," says Simon. "I wasn't looking for anything. Something was looking for me. It came from the ether. From the subconscious. It's a line for fathers. Really, I don't know where it came from, but all of a sudden it was there."

A scene from the *The Graduate*, the movie that made a hit of Simon and Garfunkel's song that asks: "Where have you gone, Joe DiMaggio?"

And it was right.

"Within an instant I knew, I'll keep that . . . the non sequitur, the jump. It all felt good. It made the song feel like it was about a larger subject."

Of course, DiMaggio has only become larger and more mythical, and perhaps, more meaningful, with age. "Over the years, I've seen him two or three times. I always go over and say hello. I never asked him for an autograph or to sign a ball or anything like that. He's shy, very polite, always asks how I'm doing."

And now comes the point where Simon asks how DiMaggio is doing.

He has been in Regional Memorial Hospital in Hollywood, Florida, since October 12. A cancerous tumor was removed from his right lung, and he remains in intensive care, recovering from a lung infection. On Wednesday, his two great-granddaughters visited his room to sing "Happy Birthday," DiMaggio's 84th.

Richard Corkery, Daily News

Joe DiMaggio attends the 1993 Baseball Hall of Fame
dinner at the Waldorf Astoria Hotel.

Simon isn't comfortable with the news. "I just happened to write a song," he says. "We're linked by one tiny little venture, one line. And I'm grateful. But I'd prefer he lives to 94 and the line fades away."

Besides, in the songwriter's estimation, there's something grotesque about a nation anticipating the loss of a famous icon.

Of course, Simon is famous himself. "Fame is poison," he says. "You take too much, you die." As examples, Simon cites Presley, James Dean and yes, the former Mrs. Joe DiMaggio, Marilyn Monroe.

"But if you take a little bit of the poison, you start to see things," says Simon. "I don't know what DiMaggio has seen. He's kept it to himself.

"And I think that's a good thing. That's dignified.

"You know the saying: those that tell don't know, those that know don't tell.

"DiMaggio knew."

But he's never felt the need to issue any public proclamations, or mercenary confessionals, to cheapen the awe of men who had seen him as children. It's enough to have been Joe DiMaggio. ■

Joe DiMaggio Day, Yankee Stadium, September 27, 1998

"Baseball isn't statistics, it's Joe DiMaggio rounding second base."
—Jimmy Breslin

Chapter 13

An Icon Forever

*M*any have called 1998 one of the greatest years in all of sports. Sports fans around the world witnessed college football's split championship, Elway's Super Bowl march, Dale Earnhardt's Daytona triumph, Nagano's Winter Olympics, Mark O'Meara's double Majors, Detroit's Stanley Cup repeat, Jordan's championship shot, France's World Cup miracle, and Real Quiet's triple crown heartbreak. It seemed as if each week in 1998 brought us a new sports milestone.

But above all, there was baseball.

The historic home run race between Mark McGwire and Sammy Sosa raged daily, sometimes even hourly. Cal Ripken ended his Iron Man streak. Baseball welcomed two new teams. Kerry Wood struck out 20 Astros. The League named a new Commissioner. Roger Clemens notched his 3,000th strikeout. Harry Caray's life was celebrated across America. Yet, with all these extraordinary events, it was the Yankees who dominated the national pastime with David Wells' perfect game, a record 125 victories and a World Series sweep. Champions again, for the 24th time in franchise history.

But when Yankee fans, players and the media look back on 1998, one of the most emotional memories of the year will be Joe DiMaggio day at Yankee Stadium on September 27, 1998. That day, Joltin' Joe basked in the adoration of the cheering crowds as he was presented with replicas of his missing World Series rings.

Unfortunately, it was only a few short weeks thereafter that the great Yankee Clipper took ill in a Florida hospital. Ravaged by cancer and a lung infection, DiMaggio's condition became so grave that he was given last rites.

For 99 days, all of America watched as reports of DiMaggio's health changed day to day—often with reports that DiMaggio lay in a coma, near death. When DiMaggio finally awoke from his coma, and true to his lifelong zeal for privacy, he promptly ordered that no further reports on his hospital stay be released. Despite this order, word leaked out that even from his hospital bed, DiMaggio had initiated what is sure to be one of the biggest baseball stories of 1999: The end of the 14-year feud between Yogi Berra and George Steinbrenner.

Finally, on what would have been his 100th day in the hospital, DiMaggio was released to his home in Hollywood, Florida. DiMaggio's courageous battle made front page headlines and served once again as a reminder that the title of baseball's greatest American Icon will always belong to Joe DiMaggio. ∎

DiMaggio in Florida Hospital After Surgery

By Bill Madden
October 16, 1998

Baseball legend Joe DiMaggio is in the intensive care unit of a Florida hospital after undergoing surgery, the *Daily News* has learned.

The Yankee Clipper, 84, fell ill earlier this week and entered Joe DiMaggio Children's Hospital in Hollywood, Florida, where he underwent an unspecified operation, according to a knowledgeable source. A few years ago, DiMaggio had a pacemaker installed to correct a heart condition.

A spokesman for the hospital said it is not hospital policy to give the condition of any patients there, adding, "I can't even acknowledge whether or not a person is even here."

However, the source told the *News* that DiMaggio had undergone surgery, adding, "By the mere fact that the man is 84 years old, has a pacemaker and has had surgery, he is in critical condition."

DiMaggio's illness comes at a time when Yankee owner George Steinbrenner has been involved in a brouhaha with Major League Baseball over having the Yankee great throw out the first ball at the opening game of the World Series tomorrow. Baseball officials, with Mayor Giuliani's blessing, had long ago lined up Cubs home run king Sammy Sosa, a native of the Dominican Republic, to throw out the first ball. DiMaggio has traditionally been accorded first-ball honors by Steinbrenner at all big Yankee games, such as Opening Day and the World Series.

Another source confirmed to the *News* last night that DiMaggio has been ill for more than a week and would not be able to attend the World Series. ∎

John Roca, Daily News

Joe DiMaggio's name graces the walls of the children's wing of Memorial Regional Hospital in Hollywood, Florida. DiMaggio was put in the intensive care unit after surgery.

The Tie That Binds

By Mike Lupica
October 18, 1998

It seems as if he was just here the other day, being driven around Yankee Stadium in that '56 Thunderbird convertible, being handed replicas of old World Series rings by Scooter Rizzuto. It wasn't much of a ceremony. Chicago had done much better for Joe DiMaggio the same week. But you can never go wrong having DiMaggio back at the Stadium, seeing him on that field. We all told him we'd see him at the World Series.

DiMaggio admitted that day that he has no powerful connection to this Yankees team, because he hadn't seen enough of it. His connection is to all the Yankee teams, to everything people felt as they walked into the Stadium last night. DiMaggio's connection is to the whole big idea of the Yankees in the World Series.

He played 13 seasons. He played 10 World Series. When he opened the Balfour box three weeks ago and looked at the rings George Steinbrenner had bought to replace all the ones that had once been stolen from DiMaggio, someone said, "That's a lot of World Series to remember."

The old man smiled and said, "I remember the one we lost," and then was telling a story about 1942.

Another day at the Stadium for Joe D. Another day to stand around and talk with him about the first October for him, in '36. And '42. And what it had been like for him to swing a bat at the Chicago Commodities Exchange and have the whole place stop, the way ballparks always did when DiMaggio had a bat in his hands.

So it was not just another day at the Stadium for me. There are still parts of this life that you can't believe. One of them is talking baseball for a little while with DiMaggio. My grandfather's dream ballplayer. My father's. My uncles'. I come out of all that. There was Mr. DiMaggio, as my father called him, and then there was the rest of them.

Keith Torrie, Daily News

Yankee manager Joe Torre presented the legendary Joe DiMaggio with the Mayor's Proclamation designating September 27, 1998 as Joe DiMaggio Day.

Yankee greats of the past listen as former manager Casey Stengel (center) recalls old times. Standing from left to right are: Allie Reynolds, Tommy Byrne, Joe DiMaggio, Vic Raschi, Tom Henrich and Bill Dickey. Flanking Casey are Phil Rizzuto (left) and Yogi Berra.

I have gotten to know him over the years when he has shown up to throw out another first pitch. Or at Oldtimers Day. Or Joe DiMaggio Day. Several years ago, my sister met him in San Francisco, by chance. She was six months pregnant at the time, having her daily walk along the water, and a guy on a bicycle nearly ran her down. A man behind her said, "Are you all right, young lady?"

DiMaggio.

She told him she was fine, introduced herself, the two of them walked together for a while, talking about everything. She didn't want an autograph from him, or anything. They shook hands when it was over and he told her how much he had enjoyed himself. Every time he has seen me since, he has asked after her and mentioned the day.

Once I went and sat with him at Fort Lauderdale Stadium, on the day of his charity baseball game to benefit the Joe DiMaggio Children's Hospital. I was writing a magazine story. DiMaggio was full of stories that day. When he is in that kind of mood, you just let him go, from Joe McCarthy to Mickey Mantle hurting his knee in the Stadium outfield in the World Series of '51. Mantle's first, DiMaggio's last.

"All he knew was pain after that," DiMaggio said.

He is one month short of his 84th birthday. He is in pain, most of the time, because of arthritis. It has bent him over, shrunk him, because it does that even to Mr. DiMaggio. Now comes the word that he is sick in a Florida hospital with pneumonia. It is why the World Series started at the Stadium without him last night. Sammy Sosa threw out the first pitch. Really, it was the biggest pinchhitting job of Sosa's life. ∎

Joe D. Tumor Removed

By Paul Schwartzman
November 26, 1998

Ending weeks of secrecy, Joe DiMaggio's doctor yesterday revealed that a cancerous tumor was removed from the Yankee legend's lung last month.

Dr. Earl Barron also said DiMaggio appeared so near death 10 days ago that a priest was called to give last rites.

But the legendary ballplayer's condition has improved in the days since, and he spent yesterday —his 84th birthday—with family in his Florida hospital room, his breathing assisted by a respirator, Barron said.

"For a while, it was touch and go, but he has been showing steady improvement," the doctor said.

"I don't want to paint too rosy a picture," he continued. "He's an elderly man, but what I have seen suggests that he will recover."

The doctor declined to say when DiMaggio could return home, but he said the Hall of Famer would remain in the hospital for at least two to three weeks. "That's the minimum," Barron added.

When DiMaggio was admitted October 12, his friend Morris Engelberg told reporters that the Yankee Clipper was being treated for a pneumonia.

In fact, Barron said yesterday, DiMaggio was admitted for surgery to remove the walnut-size tumor, which had been discovered during a doctor's visit in September.

"It was not disclosed because of his wishes," Barron said.

DiMaggio's condition was stable after the operation, but he soon developed a lung infection and had to be put on a respirator. Doctors performed a tracheotomy October 20—putting a small hole in his trachea—to help him breathe.

As a result of the procedure, Barron said, DiMaggio "can't talk—he motions with his hands, sometimes he writes things down."

DiMaggio's worst moment came November 16, when his blood pressure dropped so low that Engelberg summoned a Catholic priest to stand by in case he had to perform last rites. Within hours, DiMaggio improved.

The mystery surrounding DiMaggio's health has provoked frenetic speculation that culminated earlier this week with two television stations reporting that DiMaggio was fighting lung cancer, and that he had suffered a heart attack.

Engelberg denied the report Tuesday, although he refused to say whether the former Yankee had had a tumor removed from his lung.

DiMaggio, Engelberg said yesterday, allowed Barron to talk about his condition to clarify the details. ■

Always active before his latest surgery, Joe DiMaggio shows former Giants coach Ray Perkins that he can drive a golf ball as well as he drove a baseball.

Dan Farrell, Daily News

Joltin' Memories
As Joe Rallies, fans take D-light

By Mike Lupica
December 9, 1998

For a change, the news from Florida was good about Joe DiMaggio, and so it brightened an otherwise dark, dreary day in New York City. The old man has been in the hospital since the World Series. It is why he was not at Yankee Stadium, where he belonged, throwing out the first ball of the Series the way he always throws out the first ball of the season at the Stadium. First we heard it was pneumonia and then we found out it was cancer and until yesterday, it seemed to be only a matter of time before we said goodbye.

For now, this week, he comes back. The doctors say they can't explain why he is getting better, just that he is. There was always a lot you couldn't explain about DiMaggio, because that is the way it has to be with magic.

My uncle Sam was the first in our family, of all my father's brothers, to see him in person, before DiMaggio went off to the service in 1943. My uncle was stationed at Fort Slocum in New Rochelle, and when the Yankees were in town, he would get to watch DiMaggio play ball two or three times a week.

"My buddies wanted to be close to home plate," he was saying the other day. He is 82 and full of bright memories about DiMaggio at a time when those memories seem more important than ever. "I wanted to be out in the bleachers. Joe was out there."

There have been so many memories of DiMaggio these past few weeks, as he has fought for his life. They come in letters and through e-mail. Mostly they come from men of my uncle's age, my father's age, telling some story about how DiMaggio, the most distant of our sports stars, touched their lives as surely as if he had walked through their front door one time.

"No matter what happened in the game," my uncle said, "Joe never disappointed you. He always did something that made you just shake your head and cheer your head off."

I was talking to Marvin Miller, the great union man of baseball, yesterday, about all things from Roger Clemens to the NBA players, and suddenly he was talking about DiMaggio, the first time he ever met him, back in the '60s. It was right before Miller was about to become executive director of the Major League Baseball Players Association, and he was in Fort Lauderdale to talk to the Yankees, and DiMaggio was there in spring training as a hitting instructor.

After Miller spoke to the Yankees, he was on his way to the field to watch them work out, and suddenly there was DiMaggio, who put out his hand.

"I'm Joe DiMaggio," he said.

Miller laughed yesterday at his own DiMaggio memory.

"As if I wouldn't know," Marvin Miller said. "As if anyone wouldn't know."

They sat in the dugout and DiMaggio asked about health benefits, because his had run out. And then Miller remembered DiMaggio showing him the shabby condition of the uniform he was wearing that day. No. 5 in pinstripes, one of the most famous numbers in all of sports.

"The sleeves were threadbare," Miller said. "He turned around and showed me the holes in the back. Then he said, 'You'd think the Yankees could do a little better for me than that, wouldn't you?'"

Miller talked yesterday about how it has only been in the '80s and '90s, perhaps because of all the crazy nostalgia that has come back into baseball, that DiMaggio once again has seemed to become bigger than life. By the time Miller met him, DiMaggio had been retired 15 years, and the Yankees were in decline. Somehow, impossibly, it seemed that the country had forgotten Joe DiMaggio.

"I wondered if even he thought that," Miller said. "There were times when I wondered if he fully comprehended the power of his own celebrity. But the people who came into contact with him always did. I remember a time in the '60s when the winter meetings were in Mexico City, and we had our executive board meetings there at the same time. There was a big party one night, and no one knew Joe was coming. But all of a sudden he walked into the room and everything stopped. The people on the dance floor stopped. The band stopped. Everything. Just because, well, it was him. He's always been the focus of the room."

That is DiMaggio, even now, 62 years since he made his debut in center field for the Yankees, nearly half a century from his retirement. He is still the

focus of every room. Lately it is a hospital room in Hollywood, Florida. For more than a month, there has only been bad news, about cancer and fevers and blood pressure and intensive care and the last rites of the Catholic Church. Over the weekend, it seemed we were about to lose him for sure, lose one of the few giants we have left. But for the time being, he comes back. For today, anyway, he surprises the doctors and us all.

Tomorrow, we can go right back to the stories about Clemens, about the lockout in the NBA, about these dreadful football officials. Today the news is about Joe DiMaggio and it is good news. There is still a magic to him. He still makes you shake your head, and want to cheer. ∎

Pat Carroll, Daily News

Monuments in centerfield at Yankee Stadium honor Babe Ruth, Miller Huggins, Lou Gehrig, Joe DiMaggio, Mickey Mantle, Thurman Munson, managers Edward Grant Barrow, Joe McCarthy, Casey Stengel and former owner Jake Ruppert.

Joe D. Demands Privacy

No More Press, Says Clipper

By Bill Hutchinson in Hollywood, Florida
and Corky Siemaszko in New York City
December 14, 1998

An angry Joe DiMaggio yesterday demanded "no more press" after furious family members complained the Yankee great's doctor has been releasing too much information.

Some relatives were so angry they wanted to fire Dr. Earl Barron, who dodged the hook by agreeing to abide by a news blackout, sources close to DiMaggio said.

"Dr. Barron has been, we feel, making unnecessary statements," said the stricken slugger's brother, Dom DiMaggio, making his first public statements since Joe fell ill.

"His releases have been accurate, but not as private as we would like.

"I guess the feeling is there's been so much information put out that we might as well have a television camera put in Joe's bedroom," added Dom, a former Boston Red Sox outfielder.

The notoriously private Joe D. made the demand yesterday after surviving what appeared to be a fatal coma Friday—a "dramatic turnaround" attributed by doctors at Memorial Regional Hospital in Hollywood, Florida, to a change in the Yankee Clipper's antibiotic treatment.

DiMaggio made his feelings known when he was briefly taken off his respirator.

"We allowed Joe to talk this morning," Barron said. "He was very angry. He said, 'No more press.'"

> "I guess the feeling is there's been so much information put out that we might as well have a television camera put in Joe's bedroom."
> —Dom DiMaggio

The 84-year-old Hall of Famer was suffering from an out-of-control infection and a nagging bout of pneumonia that put his life in peril.

Barron, who had been using a 0-to-10 scale to help reporters gauge the severity of Joe's condition, said the slugger's chances of survival had gone from a 0.5 or 1, "to a 4 or a 5."

The doctor also confirmed a *Daily News* report that DiMaggio's attorney, Morris Engelberg, and Dom had signed a "do not resuscitate" order to be used in the event that Joltin' Joe's heart failed.

That and other statements attributed to Barron infuriated DiMaggio's kin, who complained when they spent Saturday with the slugger. Joe was well enough to sit up and watch TV with relatives.

Barron declined to talk about his discussion with the family and said there would be no more regular updates on DiMaggio's condition.

Dom, who, along with other relatives, flew in from San Francisco to be at his brother's bedside, said all they want is for "everyone to please give Joe his privacy."

"These happen to be very, very sad days for me and every member of our family," he said. "I would like to ask everyone around the world who adores Joe, continue to pray for him." ∎

Yogi, Boss Lovefest Prompted by Joe D.

By Bill Gallo, Owen Moritz and Bill Hutchinson
January 7, 1999

The emotional reunion that ended the 14-year cold war between George Steinbrenner and Yogi Berra was triggered by none other than the Yankee Clipper—Joe DiMaggio.

During a 45-minute meeting in his Florida hospital room, the ailing baseball legend implored the Boss to bury the hatchet and end the feud, said Dr. Rock Positano, a long-time DiMaggio friend.

Sources told the *Daily News* that Steinbrenner had already been leaning toward making a gesture toward Berra—but DiMaggio pushed him to go all the way.

"It shouldn't be a personal thing," DiMaggio told Steinbrenner, according to Positano.

"It should be first for the fans, then for the game, then for the Yankees. That should be more important than two men having a feud."

Yogi Berra and Joe DiMaggio relax in the Yankees' locker room after clinching the 1950 World Series against Philadelphia. Nearly 50 years later, it was DiMaggio's plea to Yankee owner George Steinbrenner that helped end the 14-year feud between Yogi and the Boss.

Charley Payne, Daily News

Steinbrenner, 68, took DiMaggio's words to heart and got the ball rolling to Tuesday's mea culpa meeting with Berra, 73.

Yesterday, DiMaggio—who was in a coma and near death on December 11—was happy to hear the pair were talking, Positano said.

"Joe definitely had a hand in it," said Positano. He added that DiMaggio's brush with death "shook up a lot of people."

> "We lost Mickey [Mantle], we almost lost Joe [DiMaggio], we didn't want to lose you."
> —George Steinbrenner to Yogi Berra

Steinbrenner's spokesman, Howard Rubenstein, confirmed the Florida meeting took place.

Joltin' Joe's near-death experience upset Steinbrenner. During his Tuesday meeting with Berra at the Yogi Berra Museum in Montclair, N.J., the principal owner of the Bronx Bombers referred poignantly to DiMaggio's illness.

"We lost Mickey [Mantle], we almost lost Joe [DiMaggio], we didn't want to lose you," Steinbrenner told Berra.

The grudge started in April 1985, when Steinbrenner fired Berra as manager but didn't do the dirty work himself—he sent underling Clyde King to give Berra the bad news.

Berra, who was succeeded by Billy Martin, declared a personal boycott of Yankee Stadium for as long as Steinbrenner owned the team.

He stuck to his vow—he didn't even show up at the Stadium in July 1988 for his plaque dedication in revered Monument Park.

But the cold war melted Tuesday when Steinbrenner told Berra, "I know I made a mistake by not letting you go in person. It was the worst mistake I ever made in baseball."

"I made a lot of mistakes, too," Berra responded. They hugged, shook hands and even talked about Berra's coming back to Yankee Stadium, perhaps for a Yogi Berra Day.

Berra's nine grandchildren would love that. They have never seen granddad at Yankee Stadium. ∎

Gerald Herbert/ Daily News

George Steinbrenner and Yogi Berra bury the hatchet at the Yogi Berra Museum in Montclair, N.J.

DiMag Home From Hospital

Long battle against lung ills

By Bill Gallo and Bill Hutchinson
January 19, 1999

Yankee Clipper Joe DiMaggio yesterday capped a remarkable medical comeback when he was released from a Florida hospital and sent home after 99 days in intensive care.

DiMaggio originally was scheduled to be released from Memorial Regional Hospital today. But he was so eager to get home, his doctors decided to let him out a day early, a hospital source said.

The 84-year-old Hall of Famer was said to be happy to be back at his Hollywood, Florida, home after being hospitalized more than three months with lung cancer and pneumonia.

He will have nurses monitoring him around the clock, according to the source.

Yankee boss George Steinbrenner called DiMaggio's return home "a great moment in Yankee history."

In early December, DiMaggio was in a coma, and his prognosis was so dire that his family signed a "do not resuscitate" order and called in a priest to give last rites.

Now, DiMaggio is confident he'll hear the crack of a bat and smell the fresh-cut grass of spring

> Yankee boss George Steinbrenner called DiMaggio's return home "a great moment in Yankee history."

baseball, said his attorney, Morris Engelberg.

"He's looking forward to opening day in Yankee Stadium in April," Engelberg said.

Steinbrenner said he was overjoyed to hear the news and said he'd like Joltin' Joe to throw out the first pitch when the Bronx Bombers play their first home game April 9 against the Detroit Tigers.

"Personally for me, and certainly for the fans, this is a great moment . . . Joe DiMaggio will throw out the baseball to open the season," Steinbrenner said.

DiMaggio's granddaughters, Paula and Cathy, were at his side as he sat up in his own bed and enjoyed hearing them call him "Big Joe," a source said.

Doctors hope DiMaggio's rebound will be speedier at home, the source added.

"Mr. DiMaggio wishes to express his thanks to the doctors, ICU nurses and staff at Memorial Regional Hospital for helping him recover from infectious pneumonia, as well as to the 250 million people out there who are praying for him," Engelberg said. ■

Why DiMaggio's My Hero

He gave dignity and worth to everything he did

By Gaeton Fonzi
December 13, 1998

In my youth, I disguised myself as Joe DiMaggio. Despite the couple of decades' difference in our ages, we had a lot in common. We were both tall and lanky, with slightly stooped shoulders and dark hair, dark eyes and an aura of shyness we hoped females would interpret as an intriguing sensitivity.

We also shared an Italian ancestry and were blessed with generous Italian noses. We were both serious guys, and I even tried to model my facial expression to DiMaggio's, an expression writer Gay Talese described as "sad and haunted as a matador's."

But what I relished most about my disguise was the similarity of our swing. We were both long-ball hitters. We would get in the batter's box with the same quiet solemnity, hold the bat low on the handle and shoulder high, straight and steady — no fancy, twirly gyrations for us — and then, in one sweet swift motion, uncoil our wiry bodies, extend our arms and whip that bat around with such blurred speed and sureness that you knew immediately from the sound where that ball was going.

"Going, going, gone!" Mel Allen's cry on the radio echoed for both of us.

With DiMaggio, it usually went into the left centerfield seats at Yankee Stadium. With me, it went over the stone wall that ran along the left edge of the lopsided, weed-strewn lot that sat atop a curve along the Jersey Palisades.

DiMaggio never had to retrieve his home run balls. I did mine because we had only one ball, and once it went over the wall it wound up on River Road, about 200 feet down the boulder-strewn cliffs. It required a 10-minute timeout to get it.

Now, as I'm writing this, DiMaggio is 84 and trying to recover from lung-cancer surgery. My friend Doug and I were talking about that the other day, and I mentioned that DiMaggio was one of my heroes.

Doug, who was still a toddler when DiMaggio and I were in our prime, said, "You know, I could never call any sports figure a 'hero.' That priest who gave his life to save some Jews in the Nazi concentration camp, he's a hero. But a guy who played a game for a living, he's a 'hero'? No way."

Doug's right, of course. Yet "hero" comes naturally to mind when I think of DiMaggio.

Joe was, of course, a titan at the plate — his record of hitting in 56 consecutive games has stood for 57 years and may be the only major

TV Report that DiMag Dead is Error

By Bill Hutchinson
January 25, 1999

NBC News briefly sent shock waves throughout the nation last night, erroneously reporting that Yankee great Joe DiMaggio had died.

Due to a technical glitch, the network sent out the false bulletin to its East Coast affiliate stations, which flashed the news to millions of TV viewers at about 7:30 p.m.

"This is an NBC News Special Report. Baseball legend Joe DiMaggio has died at his Florida home. He was 84 years old and had . . ." The message was then cut off.

Within minutes, NBC officials realized the mistake and corrected the report.

sports feat to remain unbroken — but he was also one of the best to ever play center field. He appeared to spring toward the direction of the ball the instant it left the hitter's bat. Once, I remember seeing him spin around at the sound of the hit and, with his back to the plate, run full speed out to deep center. Without ever turning his head back, he instinctively swiped that ball the instant it was in reach.

I'm sure thousands of fans still have that image of DiMaggio and that miraculous catch locked in their memories.

But great reflexes don't make a guy a hero. What does? In DiMaggio's case, it was the ability to give a sense of serious dignity and worth to the fantasies of thousands of kids on the weed-strewn lots of America.

That spark of class and dignity DiMaggio gave to simply doing his job was gleaned by every hardworking trucker, coal miner, waitress, teacher, sales manager, stockbroker, top exec or hireling who ever watched DiMaggio on or off the field, watched him simply doing his job, without grandstanding, without arm-pumping exhibitions of narcissism.

Class. Dignity. In these times of whining, ego-driven, multi-millionaire athletes, round up the top 100 professional players in any sport and produce one who can match DiMaggio in those categories.

That DiMaggio's image became something of a cultural icon after he left baseball attests to the substance behind it. "Where have you gone, Joe DiMaggio?" the nation repeatedly asked in song, although we knew exactly where he was. For a while he was back in his hometown of San Francisco, living with his widowed sister Marie in a three-story stone home not far from Fisherman's Wharf, where his brothers ran DiMaggio's Restaurant.

It was the wharf to which his father had brought his wife and family of five boys and two girls in 1915 from Palermo, Italy, to pull a tough living from net fishing the ocean beyond the bay.

Then we saw Joe in the only way so many of our younger generation know him, as a television pitchman for Mr. Coffee coffee maker. And even to that he brought a touch of class. No exaggerated gestures, no loud hype, he simply told you that Mr. Coffee made very good coffee.

I used to think it would be nice if I could tell DiMaggio what I thought of him, not only as a ball player but as a good, decent man and how at one point in my younger years I was him. I never thought I'd get the opportunity. Then one night I met the man.

It was my friend Martin Margulies who introduced us. To this day, I don't know why I said what I did, but my very first words burst forth in an excited stammer: "I was almost on your radio show, but Irwin Cohen got picked instead of me!"

DiMaggio looked at me funny. I tried to

Fellow ball players gather around Joe DiMaggio as the dazed Yankee revives after colliding with second baseman Joe Gordon in a 1938 game with the Senators in Washington, D.C.

on your radio show, but Irwin Cohen got picked instead of me!"

DiMaggio looked at me funny. I tried to explain. I remember telling him our team had won the town playoffs, and as a prize the Recreation Department had taken us all to Yankee Stadium and then after the game to a radio studio for a kids' quiz show that DiMaggio used to have, and while we were standing in the hallway waiting to be seated, some guy came down the line and picked every sixth kid to be a contestant, and I was the fifth kid, and Irwin Cohen, our second baseman, was the sixth, and Irwin got on and won a bike, and I didn't.

Joe didn't say he remembered me or Irwin Cohen, but he said he remembered enjoying doing that show. We talked for about 10 minutes before someone else came over and took his attention.

As we were driving home that evening, my wife, Marie, turned to me and said, "I've never seen you act the way you did tonight."

"Act? Like what?" I said.

"I've never seen you so excited," she said. "The way you were stammering and almost jumping up and down. It was like you were a kid who had just met his hero."

She went on and on, but I didn't hear anything else she said. The roar of the crowd drowned her out as I hit a long one into the left center field seats at Yankee Stadium. ∎

Daily News

New York's greatest center fielders (left to right): Duke Snider, Joe DiMaggio, Willie Mays and Mickey Mantle.

Timeless Classics...

Joe
DiMaggio
and the
United States
Postal Service

UNITED STATES POSTAL SERVICE®